Feigning

Feigning

ON THE ORIGINALS
OF FICTIVE IMAGES

Eva Brann

PAUL DRY BOOKS
Philadelphia 2021

ON THE COVER

The painting of the disheveled weeping willow—I call it my poodle tree—is hanging in my house. It was done for me by my painter-friend Albert Sangiamo (reproduced in his *Drawing and Paintings*, p. 380). When he delivered it, uninhabited, I said: "Abby, it needs birds." So he came with his paint box and palette and put in the birds.

The photograph of a miraculously similar-looking (doctored, it turns out) real tree belies both my subtitle and my thesis: I don't think Abby's painting is the portrait of a real tree, as it actually *is* a "fictive image." But the very point of *Feigning* is that the originals of such invented images live in their own realm, which is not reality, not nature, not the sandy stretch of the photograph. Yet the photograph and painting together were too full of intimations to pass up.

E. B.

First Paul Dry Books Edition, 2021

Paul Dry Books, Inc.
Philadelphia, Pennsylvania
www.pauldrybooks.com

Printed in the United States of America

Library of Congress Control Number: 2021947979

ISBN 978-1-58988-161-7

To my parents,
EDGAR BRANN, MD
and
PAULA SKLARZ BRANN
and
my brother,
*WOLFGANG "BILLY" BRANN**

*by memory from a misplaced family history:
Ben **R**abbi **A**kiba **N**achman from **N**emowitz

When life hands you a lemon,* make lemonade.

The American Heritage Dictionary:
"lemon . . . 3. Informal. One that is unsatisfactory or defective." My replacement for the car example given: "The COVID-19-forced online Spring class was a lemon." So take time off, live frugally, and scribble tart-sweet drafts.

Contents

The Project's Words

The incitement was a desire to know what I might mean when I say what I do say. "Mean" has a double sense: What *I* mean, what is in or on my mind, and what the *words* intend, "stretch toward," on their own. Several off-the-cuff responses won't do, not because they're false but because they're diversions. The chief culprits are: 1. It's what people would say if they came on the subject. You're using the words as we all do, intending them as they're commonly intended, and connecting with others as people do. That's a diversion, because now the question is diverted to the plural of "I," to "we." What do *we* mean? 2. *You* don't mean, don't have anything "in mind." Your brain initiates the speaking activity. That's a diversion, because the question is: *What* incites the brain? And 3. You say and mean what your environment, your time, or expert opinion says. That's a diversion, because then I might ask: "Who are these agents actually, those worlds, times, opinions? Can anything *act* but a human being?

These responses effect diversions by handing off the inquiry 1. to the practical effects we achieve with our speaking, 2. to three pounds of warm, wet flesh, 3. to the influences I yield to. These are diversions because they can't answer my question: What is it that turns up in my mind as an impending, an incubus-like preoccupation, as well as a delight-promising inquiry?

I'll say below why exactly these replies strike me as, in rising order of dissatisfaction, inadequate, absurd, or shameful.

A. Mental Imagery

The particular term I often think of and talk to students, colleagues, and friends about denotes the images of the imagination—mental imagery, that is, and artificial images like paintings or diagrams or on-screen pictures.

I would like any possible reader to believe me when I say that this is a soundmindedly schizophrenic enterprise, on the one hand driven by a belief that my findings can't be otherwise than I hope, on the other by the conviction that if I get nowhere, having to conclude that an answer is impossible or undecidable, I have to give in and chuck the thing. Notice that this is a nice paradox, a spawn of logic at odds with itself, a mode I love. The paradox is that I am begging the indulgence of readers, who, did I require it, would not have a book to indulge.

Finally, the end of foot-dragging. Here is the issue: It is a part of the dictionary meaning of the word "image" and, I think, readily agreed to by people, that "image of," noun and preposition, often go together and that "of" here means "derived from," and so "related to." Thus an image is by its nature, *ab ovo*, "from the egg" as the Romans say, in an essential relation, one that determines its very way of being.

B. Copy

An image is a kind of copy.* It is also a re-presentation and

> I say "kind of" because there are copies that are arguably not images. It's an interesting set of problems, actually: some copies are reproductions, like xeroxes; we readily say that they are images

of the original put on the screen. But if you stuffed it in with ten copies, could you always tell which is which? When my partner-in-crime in high school, Mary Wrzychesekowski, copied, against edible remuneration, my math answers, were these then images of my originals (whose originality wouldn't have been that great an asset, giving us both away)?

an imitation. It is a *copy** as occurring in quantity while the

Latin *copia*, "copiousness."

original is singular; it is a *re-presentation*, as being a second and secondary presentation;* and it is, above all, an *imitation*,

Latin *re-*, "again."

cognate in etymology and meaning with "image."*

Root: *im-*, of obscure origin, (o.o.o.).

C. Original

I have insinuated the term *original* into this discourse. It is the very object of my inquiry, which I'll now formulate (not for the last time):

> *What, how, and where is the original implied*
> *by the very being of an image?*

D. Chapter Summary

Chapter One, in which I specify two kinds of inquiry—Problems and Questions—and formulate some problems, perplexities for which there is expectation of a resolution, and a question, which is perennial and, just because it is irresoluble, of deeper interest. The concern with the originals of fictional images is such a question, but there are preliminary problems to deal with.

Chapter Two, in which I set out what appear to me to be evasions of, or non-responses to, my concern, particularly those presented in terms 1. of mind-from-brain emergence, 2. of human creativity, and 3. of rejected transcendence. I'll claim that these critiques are the effective prelude to posing serious queries.

Chapter Three, in which I try to think out the ontology, "the account of being," of images, be they imaginary (as are fictions of unrealities) or imitative (as are copies of real things). In sum, the fundamental terms of the inquiry are subjected to the so-called "What is X?" question. To inquire into the originals of images without this somewhat arcane preliminary (which I'll do my best to make plain) seems to me facile.

Chapter Four, in which I finally face the question with the actual intention of finding an answer—not, however, to settle, to quench, the inquiry, because a genuine question is more than just being snaffled by a puzzlement. It is a locus of inextinguishable flare-ups. Instead I hope to formulate possibilities, that is, to find descriptions of these originals that have specificity and locations that have topographies.

Here's encouragement in this quest:

Oxford English Dictionary: "Original: (1624) Of the Image there must needs be some original." (From a work on transubstantiation by a divine, Thomas Gataker. He went to St. John's College, albeit in Cambridge.)

When I submitted *Iron Filings or Scribblings* (2019) to Paul, my publisher, I said: "This is my last one." He said "Ha!" So the next one, *Pursuits of Happiness* (2020) became my ha-book. Now here's *Feignings*, the ha-ha-book—two beyond my life's book budget. Here's wisdom:

. . . [B]e admonished: Of making many books there is no end; and much study is a weariness of the flesh (*Ecclesiastes* 12:12).

I interpret the Preacher's gnome: "Be warned: Who writes books is taking a holiday from reading them." So eight fat, buxom books are sleeping on their sides on top of my most cherished records—Bach to Buxtehude—gifts to tide me over COVID-19, reproaching and beckoning, both.

Note, if you will, that the five parts, Preface through Chapter Four, are short and long in alternation, depending on whether I myself am clear about what's to be said or confused and casting about for a fit formulation. Of human love it's true (not even so very true) that "love is not love / Which alters when it alteration finds," but of object-love it's otherwise; inquiries need to march or meander with the subject's pace, to bend "with the remover to remove" (Sonnet 116).

CHAPTER ONE

The Inquiry's Frame

A. PROBLEMS

We feign, harbor figments—of the imagination; falsify reality—misconstrue things and their thinghood; compose fictions—in writing, painting, acting, whatever has the power of
representation; make believe—pretend to opinions we don't
have; counterfeit money—or our right to it; create works and
worlds—as if we were divinities; feign innocence—when
we're guilty as hell.*

> Three times I've said "we" and implied it twice as often. Who's
> "we"? Not me. Counterfeiting, acting, creating isn't much in my
> line, partly because these activities require competences and gifts I
> don't possess, partly because some are unethical. "We" is an Amer-
> ican speech tic in accusatory settings: we strive to be inclusive—
> with mental reservations; so "we" often means "you."
>
> Note that the verbs tend to end up as nouns: fake, counterfeit,
> make-believe, which is to say that the mode of doing infects the
> deed and the way of making taints the product.

What *is* the problem of problems? It is that this—to me
centrally and gloriously human—ability, that of imagining in
its two aspects, bears the taint of badness, of wrongdoing.

The two aspects of which I am thinking are, expressed
as *activities*, processes of imaging and of imagining, and as
products, things imaged and things imaginary. Examples
would be a photographical portrait, which, even when pho-

tography is declared an art form, is still intended to present the sitter in her truest being, as against, say, the Statue of Liberty, a woman the like of whom has never (one hopes) walked the earth. Put in words: the difference between a more or less faithful copy and an intentionally innovative invention.

Both of these modes of image-making are under an aboriginal disgrace, their peculiar original sin. A copy is ineradicably tarnished by its secondariness and dependency; by its non-uniqueness and inherent multiplicity; by its indeterminacy of enlargement or diminution; by its unreality and consequent devaluation; above all, by its uncertainty regarding verisimilitude, its questionable truth-value, if it proposes itself as truly mimetic, that is, imitative.

Sooner or later I'll have to beg the reader's indulgence for my etymologizing, and to hold myself harmless in this aspect: To begin with, etymology, "word-truth-accounting," is a very finicky study from which, to my present sorrow, I cannily escaped in graduate school, being then fixed on the visual reality of the shining Greeks rather than the speculative linguistics of murky Indo-Europeans. Without real competence, I nonetheless have both a fascination with and dubiousness about this study. What a word used to mean and what cognates it spawned seems to me somehow (a very flabby modifier) illuminating. Yet the appeal to initial or just old meaning seems to me to have little force when it comes to inquiring into the depths of human being and thinking (such as is called philosophy). Etymology is an incitement, not a teaching. And the use of word-truth in this way by a certain philosopher of the last century seems to me plain shoddy: Why should a very early sense in a context lost to us be more revelatory than an evolved later meaning? Was *homo erectus* wiser than *homo sapiens?**

> Not that earlier isn't sometimes better. For example, Aristotle has, in my experience, more insights per page than most of my six-thousand-some much later books, but that's not, I think, because

he's Greek (in any case, he's from the sticks) or ancient, but because he's he. Someone like him could be in our kindergartens now. I had my eye on a kid in one I volunteered at.

I diverged in the text to etymology, driven by the word "mimetic" above. It is Greek; *mimesis* means "mimicry," "imitation." The second Greek word to my purpose is *eikasia*, which means image-recognition, from *eikon*, "image," and an ending denoting activity.

The Latin terms associated with feigning (participle) and feignings (noun), that is, terms for activity and product, are more numerous and etymologically forthcoming—see below. But *mimesis* and *eikazein*, the verb for imaging, are wonderful in their etymological impasse. Neither seems to go beyond Greek: my etymological dictionary says "*rein griechische Schöpfung*, "purely Greek creation," for *mimesis*.

So Greek speakers originated their imagination-vocabulary, perhaps, to grow wildly speculative, because these folks felt themselves to have a closer, more "special" (species-specific) relation to this capacity.*

> One of my dictionaries has an abbreviation I love for such an impasse: "o.o.o.," meaning "of obscure origin," a phrase referenced above. It seems pertinent to me that the Greek-derived image terms in English, "mimetic," "iconic," belong to scholarly, not to ordinary, speech, unlike the Latin cognates that everyone uses. Probably, then, the Greeks, who cared about words, had a "special," not lazily transferable, a species-related, relation to our capacity for making imaging (copying) and imaginative (imaginary) images.
>
> The translation above of *eikasia* as image-recognition follows Plato, *Republic* (509e, 511e). *Eikasia* in this usage is a nonce word, perhaps devised by Plato. It is composed, as I said, of the stem of *eikon*, "image" and *azein*, an agency-indicating verb ending.

Before I get down to business, I'd like to say a word about these annotations that appear in mid-text. I call them midriff-notes, as opposed to the endnotes that appear in the rear of the text and the footnotes that stand below it. I think I invented this form, lest it seem that this writing is to be taken earnestly as a straight shot for a determined target. No, I'm thinking things out. But on the way come sub-thoughts and side-issues, which intrude themselves as curlicues that break up the linear thinking-through and offer themselves as arabesques to the off-putting austerities of a logical development. So these might as well show up as they occur. After all, we old ones are under self-imposed lock-up, being for once (I might say as a teacher) more endangered than endangering. And this writing is, on the one hand, the occasion for attending seriously to *the* question, almost rising to a theological concern, of my life; and on the other, a divertissement—for which there's world forgone and time enough.

So back to A. The Problem. "Problem" is a Greek-derived word (*problema*) meaning "something thrown out before." Long ago I discovered an antithetical pair that has clarified many a perplexity for me: There are *problems* and there are *questions*. A problem requires solution, resolution. You solve it and it's history, terminally unarousing. Lots of ingenuity-imbued time may go into it. For example, you have a math problem to solve. Well, look up the answer given in back (at least in my old math books), work back from there, and forget the whole thing. Or, there's a problem with your neighbor: ratchet up your courage, lodge a mild request to turn it down. Done with. Or, I'm a happy home fixer. Pictures go skewwiffy: use two nails. Paint is flaking: smack on the latex and feather it, *etc.* I like problems but can't give them my deepest respect.

The older you get the more childhood tags return as guides to life. Here's one: *Wer A sagt, muss auch B sagen,* "Whoever says A has to say B as well." I've said A, so now I must say B.

B. THE QUESTION

My favorite book on etymology, Partridge's *Origins* (sometimes, I suspect, more brilliant than reliable), says that the origin of "question," from the Latin verb *quaerere*, is acoustic, a plaintive cry for help. So a problem presents itself to you, or better, your world does the presenting; a question, however, comes from within.

If you are given an impossibility proof for the solution of a problem (such as exists for the squaring of the circle) you stay away from the problem; it's no longer properly a problem. But if you have an intuition that the perplexity might have persisted merely because even plausible attempts through the years have not found acceptance or because your own progress seems asymptotic (that is to say, you get closer and closer along the curve, but never reach a crossing with the axis it's approaching), you declare the question "perennial." Then, if it was really a problem for you, if you expected a solution, you let it go—you might even look for an undecidability proof. But if it was a question, you carry on, almost *because* you suspect it of never yielding a solution. You think that this impossibility is *your limitation, not the matter's opacity.* This belief is a secular version of the Christian *Credo quia impossibile,* "I believe because it's impossible." (A version of a Tertullian passage, early third century.) To me it says that you have faith in the fallout of your inevitable failure—not because it's a salutary exercise, but because it keeps us in the porticos of realms most worth exploring. Nonetheless, the "plaintive cry for help" has something to it. There is some dis-ease in this questing, querying, inquiring, an activity that concerns finalities and never finishes.

But a word comes to mind that gives the condition a brighter turn: wonder. Wonder is hopeful deprivation, *expectant ignorance.* Problems put you to work, which is life's best anodyne, but questions make you reflect, which brings me back to myself, and that's life's homecoming.

C. Feigning

In order to frame the Problems, I will subject the reader to one more etymology, that of my title, "feigning" itself. It is an amazing verb. Its root goes back behind Sanskrit to Indo-European *deigh*, an ancestor of items as apparently disparate as dough and *teichos*, Greek for "wall." My Latin dictionary has some two dozen different meanings for the Latin version, the verb *fingo*.

The basic sense seems to be the doughy one: aboriginally, "to feign" is to shape basic material (dough being as basic as it gets) by kneading it into loaves or figurines.*

> I just opened a bag of graham crackers, each in the shape of a big-bellied teddy bear.

The *teichos*-wall (compare German *Teig*, "dough") seems to derive from the dough-like cement called putty with which an earthen wall would be plastered.*

> "Paradise" is cognate: a walled safe-haven.

Here are the principal parts of the Latin verb for "feigning." It is a transitive verb, meaning that it takes [something] as an object:

> *fingo* (first person, active, indicative): "I make . . . by shaping [something]."
> *fingere* (infinitive, present, active): "to make . . ."
> *finxi* (perfect, active, indicative): "I made . . ."
> *fictum* (perfect, passive, participle): "[something] made . . ."

Of these, *fingo*, "feign," and *fictum*, "fiction," contribute to the meaning sphere of feigning. To take the participle first, *fictum* means something made, hence something made up, hence the whiff of devilry about it: The maker-up projects into the world a novelty, a non-being, a phantasm, and with it delight, delight in the charm of newness, the freedom of innovation, the enlargement of a world worn down by familiarity. But this delight is complemented by danger, danger from the manipulative, possibly evil, falsifying intention of the maker-up of a *fiction*.

Then the even more complex *fingo*, not a thing made (*fic-tum*) but a personal doing: "I, you, he feigns." An old use of "feigning," never quite lost, was associated with imagining, with having and projecting mental images. This meaning was, apparently, only an afterthought, in any case secondary, when the root meaning of a physical shaping from doughy material was still active. Then, as is the way of Western speech, the physical sense gave way to non-sensory meanings.*

> Producing food for thought. If you approach certain terms from our present-day position, they are dead metaphors. For example, the Greek word for soul (a topic I'm about to take up) is *psyche*, assumed into English as a technical term, as in "psychology." The original meaning of *psyche* comes from a stem with the sense of a cooling breath as does that of "spirit," which is preserved in "respiration." Thus soul and spirit are inactive metaphors, meaning we employ them unconsciously. Metaphor is a figure of speech that often transfers, "carries across" a sense from our place, here the material world, to the other, the spiritual realm. We moderns will tend to think that they *are* metaphors, though in rigor mortis. But those who first used "psyche" to express the image of a cool, life-bearing breath, and "spirit" to signify the same—they meant it, I think, whether literate or not, literally: cooling, drying, life-giving in- and exhalation; when the last breath hisses from the mouth, we're a corpse. Nowadays, post-Harvey, it's when the last heartbeat lub-dups through the stethoscope.
>
> One more word on the etymology of "soul": the word is said to be o.o.o. There have to be some words that don't originate from words. What was he, she, it (could have been a child) thinking? Perhaps: "Here's an apprehension"—of course in "mentalese," that is, preverbal discerning awareness. And next, why did the sibilant "s" and the liquid "l," why did "soul" (the vowels differ in different languages) seem the right enclosing consonants? Who knows?

So what etymology illuminates here is a possible, surely highly speculative, sequence: Human beings early on conceived of shaping stuff into figurines, figures as a kind of counterfeiting, faking.

There is also an incidental implication—that our forebears were not acutely self-conscious, for then they would have wondered if a mental image must not always precede a material figure, especially if deliberate deception was involved.*

> Though I've heard arguments that, for example, in sketching, true spontaneity is best. Consequently, instead of recurring to a deliberately summoned mental image, we should let our hands do their work. The results I've seen are not encouraging to this theory; they tend to be "abstract," in the sense of "withdrawn from a representational context and so in-significant."

Thus etymologies do seem to help set up the *problem* of feigning in terms of inviting a solution. Is the early sense that figural shaping is a kind of deception, even if it's nothing very obviously representational, like loaves of dough, still alive in artists, as we call people who are quite normally referred to as "creative," that is, as god-analogues? For they make images and breathe life into them or design shapes that are good at appealing to the senses independently of any objective reference.

"God-analogues" presents a problem in Scriptural interpretation that comes to the forefront precisely because in the Old Testament human being, man, is presented as having been made, on the sixth day of the world's creation, in the *image of God*. If you believe this to have been our origin, the actual process, the *How* of it, will be of deep interest to you. Oddly enough, if you are apt to think that God's creation of man was conceived in the image of human feigning, the process will be even more engaging, as telling how a very grand author, the scribe of Scripture, a fellow human, thought that human feigning takes place. As it happens, Genesis 1:1 and 2:7, that describe the elements of God's feigning, are arousingly puzzling.

In Genesis 1:26–27 God speaks, probably to himself: "Let us," he says, "make man in our image, after our likeness."*

> Thomas Mann, in the Prelude to *Joseph and His Brothers,* a novel of over eighteen-hundred pages fleshing out the fifty chapters of Genesis, invites me to interpret "Let us" differently: God tells,

even asks, the concurrence of the angelic host that is highly displeased with His intention to introduce a new species as rivals to the angelic order. They are jealous, He is self-willed. They are resentful, He is autocratic. The Germans say *selbstherrlich*, "Himself the [sole] ruler."

Later, in Genesis 2:7, we are told: "And the Lord God formed man of dust of the ground, and breathed into his nostrils the breath of life"; and man "became a living soul." This sounds as if God first made a—discarnate—image of himself, that is, similar to himself. And then he made a body of earth-dough and imbued this man-shaped loaf with His own breath by which to live. So a corpse preceded the living body, while an image of God existed first, separately.*Here's a set of consequent

A similar question arises in the Mayan creation epic *Popol Vuh*. I discovered this really fascinating work because I was asked to be Mr. Liam Marshall-Butler's advisor on his senior essay, so I am grateful to him for this all-too-late discovery.

The *Popol Vuh* was composed in the mid-sixteenth century by anonymous members of the Quiché-Mayan aristocracy, soon after the Spanish conquest, to preserve the religious traditions of the Quiché, the Mayans of Guatemala, in the face of the forced Christian conversion and the systematic destruction of Mayan hieroglyphic books imposed by the Spanish.

The Mayan hieroglyphics were not only pictographs but also represented sounds. Thus the Mayans were the only literate Mesoamericans, since they had the makings of an alphabet, and so the authors of the *Popol Vuh* were in possession of *written*, that is, verbal, records. (*Popol* refers to a "mat;" a woven mat, signifying the unity of the community, denotes a royal throne; *Vuh* means a Mayan codex.) All my material comes from Allen J. Christenson's introduction to and translation of the *Popol Vuh* (2002), lines 1–906.

Although the *Popol Vuh* is a verbal account—and herein lies its relevance to my inquiry—the authors thought of it as an *ilb'al*, an "instrument of sight," an envisioning (the apostrophe marks the glottalization of the a, as in "bottle"). That is, I conjecture, because half-living images, *effigies*, play a major role in the Mayan genesis: it is, almost risibly, similar to the Hebrew Genesis. (I'm without the learning to support my suspicion that the Mayans composed the *Popol Vuh*, being forced converts, under the influence of Genesis: a similar pre-creation watery waste, creating divinity, failed humanity, exterminating deluge.) There is nothing laughable about these, but the Mayan presentation of mankind as images is a grotesque parallelism.

This is the story. The two creation-divinities are named Framer, "Composer," and Shaper, "Moulder"; the latter is neatly translatable as "Feigner." They create in succession animals, a "mud-person" and finally a herd of "effigies," mobile manikins. Like the Biblical God, these creators want to receive sacrifices and worship; for the latter their creations need to be verbally articulate. But all three creations in sequence fail. "They don't speak"; the animals "squawked and chattered and roared," the mud-man falls apart, but the effigies, carved of wood, seem the worst; they don't remember their gods, crawl around without purpose, are rigid in body. "Their faces were masks"—as do we COVID people.

Here's the problem. Like the mankind of the Bibles, these Quiché people are images. We are made in the image of the Creator (Genesis). But of whom is this wooden generation the image? They're a bizarre race. In their making the Framer and the Shaper intended "people"; but did they have a verbal pre-conception or a visual mental image? The effigies are finally drowned, but they are first toppled by a full-scale revolt, not only of their fellow-failures whom they have tried to dominate, but—and this is purely wonderful—of the things they've made, used, and abused, including their blackened cooking pots. This rings true to me; in an essay, "Thing-love," I once asked myself about the inner life of objects, particularly of artifacts like pots (more elegantly, vases), and, above all, of books.

So there's no answer telling just of what these wooden figures are effigies, "shaped-out-of's." That bastardy is the source of their bizarreness, for Biblical humanity derives not only its subjection but also its dignity from its divine similarity. Two facts, too good to leave unmentioned: One, the Quiché's title for an artist was *Toltical*, a Toltec from Tula. I have a warm spot for that town (not far from Mexico City) because it was to Mayans and Aztecs what Athens is to those of us moderns interested in our psychic origins. A pertinent couple of Aztec lines (*Popol Vuh*, note 102):

> The Toltic were truly wise . . .
> They conversed with their own hearts . . .

So they not only had the craft to make things of beauty but the intellect for self-consciousness—like the Greeks.

Finally, apropos nothing, but cited for its encompassing truth:

> From within heaven they come,
> The beautiful flowers, the beautiful songs.
> Our longing spoils them,
> *Our inventiveness makes them lose their fragrance.*

(My italics: There goes our vaunted human creativity!)

problems: First, generally: How is it possible to image a being that is not visible (though audible)? Second, more concretely: How can we be the image of a divinity whose difference from the pagan idols is precisely that the latter are, *like us*, made of earthly material, albeit gold, and image natural beings, albeit below humankind, like calves (Exodus 32:4)?* Third, regarding

"Idol" from Greek *eidolon*, which is, in turn, from *eidos*, "visible form" and an ending signifying that the form is a phantom.

the process: Is it God's breath that infuses this proto-image into the corpse?

A summary solution to these problems seems to me to be as follows. First, this imaging has to be non-figural, that is, non-spatial, qualitative, that is, more of the spirit than the body. This understanding, that what is God-like in man are qualities of soul, is supported in commentaries. Second, all the light chatter about creativity perhaps has a deeply respectable source in the New Testament. It is the mode in which human beings, legitimately after all, think of themselves as world-makers: secondary worlds, artful images—human-made, imaging God's image-making. Third, the solution to the "breath of God" problem will be attempted in the next paragraph.

So here's the third problem area. The text, which my various Bibles do not question, says not that God encouraged himself to make an image of Himself, but to make man "*in*" his image and "*after*" his likeness. This locution, taken literally, sounds as if the Divinity first produced an image or likeness of Himself into which or according to which He then worked the dough, the dust-clay, such that it could be a human body. Probably he infused his self-image into the dust-body by breathing into its nostrils.

I had my suspicion and found it supported in the *Soncino Chumash* where "in our image" is explained thus: "in the *mould* which We have prepared for his creation (my italics)."*

The *Soncino Chumash* is an edition of the Pentateuch with a collection of classical Jewish commentaries. I bought it more years ago than I can recall, not knowing that one day it would give me just what I needed.

"Mold" means matrix, which is by definition a maternal setting for within-ness. So what is this mold which precedes, which is to *receive* the human creature? I speculate that God is represented as going about his creating just as would a human artist: summon a mental image, project it into the world as a pattern, a paradigm.*

> From Greek *para*, "beside" and *deiknynai*, "to show." Often it's a drawing, sometimes a mini-model, sometimes a set of specifications.

And when the material, the "mother-stuff" "out" of which the creature is made, is cast into the mold or matrix, the shaped creature has come into being. Take note: not the body ensouled but the soul embodied—just as human works of art eventuate.*

> Of course, sometimes the material might beckon to be shaped a certain way. Is that the primary art, the matter-guided art? I think not.
> The above account of world-making is close to the one followed by the divine Craftsman in Plato's *Timaeus*.

This account is, however, at odds with an understanding of divine creation as *ex nihilo*, "out of nothing." For it puts between the maker and his product *two* stages of image-making. One is the preparation of the material to be shaped "in" these images, the other is the mental image and its embodied realization.

It seems to me that workers in the fine arts who wish to be creative think of themselves more as creators *ex nihilo* than as craftsmen working from images, internal or external. Another way to put this is that they intend to put something *new* into the world, to produce novelties. This ambition is expressed in the genre-title of one truly new type of literary work, the Novel, which, contrary to ancient myths that furnished time-out-of-mind plots for the dominant ancient literary genre, Tragedy, is based on the kind of news found in newspapers—not concerned with royal heroes and their fate but with ordinary individuals and their circumstances.*

> As ever, this generalization doesn't quite work. One might claim that Epic, particularly the *Odyssey*, is novelistic. But Odysseus's encounters are with beings of mythical stature; most have divine ancestry, as does Odysseus himself, the great-grandson of Zeus.

The problem with news, with novelties for the avidly curious, is that "novelty" itself has a derogatory taint: novelties are mass-produced trinkets. And more deeply, novelty, even unintendedly, denigrates present existence: The desire for novelty implies that what is, is actually, is now, is to be trumped by what has eventuated *just* now; it intimates that progress implies contempt for present being as the eminently superable. Novelty vitiates the only time for actual life given us, the present. It is the keynote of modernity, "just now-ness," and not a happy era in which to *be*.

Solution: Just to realize what a devotion to newness (cluelessly called "change" these days) implies is to be cured of excessive progressivism—unless you're bitter about your condition—in which case you'd better *imagine* alternatives *very* vividly.*

> For example, you wish—I've heard this—our present president might die of the virus. Well then, besides our being afflicted with a humanly unworthy desire, we'll have a president who doesn't even have the moderating grace of an unpresidential appearance.

Once more: The god-analogue problem (whether it is our god's or another's) might be soluble by thinking through our limitations: Can we encompass intellectually what is not imaginable? Can we deeply care for what is not embodied? The novelty problem is approachable by finding and practicing the temperamental discipline that helps us stay devoted to stable beings, to convert curiosity into *interest*.*

> That discipline, thoughtfulness, was given us, I think, so that we might formulate the mystery of things: clarifying involvement.

Back to the problem of problems, the taint of wicked-
ness attaching to feigning, although its dough-shaping origin is so innocent. Some of the evil-doing is quite concrete.
For example, here's a locution from the terrible Thirty Years
War (1618–48): *einem den Beutel fegen* (cognate to "feign"),
"to swipe someone's purse."* It is said to be thieves' argot, so

> Another pertinent relation in German: *tauschen*, "exchange" and
> *täuschen*, "deceive," as if change even (or perhaps particularly) as
> reciprocity was next to deceit.

something about the word must have invited the unlearned
ear to sense its inclusion in the sphere of duplicitous terms,
feigning, fiction, imitation, mimesis, image, imagery, imagination.*

> The *im* root of the last five terms seems to be o.o.o.

What makes these a meaning-sphere? They are all beset
with a double duplicity. The first is that they produce, or are,
copies, affected with existential secondariness, with derivativeness. Something, the *original*, came before and lent itself
to being reduplicated—but with a defect, be it the mere fact
of not being original, of being an epigone, "late-born," be it
the substantial feature of lacking the qualities of the original. Take the portrait of a Dutch burgher in the seventeenth
century. The picture has existence; he's dust and ashes. The
portrait commands an enormous price; the burgher's whole
estate probably couldn't buy it. The picture is famous and is
itself often imaged; he's obscure—was in his time and is in
ours. *But* when he was among us, he wasn't two-dimensional
but probably pretty voluminous and full-size to boot, though
maybe narrow in soul. So here's his picture flat as a pancake
that he's sat for and paid for. He's unquestionably primary, so
why go on? Add even music and motion. It's still not up to the
mortal original.*

> There are those who foretell a future when virtual images will be
> indiscernibly different from originals. No doubt they'll invent a

Turing test by which to tell image from reality. I propose this one: an hour sequestered with this virtual monster and you'll be overcome with a *horror imaginis* much like that *horror vacui*, the instinctive shrinking from pure emptiness, which is unreasonable, for what harm can empty space do you? And if you're locked into a vacant room, it's not empty because there'll be walls to palpate, and a floor to feel beneath your feet, and resonances to produce. The company of a virtual being, plausible but unreal, seems to me far more horrible than emptiness.

The terrifying duplicity here is that a copy pretends, so to speak, to be the original.* The locution is, to be sure, an

Of course, if there is a maker, the intention is the maker's. Then there are natural deceptions, such as that of the insect called a walking stick, which imitates an inedible twig. To attribute an intention here would be to be sucked into the black hole of contention between evolution and intelligent design.

anthropomorphism, but I mean just that: perfect images would be dangerously seductive, not only in having been made to cause you to forget their secondariness in technological marveling, but even to convince you that they tell truer truth about the subject than the still-life itself, or the sitter, or the scenery.

So the first duplicity has to do with the pretense of necessity, the compulsion to belief, that is, one might say, virtuously inherent in images. The second duplicity is the opposite; it concerns an outright propensity to deceit of copies, their claim to re-*present*. So the former is aesthetic in the older sense of relating to the ways of perceiving, but the latter is moral in the normal meaning of intentional right or wrong conduct.

Thus there is often something wrong when the images are given priority over originals, as when shy or inept, essentially isolated, people lose themselves in image watching, or, more ominously, in autocratic countries where the image of the leader, who might be unimpressive in person, watches over people's work or private lives from a picture obligatorily hung. Or when an image is modified to tell lies about the original. That might be relatively innocent, as when snapshots are enhanced, but it can be plain manipulative, as when essentially dingy environments are gussied up to shining splendor, exemplified by the Russian "Potemkin villages." But why give examples for deceits we all know and have probably assisted in?

These are soluble image problems. The first set is soluble, as are most problems of perception, by attentive thinking, the second, as are most moral perplexities, by refusing to collude.

The problems always tend to obstruct the question, because unless we're terminally supine, we're driven to be doing something about something, rather than allowing ourselves just to be, that is, to think.*

> Being ignorant of, and therefore opinionated about, Eastern wisdom, I want to forefend any reference to it when I render the sum total of my elderly conclusions thus: "Do less, think more." (Actually, it's out of Aristotle's *Nicomachean Ethics* IX 4, 8.) Also: "Say less (and what, oddly, needs saying in addition: keep it short) and muse more"; "Be nice, if at all possible, if not, raise an eyebrow, perhaps even two."—Mordancy charged with love; this is why Jane Austen is *the* admiration-charged love of any life with literature. Well no, perhaps Odysseus as well—Homer's stand-in, the teller of his own odyssey.

Here, again, is the question subverted by the problems: *What, how, where are the originals of mental images?** The

> I had hoped to find a consideration of my question in Johann Wolfgang von Goethe's *Wilhelm Meister,* a work written, it seemed, to contain it. *Wilhelm Meister* traces the development of Wilhelm as artist through the traditional stages, from apprentice through journeyman to master. In the musings following Chapter 11 of *Wilhelm Meisters Wanderjahre* I came on the following:
> The Question—Whence does the poet get it?—again reaches only the What; about the How no one learns anything from this.
> I think that by "the How" Goethe means the artistry as distinct from the subject, "the What." So he too is deflecting the question of origins into the problems of production. By the What he seems to mean literary and historical sources, not ontological ones.

setting of this three-in-one question is the hypothesis that mental, internal imagery is ultimate—all material external image-artifacts are derivative from these; they are the originals. For it can't be "turtles all the way up": Once we're in the soul, the answer, treating the question as a problem, will be either 1. Mental images originate in our brains. As I've intimated, I'll try to persuade a friendly reader later on: if you believe that, you'll believe anything. Or 2. We are in the Biblical sense creative, able simply to magick the "molds," the primary images, into being, capable of spiritual spontaneous generation. If there are fellow-humans with such capabilities, they would have souls so qualitatively different from my own that I would then be at a loss to understand why their products speak to me so directly. The resolution to the problem of human creativity lies, I think, in a proper sense of human limitation.*

> I am thinking of a sober assessment of our time-and-space determined incapabilities—a sensible modesty which is poles apart from self-abasing, virtue-signaling humility.

There is also encouragement to raising the question. Eccentric as it may seem, I am supported by the testimony of one who might be considered an expert: Homer, to me the poet of poets. For the making of both his epics he calls on agencies beyond himself: "Sing, goddess, the wrath" and "Tell me, Muse of the man." Homer is invoking Olympic deities as the keepers of the originals that the epics (from *epos*, word) image in words.

Here, in contrast, is Wallace Stevens in "Of Modern Poetry," speaking of the pre-verbal poem in the poet's mind and its search for "What will suffice. It has not always had / To find: the scene was set; it repeated what / Was in the script." This script is what the divine Muse brings to Homer: the original. But right away there's a problem. The Olympic original is for this modern poet already a script, verbal, written. For

my part, I can't imagine the mountain of the gods housing
a library; most of those Olympians couldn't read.* But they

> I've never seen an ancient image of a Greek god reading a book (as I
> might have, since I was, in early life, a Greek archaeologist).

could look down or go down into Hades (where dead Achilles
was once visited by living Odysseus, *Odyssey* xi 467 ff.) to see
the heroes—if not in the flesh, at least as fairly voluble shades.

I have spoken of the soul in various ways; now is the
moment to lay out the psychic territory I have in mind. It
seems to me to be a metaphorical description that most of my
fellow humans might go with.*

> One last time: I'm persuaded that our languages (I mean the ones
> with Indo-European roots) have *no* words for non-physical being.
> The o.o.o. (recall: "of obscure origin") words give the appearance
> of not having a physical etymology (though, to be sure, that word
> history may simply be lost). I just can't imagine that this linguistic
> fact—that such words are all, insofar as we know their developing
> etymology, dead metaphors—is not a reflection of a primary exam-
> ple of the human mental limitation referred to above: we have no
> way to think of the spirit but by physical, by material metaphors.
>   But no, that's upside down: Far from being a limitation, it's a
> latitude allowed us by our remarkable mental constitution. As we
> can imagine whole beings not pieced together from namable parts,
> settings with atmospheres not adequately describable, so we can
> think thoughts beyond visualization. In other words, the psychic
> territories I'm about to describe mutually exceed each other—
> which is a mark of mental "modularity," of the discernible separa-
> bility and occasional predominance of our faculties.

So the metaphor summons a topology, a description of a
place that has its own furniture and functions. Up front are
the sensory organs that channel perception, that is, sensation
organized into objects and their backgrounds. (As attention
shifts so can the priority of things or settings.) So sensation
seizes the outside and projects some version of it inwards. I
leave aside the truly unanswerable question whether what we
bring into this soul territory resembles its origins at all.* Yet

> By "truly unanswerable" I mean: not even decidedly indeterminable
> by an impossibility or undecidability proof of the sort that, once

discovered, resolves—in a manner of speaking—such problems as the squaring of the circle, referred to above, which thereafter you have to be mad to try to work out. In Mann's *Magic Mountain* one of the sanatorium's inmates tries just that (Ch. VII 6); calculation having got him nowhere, he decides to make the problem simple by catching it by surprise. He lays out a length of string as a circle, then pounces on it with the thumb and index fingers of both hands and transforms it into a square—and falls into bitter brooding.

I cannot imagine that nature (or its Craftsman) would be so malicious as to make us systematically misapprehend our environment; in fact, when we fail to cope with it, it's not our perceptions that seems to be mostly at fault but our judgment.

For the moment I'll skip to the middle arena, most to my point, and go way back or down (whichever dimensionality seems to fit the inquiry), wherever some sort of intuition, insight, or "at-sight" (*in*, "at," *tuere*, "look") seems to occur, some ultimate mindfulness, some consideration of finalities, and wherein ongoing thinking turns into accomplished thought.*

> The metaphor of intellectual substance expressed as depth, a third dimension, wants digging into. Could it signify the temporally stacked, accumulated and enduring, corroborations to be got to the bottom of? Or the notion of substance itself as having a kind of compactness, a metaphysical solidity and so a dimension not to be reached by scratching the surface?

That returns me to the middle territory, the human center, shared in amicable dispute by both the memory-summoning and the muse-inspired fantasy or imagination and by logic-constrained and attention-driven thinking-through or reasoning: poetry and reality. It is the place we mostly live, temporally and spatially.* Perhaps we must, at any moment,

> Kant aptly calls the account of this place the "Transcendental Aesthetic," where the *conditions* for converting sensation into knowledge, that is, *for turning externality into internality*, are located (*Critique of Pure Reason* B35).

choose between living in the imaginary *or* in the thinking mode. Opinion seems to favor the claim that we can't be in

both modes at once. But I think that they can be simultaneous, that life can be at once imaginative and realistic, even
when lived in sight of a soberly factual, perceptually plain
appearance.* Here is an example. I look around my study

> I always keep in mind that "realistic" is Latin for "thing-devoted"
> (*realis*, "pertaining to a thing," *res*, plus *-ist*, designating an
> adherent.)

which is devoted to self-sameness, or I could never just get up
and reach for one of my thousands of books, knowing it to be
in place. Hence the imaginative atmosphere is bread-and-butterish and old-shoeish: good for work. But both in familiar
and in strange places, seeing and imagining *can* immediately
leap and glom onto each other, being the same in some aspect.

So here's the other experience. I was driving with friends in
the vicinity of Taos, New Mexico. We came by a stretch in the
road, a sward whose grass had gone to hay, which flickered as
if gilded when the sun emerged. There were stands of cotton-
woods scattered over this floor of gold, and under them, graz-
ing and gamboling, a small herd of pintos: a pretty enough
sight on its own, as merely real. But suddenly, momentarily,
as we raced by, there appeared an overlaying, underpinning,
or permeating image (I couldn't tell)—its *archetype*: the scene
itself but out of some pre-perceptual memory and not identical yet correlative with the real sward—less detail, more
atmosphere; less objective, more actual.

Here was a blissful though brief inversion, the projected
mental image (for what else could it have been), though curtailed in duration and devoid of volume, assumed the function
of original.* And, of course, since it came as a reminiscence,

> Though, to be sure, that is what mental images always are to
> an artifact; one might say that they are *intermediate* originals,
> because my question is precisely about *their* origin. I would surely
> like to know whence these evanescent but unforgettable events get
> their archetypal feel. (Archetype: *arche*, "ruling beginnings"; *typos*,
> "original pattern," "impression.")

the memory immediately produced associations with the floor
of gold, Shakespeare's mason bees fashioning a dome for their
hive, "The singing masons building roofs of gold,/The civil
citizens kneading up the honey"—as if they knew, expressed in
susurrant lines, the etymology of feigning as kneading dough.*

> How is it that the loveliest lines I know, in sound and figure,
> should also fit by meaning and significance into my booklet?

A page or two more on the inherent endlessness of serious question-asking, of the forever-on-the-stocks character of
its characteristic topics.* In the experience I've just reported

> "On the stocks": of boats sitting on the timber-frame on which
> they're built and from which they're trailered to be launched—
> *if* finished. In Annapolis garages they tend to displace cars,
> which were permanently parked in driveways—to the neighbors'
> annoyance.

there is one element that particularly stymies persistent
inquiry; it won't hold still for a closer look. It withdraws
under scrutiny; the harder you try to hold on, the more eva-
nescently it behaves. Thinking about such illuminations is
standing in one's own light. This self-interference occurs in
all attempts to make the mind turn *to* itself; it's always turning *on* itself, but most unavoidably of all when one power
attempts to comprehend another, for example, thinking about
imagining. But then again, while experience is necessary, it's
also in the way. Before long you have to penetrate, go beyond
the world of examples, go below—or above.*

> The German word *Untersuchung* is pertinent here. You might think
> it means a search "under." Not so, this *unter* (prep.), as distinct
> from *unten* (adv.), is more like Latin *inter*, "among." So an inquiry
> conducted as a literal "search among" will tend to remain scholarly,
> that is, it will bring together facts and opinions to produce, usually
> minutely differentiated, additional opinions.

If you don't know a thing, look it up in a book (for me;
others may use other "delivery systems," yecch!). It will usually tell you: It's the brain that does it. The actual brain sci-

entists use a much more modest term: the brain "subserves" the images of the mind. One central switchboard is that little nut, the *amygdala* (Greek: "almond"), a module of the brain involved in emotion, particularly fear. Is there a physical illumination here concerning the fear, the suspicion, of feigning, of being fooled? So now the imagination, the agency for images, has in this module "a local habitation and a name" for the "airy nothings" that "imagination bodies forth," an imaginative function that Shakespeare—of course—assigns to the poet (*A Midsummer Night's Dream* V i 17).*

> I have, impudently, edited Shakespeare, who has "airy nothing," singular; this nothing has huge numerosity.

What the books—in fact a shelfful—tell about the brain is called "information." I'm full of suspicious aversion to it, both as the matter of learning and as the driver of judgment.*

> Information is a *sine qua non*, a necessary but scandalously insufficient condition of good judgment. —So take it in and go with your initial intuition. It's *very* biddable, is information.
>   And often deflating: it turns out that mason bees are a family of solitary workers who build domes out of spit and dirt. And continuously out of date in its bondage to the facts of reality, which regularly fall apart. That golden New Mexican sward is probably a blackish parking lot by now.
>   In one of her satisfyingly snobbish, terminally English novels (you can't get that here, since Americans look silly as snobs), Angela Thirkell says of a woman: "To dislike her was the mark of a liberal education." I say: To be information-adverse is the sign of a mind yearning to be free. Information should always be ancillary, never sovereign; it's plain dangerous to gather information without having clear intentions; it untethers you, and then you're under the influence.

I've introduced the brain solution because it means to lay to rest the question itself—where do the images of the mind's imagination come from? But it can also do just the opposite. It can raise the question: Why is it taken more or less for granted that brain action precedes psychic awareness, consciousness? Why might it not be the case that it's the reverse:

the soul's activity, that spiritual awareness, thinking in particular, arouses the brain circuits to action? It is probably insoluble as a problem.* But that is the very reason for dwelling on

> In laboratory settings miniscule time lags between brain activ-
> ity and consciousness are observed, but to the amateur reader the
> measurements seem problematic.

it, on a., the logic and temporality of brain-mind interactions
and on b., the actionable consequences of either sequence,
and on c., the possibility that the laboratory skews the subject's everyday behavior, here last mentioned but possibly first
in consequence. If the brain fires before consciousness arises,
is it obligatory on us to try 1. to accept, 2. to ignore, 3. to con-
travene the fact? If the protocol contravenes common sense,
should we assert an amateur right to an opinion? If the science appears to show free will as an illusion by showing that
the brain goes first, then the prime experiential argument for
our having a will, namely *post hoc, propter hoc*, "what comes
after something happens because of it," no longer works. Our
sense that we choose is nullified, since it's the will, now an
illusion, that comes after the determinative event, the deci-
sion—unbeknownst to us.

To return to these fleeting flare-ups of archetypes. Are they
anterior or posterior to their real, factual occasion (which, as
I've said, is itself in passage)? Are they more or less ephem-
eral, a diffusible effluvium, or an enabling condition or reality? Whence did the archetype come, where did it go? What
betokens this sense that, "but for a little" (see no. 11, end of
chapter)—a little what?—something palpable would eventuate, and why does it not?

With this squall of queries, problems morph into The Question.* It is a real one, not driven by a criterion-fulfilling solution.

> One last problem: how to hold onto the intended object of my
> inquiry. Between its first, thus freshest, apprehension and its
> final, thus most worked-over, formulation, has the object itself
> not been reshaped? I asked myself—or better, something, the

question itself, asked me: What is the original of a mental image? Meanwhile I might have complicated it, the object of the question, past recognition: images all the way up, from this flat yellow tablet and its ant-trail scribblings to high Olympus and its resident, originally musical Muses. Well, the solution is: keep rereading before barging on, to track the morphing.

Apropos complexity: I was, not long ago, much taken up with the question, Why is the duo of complexity and depth so often falsely taken as an identity? The metaphorical dimensionality of complexity seems to be the second dimension, the plane, while depth seems to be a descent into the third dimension, volume. For complexity is visualizable as a lay-out of mutually implicated elements on the same surface, and, in fact, superficial. But what superficiality really is—often ex-plication, "unfolding"—seems to be best discernible by its *antithesis*, depth. It can't be that the latter is copious, since complexity seems to have preempted multiplicity. For superficial things are various as hell—and that is not an idle simile; read *Paradise Lost*: God's heavenly realm deep in its height, is simple and single-minded in worship and obedience, while Satan's underworld is shallow in its gloom, full of ultimately "in-dividual," meaning uncuttable, terminally a-tomic, finally unassimilable, radically species-evasive beings.

How often have I called a matter "deep"—and now it turns out that, in spite of having tried, I still don't quite know what I'm saying when I claim: "The question I'm broaching is deep." One last time: Could I mean first of all that it's fleeing from me? "They flee from me that sometime did me seek, / . . . / . . . and now they range, / Busily seeking with a continual change" (Thomas Wyatt).

Where do fictions come from? The first solution-semblance, the diversionary answer, is: from mental images. So the inspiringly hopeless question now is: Do mental images have originals, and, if so, what and where are they? Mental images are, *as causes*, the originals of works of art, a condition reinforced by the etymology of feigning, which invokes a model. They are, *in themselves*, derivatives of some sort; this condition too is underwritten by "feigning," originally so innocent a term.

One more consideration: What makes for a true question? It is a shaped indefiniteness, a cloud that issues audible claps and visual bolts, while being itself impalpable.* Whether this

---

Here is my interpretation of Aristophanes' comedy *The Clouds*, which presents Socrates (who was in the audience) to the Athenians as a mischief-maker. The choral community onstage is made up of these titular clouds. I think they are Aristophanes' take on the forms, the Socratic-Platonic answer to the universalized version of my particularized question. The foundational Platonic question is: What are the originals of which we and our world are images? And the answer is: the Forms.

mental impending, this thought-vapor, can be made to have an outline and a center, as the poet gives airy nothings their habitation and their names, the subjoined effort will show. What I find myself saying here is that to be preoccupied with a question probably is more to clarify, to specify, to concentrate the question than to produce an abiding answer.*

> One thing is clear to me: Certainty isn't in it. Perhaps truly discovered truth is certain—if it occurs. But human truthfulness is already discredited if it merely intimates certainty. Cheerful satisfaction at having done—never mind "one's best"; hardly anyone does his best—as much as there's zest for at a time, plus a little pride at having probably come out the better for it, and perhaps sent some stymied students on their way—that's permissible, I think.
>
> An addition: Being in the tenth decade makes everything easier (well, whatever it doesn't make harder). I don't have to worry what people think of me because where I'm going before very long, I may have other things to harass me. Moreover, being a little more personal than is expected will be imputed to me for a mildly incipient senility—along with everything else.

Let me get down to business by way of imagining a conversation I might have with myself—or, for a little tension, with one of our students, a senior. It's September, before the virus, and he's just read *War and Peace*. He wants to know: "Ms. Brann, what did you mean when you asked us whether Tolstoy has accurately reported the music Petya hears betwixt sleep and wake on his last day on earth?* Didn't he make it up?"

> Petya Rostov is my favorite permanently-fifteen-year-old in the world. He's the most musical of all those lovable Rostovs, including even Natasha, who is girlhood incarnate.

Me: "Make what up? How?" "Well, invent him, Petya, and his music." Me: "Well, 'invent' means 'come upon him, find him.'

Where?" "In his imagination, where else?" "The boy and his music were in his imagination?" "Yes, where else?" "Both he and the angelic orchestra that plays for him?" "Don't be silly [no student would actually say that to a tutor]; not the boy himself but his image. Mental images are like angels; having immaterial bodies, thousands of them can fit on a pin or into the mind." Me: "And where's the imagination?" "I won't say 'in the brain.'" Me: "Bravo. It's a real question whether that was a sensible question I asked in our class. But here is another one, equally odd: Petya is fifteen and dies in 1812. So he was born in 1797, as I calculate it. Are 1797 and 1812 imaginary?" "No, of course not." "And Napoleon?" "Even less so!" "So how did an imaginary boy get to be born and die on real days, on a real campaign in the Napoleonic Wars?* But

Thus being in a category referred to as "immigrant objects" (T. Parsons, *Nonexistent Objects*, 1980, p. 51 ff.).

let's get back to the primary question: If Tolstoy invented Petya he must have had the material and the model from which to put him together." "I guess so." "Well, the material boy-parts, cadet's uniform and kith and kin—these materials might have come from memories of reality. But what about the model itself?"* "Well, time for me to try to answer your

In an earlier note I mentioned Plato's *Timaeus*, in which a divine Craftsman makes (not creates) our cosmos, using a model; we may imagine it as a geocentric orrery, a device with moving parts embodying Ptolemaic cosmology. As a consequence of this production history of a finite universe, we can in turn make a mathematical model of our world—for our live-in world is still Ptolemaic, earth-centered. The starry heavens are its spherical container, the earth (as later, the sun) is a still center, and the planets, including earth, are the arena of the geometric astronomy belonging to this geocentric cosmos, a specific astronomy within its own cosmology.

   The term "model" itself has a dual meaning expressive of my interest in the proper sequence of image and original. Model can mean prior in excellence as in "the very model of a proper major general" (Sir W. S. Gilbert, the librettist of Gilbert and Sullivan). Or it can be a copy diminished in size or function, such as a model railway.

fair enough question: 'What did I mean in treating Tolstoy as if he were reporting facts from the world of realities?'" So I'll go back to narration, to make my speech. (In real life we don't make speeches at students.)

No doubt like most of us, Tolstoy had a memory, for which a telling metaphor is "storage facility" and an apt descriptive term "pawnshop"—a large, mostly uninventoried but directly accessible collection, in part a jumbled heap with items coming accidentally uppermost when scrabbled around in. Some of its contents are invaluable, some pretty rubbishy. Say (I'm leaving Tolstoy out of it now) that I wanted to bring about a bicycle in my imagination. Could it happen that the second wheel I come on was hopelessly bent out of shape with the tire in shreds and the valve missing? Would I then say to myself, "Well, I'll have to imagine a unicycle." Absurd, but my point is: The notion that we piece together things from memory is most often false; the image comes as a whole, and the question returns. If the bicycle image comes from my perception of bicycles, whence come the images of sights previously unseen, of objects not pre-perceived? Remembered real things are generally no more constructed of assembled pawnshop items than fictions are made up of them—if anything less, the inventory's too seedy.

According to what model, paradigm, image, then, was Petya made, so that Tolstoy got him, to my feeling, absolutely right? I am posing the question in the hope that long-breathed fussing around will yield not an answer to lay the question to rest (which would mean, in my terms, that it was a workaday problem after all) but an alleviation of the fixation on this inquiry.

This dawn scene is, I'll now assert, Petya to a T, Petya's music, Petya's death. This is that lovable boy big as life and twice as natural.* What was this author looking at in describing

Here this turn of speech means a Petya-concentrate. The Germans say: *wie er leibt und lebt,* loosely rendered "as he lives and breathes"; I say, *more so.*

his great and final entrance into the fiction?*

> A question given warmth by the fact that the accuracy of Petya's
> portrait is clearly related to Tolstoy's affection for him. The depic-
> tion of Napoleon in *War and Peace* makes his very physicality
> repulsive, not to speak of his amoral self-regard. Nonetheless I'm
> not critiquing the imperial portrait. He is what he needs to be to
> make Czar Alexander I look good.

If I am persuaded by the foregoing that it can't be "turtles
all the way up," that images must have originals that aren't in
turn images, then they must be? exist? eventuate? be realized?
in some mode quite radically different from that of the images
of the imagination.*

> "Must" is not the right word; all this is iffy. I'm reminded of
> another childhood tagline from Lessing's *Nathan the Wise: Kein
> Mensch muss müssen*, "No human being has to have to," so much
> the less images.

"How do you mean?" asks our student, back on the scene.
"Well, the images of the imagination can be, mostly are,
quite spontaneous. But consider an image that is the product of a visualization exercise." "You mean of a deliberate
activity? Does it need a script?" "Bravo, yes." And—I'm back
to talking to myself—every lyric poem, all epic poetry and
its modern counterpart, the novelistic genre—all these are, I
would even say, are *essentially*, scripts for visualization, verbal instructions for internal picturing, that is, for producing
mental imagery.*

> *That's* how geometry books differ from novels; it's not by requiring
> obligatory diagrams. I have a book on Euclidean geometry that's
> without diagrams, albeit unreadable. So most usable geometry
> texts do have diagrams, set to the left, right, or in the middle of
> the words. An interested student will wonder: Are the words, is the
> verbal proof, explicating the diagram or is the diagram illustrat-
> ing the words? I think most of us would say that the more inher-
> ent spatiality of the diagrams (I say "more inherent" because, of
> course, narrative proofs are also set up spatially: enunciation at
> the top, demonstration in the middle, and conclusion on the bot-
> tom) make them the proper location of the geometry.

On the other hand, to illustrate a good narrative fiction, a fine novel, is an offense against the genre because it preempts the reader's primary obligation: to *see* what the writer *says*. This is the marvel of it: often the visualization shows *more* than the words tell. Homer is the master of such show-and-don't-tell: What do you see when you envision Achilles driving his spear into Hector's throat, Hector, who is wearing Achilles's old suit of armor, last seen on Patroclus, Achilles' bosom friend (*Iliad* XX 317 ff., too good not to be cited again)? Or Shakespeare: "Being your slave, what should I do but tend / Upon the hours and times of your desire" (Sonnet 57). Who among us doesn't see a telephone (or, late sixteenth century, a street door with a knocker, or, nowadays, a screen) anxiously attended on while other obligations get neglected?

The boy's back. He knows what I'm talking about. Me: "Here's a strange fact. They say that one picture is worth a thousand words. But conversely, one word is capable of raising as many pictures as there are imaging minds—maybe eight billion by the time this gets printed, if ever." "Yes, because words are terminally generic. Except for names?" Me: "Well, I'm thinking of the novel sequence that I regard as the great fiction of the last century, Paul Scott's *Raj Quartet*. Its non-villain protagonists are called Sarah and Guy, 'Princess' (Hebrew) and 'Man' (American)—pretty generic. The complex villain, incidentally, is called Merrick, merit gone wrong. Or, while I think of it, Eva, 'Life' (Genesis 3:20). So even proper names have a generic aspect."

But the reason Scott's novel came to mind is that its BBC dramatization, that is, a moving, audible illustration, bears on the question whether a public visualization is always a travesty. This one seems to me near-perfect. They got it right— and therefore were not preemptive of my participation as an engaged reader. Why is that? Perhaps first because such a scripted visualization does not mean to be an illustration of the novel but a second coming, so to speak, a quasi-incarnation. But, more psychologically, this very internal assent, when I say to myself: "This *is* the Raj and its English, the Realm and its Folk, the inexhaustible subject of some much-loved novels (chief of them E.M. Forster's *A Passage to India*, and you don't have to be attached to the situation to care for its people)—this very assent *converts the mental imagery of a responsive reading into a quasi-memory*, not exactly but almost as if I held these people in remembrance, in memory. For memory is the venue where beings that are gone, absent, or non-existent regain actuality."*

> Suddenly a thought interjects itself. While I'm writing, a cantata is in my earphones. Surely my dead friend, Beate von Oppen, is right. It's an offense to Bach and piety to use as background music these works, each of which, the secular ones excepted, is written specifically for a Christian holy day. For that matter even secular music (except that specifically intended as masking-din) should not be half attended to.
>
> Then why do it? Because, in my experience, be it central or peripheral to my attention, music is moving—each piece moving me in its specific mode, expressed in its key, its tuning. And since the soul has its own dynamic, including a law of inertia, which, in this adaptation of Newton's own version of his First Law of Motion, says "Every soul continues in its state of supineness unless compelled to change its state by musical sensation impressed upon it," it is natural to become specifically active, as in writing, if the agency principally called on, the soul, is already aroused. The music that addresses us most directly does just that. It is a wonder how accommodating serious music is to the moods of serious work (which includes being funny).

Thinking about the generality of verbal denotation* and the

> As distinct from the multifariousness of verbal connotation. These one-to-many relations make this question so vexing: How do words glom onto things? Or things leap to words?

multitude of possible pictoralizations raises the question: Are there truly unique beings, each a "nonesuch," there being no other such? If there were, how would we recognize, envision, apprehend them? But then is there anything that is *not* unique when scrutinized sufficiently closely? If there were beings terminally the same in qualitative description and other only in space and time, would these latter cease to be transcendental, that is, merely the conditions of our perception and turn into qualities of beings themselves? I mean would we say that "in a different place" implies somehow different in kind? Would or wouldn't Leibniz's law of the identity of indiscernibles apply? Try to say: If we counted them, which item would be no. 1, which no. 2? Would their order depend solely on us, say, on our habit of reading from our proper left to right?

These irresoluble queries are pertinent to my inquiry because now arises the question: Could one say that either of these indistinguishables is the image of the other? If the answer is "yes," then which? And if the answer is, as seems really obvious, "no," then what would the lesser progeny of a nonesuch look like? Could it have an image? It's a real question, because in the absence of a kind—to which a nonesuch by definition does not belong—how would we know what qualities or dimensions to abstract in order to achieve true similarity, that is, qualified likeness, lesser sameness; for "similarity" is a condition between "sameness" and "difference"?*

> "Difference" is Otherness seen from the point of view of Sameness—I think.
>
> I'll add to the first mention of this consequential pair that I'll be considering it from its logical and semantic aspect and bypassing its huge practical effect in history, the iota-controversy that rent the Christian world in the fourth century C.E. The Greek word for "same-in-being" is *homoousios*, for "similar-in-being," *homoiousios*, the difference being a *iota*, an i. This littlest of letters stood for a difference no believer could take lightly: whether Jesus was God incarnate, or only like God. Without believing for a moment that violence has any business mixing with belief—thinking so with a view of the very nature of faith—I can imagine myself getting quite hot under the collar for the side I had found myself on. And that's because the pair Same/Similar seems to me the most life-involved duo I know—more immediately so than the most fundamental pair, Being/Nonbeing.

I am about to set out more compactly the questions that seem to me to be comprised in the super-question: Whence comes the ultimate original of any image that is not just an artifact of our productive will but has quasi-self-sufficiency, some shadow-independence. But now it appears to me that

I've slighted memory by my pawnshop metaphor. I should broach the question: What is the memory's positive role in mental imaging? For example, are memories ever free of imagination?

We say, "Memory fails me." Is forgetting always a failure of memory or is it often an editing by imagination? Surely the latter, but memory does not always say "delete"; sometimes it demands "recast." The common wisdom is that memory is a site of much "individual difference." For example, I think, that people with pointillistically accurate memories tend with that very gift to foreclose imaginative activity.*

> Such moments of "photographic" memory are not unknown to me. For years, when I couldn't get to Greece, I used to have a sudden vision (and, I think, a dream) of climbing up a steep street on the unclassically conical Mount Lycabettus and seeing above me the graceful colonnade of one of those neoclassical villas the Germans built in Athens in the nineteenth century, and above, as a charming admonition to all that classicism, a small mosque, now a church. Then years later I came back along the same way up to the American School, and behold: There it was, a quite accurate original. But! Probably because the memory sits so proximate to the imagination—perhaps even each is a mode of the other—this memory was aromatically atmospheric while the street scene was dully just that, a street.
>
> Apropos Lycabettus, surely the most prominent natural feature near Athens, ever the poor anomalous peak, was ignored by the ancients. (Thus the travel writer Pausanias devotes a chapter to the mountains around Athens [I 32] and omits Lycabettus.) So tend the moderns to do.
>
> I cannot tell whether it is the work of time or of the imagination that makes even quite accurate reminiscences magical. Perhaps the magic is in the length of bygoneness—and of course, the older you get, the younger the memories: I'm on my beloved sled, no metal struts with varnished wooden slats, but all beautifully turned hardwood. It's Christmas/Chanukah (they melded into each other in my terminally assimilated home, about to be driven into a return to Judaism). Spears of grass poked through the sinking snow; inside, waiting for me, were my parents, the table of gifts and goodies, and somewhere in my memory were my Maccabee forebears, the warriors celebrated by Chanukah, sitting in caves around fires, about to defeat those Romans—as before long

would my cousins in Palestine rebuff the current encroachers. It is a lovely, unquestionably accurate, early memory with the required elements of childhood safety, joy awaiting, and storied glory.

What follows? I'm by family and fate a Jew, by thought and vocation a Greek pagan, by life and love a "naturalized" American—a triple devotion, to my mind prepared by a childhood rich in opportunities for archetypal experiences. Otherwise put: I'm for antiquity as the realm of origins and originals, be it the antiquity of childhood or the agelessness of the Ancients. Thus the Past and its particular relation to imaging will be part of this inquiry.

Since the past furnishes memory, as images fill the imagination, bygones are close cousins to images. That's how they'll enter this inquiry. Now I'll catalogue the elements that made me come to think, over fourscore or so years, that this inquiry is not just a niggling personal necessity, but possibly a capacious common enterprise. Moreover, though I know there won't be a conclusive answer, nothing like a resolution, still there might be something asymptotic, the way, say, the two branches of the hyperbola xy=1 keep approaching their axes without ever coming across or even together with them. So the curve of inquiry can approach along various paths, come closer and closer to the lines that issue from the origin; I like this mathematical simile, so I'm repeating it.

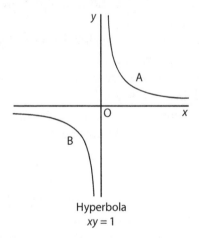

Hyperbola
$xy = 1$

Muddling the while metaphor and simile:

Metaphor says: A is to B as C is to D; the curve is to the axis as the inquiry is to the answer.

Simile says: A/B is like C/D—the geometric configuration is like the mental activity.

Unmuddling the poetic figures is a lovely exercise: they generate
quite different imaginative processes. (0 in the diagram is called
the origin. Could that mean that I'm off in the wrong direction?)

D. EXPERIENCES

Then to the elements, as Prospero says. Here are the experiences, observations, and thoughts that shape this inquiry.

1. First of all, a personal experience, the sense of "behindness," that is, of an implied aboriginality in mental and projected images. Another example: I was in the room of the
museum in Delphi that the so-called Charioteer has all to himself. The Greek guard, who had been following me around,—
could I possibly run off with or mishandle this item?—looked
at him, and at me, and said (in Greek), "You love him?" The
truth was: not him only but also a boy called Jürgen whom I
knew when I was ten, who looked like him (the Charioteer
was the elder, after all). But no, they both looked like their
type—and where was it, he?

2. The relation of this psychical sense of behindness to
temporal earliness, to the past, and why bygoneness is image-
spawning, why the past is *the* time phase of the imagination,
the place of origins and originals.

3. The fact of speech, the meaning of "image" and its use,
which implies from way back: *not* the original.* This meaning

In Partridge, image is o.o.o. (of obscure origin), that is, we can't go
behind it.

shows up in the German word for image, *Abbild. Ab* is a
propositioned prefix meaning off- or re-, so *Abbild* is a re-presentation, a secondary occurrence, as in *off*-print, see below.

4. That in human life it's "Die single and thy image dies
with thee" (Sonnet 3): no procreation, no off-spring.

5. The fact that images, be they mental or external, come
in two major kinds, one kind being the recalls from record-

ing memory or reproductions from existent objects, the other being apparently free inventions, without models visible, audible, or tangible, either in the mind or out of it. Add to these the schematic pictures, diagrams, produced by abstracting and regularizing patterns, embodied in items or incarnated by nature or craft in reality. Regarding these latter mathematicals, it's a deep, and so, unsettled, question whether they are in fact *abstracted from*, or rather *the models for* immattered things, whether they come to us by experience or from immemorial memory. In any case, the very fact that mundane images have originals in memory or in the world drives the suspicion that so must unworldly imaginaries—somewhere.

6. The very fact that humans have invented devices for recording, like light- and voice-writing (photo- and phonograph) but also have instruments like chisels and lyres for producing possible novelties.

7. The visualization from words, especially well-composed fictions, the most mysterious transmogrification imaginable, seems to have to go through some original. For words are terminally generic, though capable of intending individuals, while visual images are equally terminally unique, though capable of projecting typicality. To me this intimates that there is some atemporal noetic (intellectual) place, some possibly celestial venue like its antique counterpart at the terrestrial extremes, the *Aides aeides* (*Phaedo* 80 d)—Hades, the In-visible (*a-ides*), Un-seen (*a-eides*), the true realm of the "good and thoughtful god." There indeed, as Homer reports, the figures imaged in myths have their flittering but blood-quaffingly resuscitable existence (*Odyssey* xi 35 ff.), see below.

8. The experience of items in my world that are more like themselves than the run of the mill, while others are falloffs from their intended selfhood. These, the excellent of their

kind—we call them ideals—imply that there are degrees of closeness to an originality, since it is hard (for some people like myself) to contemplate approaches to perfection without positing the perfect being, which is no longer an instance of a kind but its very model, its original.*

> Model is here used in the sense, distinguished above, in which, say, a fashion model presents an instance of a couturier-designed gown (which is an example *even if* it is the only one) or a hobbyist fashions a miniaturization of a railway scene. Incidentally, why and when diminution increases lovableness is a topic for thought; it is a peculiar kind of imagery with its peculiar charms. So what are the effects of size in imaging? Above I've reminded myself that images are frequently smaller than originals. Might we wish to say that extreme diminution all by itself turns an image of a real thing into an imaginative, an imaginary being?
>
> A test case is T. H. White's *Mistress Masham's Repose*, which works a flipped magic by immigrating Gulliver's Lilliputians to a tiny artificial island on an English estate. Recall that the technical term for a real object that has wandered into a fantasy venue is "immigrant object." So here we have fantasy beings emigrating into real England. Once there, they turn out to be very assimilable Brits without forfeiting their miniscule magic. I would say that they pass the stress test for being properly imaginary just by reason of being 5" tall.

9. The circumstance that the geometry of our immediate life world is Euclidean. This means that we have a very simple, straightforward relation to that basic kind of imaging: a change of size (broached in a note above) without change of shape. Non-Euclidean folk (probably airy nothings) would have to engage in very complex calculations to achieve similarity and then, they being organically Non-Euclidean, it's not clear to me what the sameness of shape would mean to them, if anything. Our gift for similarity leads to a very interesting ethical question: Does difference in size bring with it a difference in character? That wonderful fiction just referenced, which dwells vividly on the relation of physicality to mores, Swift's *Gulliver's Travels*, suggests "yes." The Brobdingnagians are huge and with it large-souled and quite decent, while

the tiny Lilliputians, the "Little Thinkers" (Latin *putare*, "to think") are finicky and somewhat mean-minded.* White's

> Hegel, in his *Science of Logic*, has quantity develop quality in and out of itself (under "Measure"), but that is an argument from number, not size.

"New Lilliputians," on the other hand, lose, as I've just told, their mingy ways once out of Lilliput and become English.

10. One account of being, an ontology, claims that what appears to thought to be somehow homologous, meaning that it preserves among levels of being ratios analogous to those that effect geometric similarity, a proportionality somehow descending from a hyper-being, a "beyond-being" (as Plato calls it, *Republic* 509 b)—some such account, for all its obscurities, seems to me most promising. Call it a temperamental Platonism, it is at the root of my fascination with imaging and images and of my dogged sense that the search for their origin is warranted, plus the suspicion that this source might be not just an origin but really an original.* This original would

> An *origin-source* might be nearly beyond our conceiving. For example, it might take a lead from mathematical topology in sending down properties of images that are prior to size and shape and thus are preserved when these are removed. Of course, I cannot imagine such image properties. Or it might be a genuine Nonbeing, such as is not a merely relative negation, that is, an Otherness, but simple, ultimate, and inconceivable Nothingness. A *source-original*, however, would have some articulable qualities; for Socrates it is to be called the Good and has specifiable functions (509 e ff.), among them the emanation of gradations of images and the unifying of wholes that makes possible the founding of communities and other sorts of commonness (*Republic* 531 d).

have a character, sayable but not thinkable, of having no visible form at all, while yet being, in retrospection, somehow proportional, analogous, to its offspring-images.

11. To come back to earth, there is the somewhat startling realization that this "airy nothing" which the poet has brought down to us, that these doughy feignings are far lon-

ger-lived than I am, more vivid, more significant to my fellow
humans than I could hope to be—and certainly have more
worldly reality than much worldly reality has. Moreover,
there is that experience for which a German locution comes
to mind: *Über ein Kleines—und du wirst ihn sehen*, "Just a
little shift—and you will see him."* The intimation is that

> To be sure, the ordinary meaning of *über ein Kleines* is "soon," thus
> temporal.

only some small modulation need occur to make Odysseus
emerge, auburn-haired but now nearly bald, from my stair-
well, as he once did from his disguise in his Ithacan palace.
This experience is the sense that figures might eventuate as
their own originals.

So now to the aspects of the question: What and How and
Where *are* the originals of images? As I've said, I've already
made out for myself that it's a sensible question; I've settled in
my mind that there's a good chance that there are such originals and, hence, have obviated, overleaping myself, what might
seem to be the first question, "Can there even be such beings?,"
a question the answer to which must surely depend on the
prior question: "*What* would they be like?"* They might *be*

> This getting ahead of oneself is a feature, acknowledged as inevita-
> ble in philosophical inquiry—or any delving into an unknown that
> is suspected of existing.

but not be *beings*, if you see what I mean. Might they have
some sort of mode of eventuating, a "How" they came to be,
that fits no known ontological category, no known type of
being? Finally, do they have an assignable "Where"? In physical space "what" and "where" are usually easy to distinguish.
St. John's College (what) is in Annapolis (where)—contained,
encompassed by the container. But metaphysical realms have
a more difficult topology; it is expressible in terms of the
"one-over-many" problem: Does the realm of images, does
imagery, consist just of all the images, or is their togetherness,

their unity, even their being, something beyond their mere collection, a sort of meta-physical container?* My notion of

Somewhat as a vessel shapes its contents.

originals directs me to say that their realm is "originality," something beyond them that makes them what they are: pro-genitive in the mode of reduced similarity.

Let me end by reminding myself that besides What and How and Where, there was from the beginning the question: Are images inherently declinations, falls-off from fullness to falsity? So I'll end this section with lines from Chapman's translation of the *Iliad* (1608): He claims that

> Homer lasting, living, reigning, . . . proves how firm Truth builds in Poet's feigning.

But no, as so often, the list-thinking effort is only prelimi-nary to reality-musing engagement; it's the afterthought that matters. So here, more narratively, is yet some more experience.

Muddles differ from mysteries—*toto caelo*, "by a whole heaven." Their distinction parallels that of a favorite pair lodged in my mind. So once more: Problems and/versus Ques-tions. Muddles need transformation into the former; as prob-lems they call for *ana-lysis*, "loosening-up," and *ex-planation*, "laying out flat": the imposition of a resolving procedure—to obtain assured solutions. Mysteries require questions that pursue, quest, re-quest: the application of a receptive inquiry rather than a methodical demolition—to get, probably not answers, but surely enhancements.

All that is prelude to a very lame answer to a very necessary question: What, really, is a mental image, now not ontologi-cally, categorically, cognitively, but *really*, as an *experience*? There is no way I've read of other than the way known to me: introspection. And here's the stumbling block*: As ever,

Greek supplies the fun, as usual: *skandalon* is the word for stum-bling block. So I'm causing scandal. English is fun, too. Looking up

"scandal" my eye fell on "scarify." It's a homonym. It means both
"to make scared" and "to produce scars by lacerating the skin." OK,
but this scarring is done by a stylus and is etymologically related
to "scribbling." Which I'm doing: causing scandal by scribbling.—
Would that . . . !

albeit I'm the sole candidate to do it, I'm the very one who
can't—because reflecting on one's own mental operation is,
once again, standing in one's own light. Why is that?

It must be because mental functions and their objects are
unlike *real*, that is, "thingly," things, those met with in the
world, or even the objects of mathematics or the intentions of
words. Like-shaped boxes can really contain boxes, even very
shapely ones, like Russian dolls, can contain dolls; circles can
contain circles, not just concentric but also ec-centric ones;
words can snaffle, "intend," "be about" things. Most de-car-
nately, thinking can be about ideas.*

> This last is not what most ordinary thinking is about, and though
> "thinking my thoughts" is normal speech, if a little poetic, it isn't
> a good locution for daily thinking. I think about all kinds of stuff,
> and only occasionally about, say, a concept. Anyhow, the best
> thinking is not *about* ideas, that is, about given objects of thought,
> but it is *forming*, articulating them.

Why is thinking about mental beings so problematic? It
might be, to speak more spatially than is probably warranted,
because the container needed to encompass them must be
larger than the content. Yet the *about-thinking*, the aspiring
mental container, being a secondary, a second-degree event,
might be (figuratively) smaller, less capacious, than the primary mental object. Or it might be because thinking is, even
before being immattered by its subject, an effort-summoning
attending. So perhaps this attention is so absorbed by the first
focus that we can't keep our mind, so to speak, on the contained thought: I, the ego, technically called the *subject*, that
is, the underlying locale of thinking, interfere, in my human
limitation, with my own activity. Whatever the reason, reflection, sending out attentive mental functioning to a real

thing, turns out to bring back more definition from the object than reflection into a self-object can produce. (By "reflection into a self-object" I mean: not going out to bring back evidence from an object but turning back into oneself as one's own object.)

And so it is with mental imagery. Casual glances tend to return a muddle that calls for postponing the questions "Whence?" and "Of what?" and converting them into something more immediate, more problematic: a somewhat detailed analysis of mental imagery.

First, then, are mental images really, precisely speaking, pictures, or at least picture-like? I mean: Do they have definition in aspect and stability under attention; are they perspicuous and repeatable? Are they framed and matted, as it were, meaning: Are they delimited and do they have an underlying field analogous to frame and canvas? Are they circumnavigable, that is, can you view them from different perspectives; otherwise put: Do they have backs? Then, closer to the question of their very being, do they have thereness, give off a sense of self-existence rather than summoned presence; are they ours by *inspiration*, "breathed into us" from a Beyond, or by *invention*, "looked for and found" by us, or by *creativity*, the godlike ability to make something out of nothing?

Well, as so often, the answer is an unequivocal yes-and-no, for all three modes. The exposition of this artless answer is, as I said, from self-observation.

My mental images are somehow pictures and somehow not. I seem to myself to "see" the villa of my birth: *Berlin-Dahlem, Hittorffstrasse 8.** Yet surely nowhere in my mind is

> With its lovely house number 8, *acht* and *Acht*, homonyms meaning "eight" and "attention" respectively. So are "8" and "ate" homophones: "8 students in class today—three occultations and a belly ache."

the house itself to be found. So it's perforce an image. Yet where and how? Not in a distinct environment; not sharply

bordered or tethered to a supporting material; not clearly out-
lined, not reliably recalled; without natural solidity offering
a sense of thickness and assurance of other sides; not clearly
either of my making or anyone's sending or really existent,
that is, here and now.

Yet this is undeniable: Here's something in some field.*

> I forego here considering the individual differences that bedevil
> cognitive theories. Some people claim not to have mental images;
> they may be simply inattentive. It used to be thought that women
> and children have them; not real men who have logic instead.
> It's not as silly as it sounds, since there is a faint possibility that
> image-seers are mistaking visibility for sightless knowledge so
> that these men took seeing for thinking. The converse is common;
> though it is not so much a categorical mistake as a figural help-
> meet, a metaphor: knowing is seeing—seeing invisibles that have,
> figuratively, looks. It has Platonic ancestry: the "Forms," proba-
> bly inspired by the fact that in Greek "to know" and "to see" have
> the same root: Fid. (The F stands for the early digamma, something
> like V.)

Moreover, that Kantian "productive imagination," or some
power, either brings it forth in its own time or by my incitement in my moment. When I evoke (or invoke) an image, I
can do it with eyes open or closed. The open-eyed imagery
tends, in my experience, to hover more distantly in the back
of the internal image-field; it tends toward being more knowl-
edge-like; in it, intention, which is a thinking, is more prominent.* To summon detail, I think most of us will close our

> I'm a bit ashamed of using "tend," a weasel-verb, but sometimes it
> fits: for an incipience before full motion.

eyes, and a quasi-visual field, full of light-traces and luminosi-
ties will appear. Like external pictures, internal images can be
amended, though with far fewer entanglements.*

> Including legal ones. There seems to be case law about painters
> demanding access to their bought work so as to make changes,
> and owners altering paintings without the artist's agreement.
> My painter-friend Abby Sangiamo painted a wind-tossed willow
> for me, the one on the cover. I thought of it alternatively as my

poodle-tree and my Struwwelpeter-tree. I demanded a bird to sit in it. So he came with palette and brush and settled a cardinal where I pointed and then added a pallid consort on his own. For me it was a volatile bird in a rooted tree; for him it was a red highlight in a green picture. The episode left me with a question: When is a painting finished? Does the painter, the picture, or the possessor have the say? The best option would be the middle one, but even then: who's the judge?

The most wondrous experience for me is when mental image and real world glom, effortlessly, onto each other. It can happen in two modes. Marianne Moore speaks of "real toads in imaginary gardens" and Mary McCarthy similarly of "real plums in imaginary cakes." Or it can be the inverse, say imagined players on real fields: "If you build it, he will come."*

Moore in "Poetry," McCarthy in *Not Forgotten.* "He" in "If you build it, he will come" is "Shoeless Joe" Jackson, involved in the Black Sox gambling scandal of 1919, when he and seven teammates were accused of throwing the World Series and barred from the Big Leagues for life. That loveliest of novels, *Shoeless Joe* by W. P. Kinsella, was recommended by my colleague Joe Sachs, a sternly particular reader. It tells the story of Ray Kinsella, an Iowa farmer, who builds a baseball diamond on his land, bidden by a ballpark announcer's voice he hears as he is sitting on his farmhouse verandah. He gets to work, and one night "he" comes; Shoeless Joe appears out on left field, he and the teams, and they play a game— dreamed-up players on a well-honed lawn. (In those days the field was clipped and rolled grass.)

When I sat in the dean's office in the nineties, I posted the promise on my—always open—door, for all of us to see: For those functioning in Power Alley (not my term, but our wicked students') and for students coming to visit the dean (good) or summoned to see her (bad). For us functionaries I wished it to mean: get us the best learners (estimated not by grade averages but by the ardent desire to be with us). For the students it was meant to mean: read passionately and "he," say Socrates or Madison, will come to roam our campuses, as will "she," say Elizabeth Bennet or Natasha Rostov, come to frequent our Great Halls (in the plural: Annapolis and Santa Fe).

My own best loved mixed mode is the over- or underlay of a real scene by a mental image, an experience I will dwell on later. It is the sudden golden glimmer on daily drabness, when an image settles on a scene—the be-magicking of the view by a vision.

Is a summary of this imaginative experience possible, when the phenomenon is at once terminally evanescent and toughly there? I'll try.

If you train your attention on your mental imagery, it recedes and grows dim—the shadow of a shade, more awareness of a shape than prominent figure. Left to be, it can become quite rounded out and saliently detailed, up to scary, hallucinatory vividness—moreover, speaking in sonant voices. Mental images can be sent a summons, a verbalizable invitation, so to speak, and they present themselves in the mental field. But *what* arrives is not uniquely determined by our call; words cannot be uniquely translated into mental sights.* Effort is, to be sure, effective; internal images can

> Nor mental visions into external works; artists complain that they couldn't quite capture their "intention," meaning "the way they see it."

be modified, amended, rectified, somewhat as can externalizations.* But each realization, "thing-becoming," lacks the

> Which have their own perplexities, see third note back.

fugitiveness of the image, thus showing that—strange to say—*evanescence is of the essence* in a mental image. Not as a sort of negative liveliness but rather precisely as an inherent deficiency—that of *not* being an original, of having cast loose from the stability of originality: an image is in its very being *not* the genuine article: What keeps it going is similarity, but its metaphysical backstop is Nonbeing.

One more fact of experience—universal, I'll conjecture: Much imagery is passion-charged—or maybe feelings are image-fraught. Is one affect in the lead? Images are summoned to stir up the temperament, for example, to engage in

advocacy, often with an ideological bent: that so-called con-
sciousness- or awareness-raising, and to induce that display of
virtuous indignation called outrage, which is currently much
valued.* They are surely also used to aid erotic arousal: then

> I heard an anchor say to a guest on TV: "Thank you for your out-
> rage." (!)
> *Outrage*, "beyondness," from *ultra* plus "age," a nominal ending,
> so nothing to do with rage but with temperamental excess.
> All the raising of sensitivities has finally gotten its neolo-
> gism: wokeness. This hyper vocabulary displaces (not, of course,
> entirely) an older, more modest and more moderate language of
> decency, fairness, candor, humanity.

they're in the lead. But sometimes the passion, emotion, feeling incites images: fellow-travelers, so to speak, of affect.*

> *Affect*: "do-to-ness," the most general term for this human capac-
> ity, distinguishing it, as essential passivity (not ever to be con-
> fused with lethargy), from essentially active cogitation (Latin *com*
> plus *agitare*, "to act on [in the mind]." The old antithesis of pas-
> sive affect and active reason is too complex for mid-note brevity).
> *Passion*: "affect as suffered"; *emotion*: "affect as expressed"; *feeling*:
> "all-overish sensation." ("Feeling" is cognate with "palm," so ety-
> mologically aroused by touch.)

What brings imagination and affect together?* Surely it can

> I should register here that at moments of high intimacy they may
> in fact diverge spectacularly. I'll put it in this way: In love or lust,
> imagination is the most discrete and the most shameless adul-
> terer or double-timer ever. Imagination is licentious and libertine
> because it is shielded from opprobrium by inwardness.
> Moreover, ontologically (see above) images are beings—yet com-
> posite with nonbeings. The consequence is—and who hasn't taken
> advantage of this aspect of the imagination?—that, practically
> speaking, its deeds are deedless, its actions inactive. Not only are
> they inaccessibly secreted, they are also, often, their own end.

go in either direction: the mind's eye incites the heart's beat,
or the converse. Here's corroboration from the Master of All
Love-Lucubrations:

With my love's picture then my eye doth feast,
And to the painted banquet bids my heart;

Another time mine eye is my heart's guest
And in his thoughts of love doth share a part (Sonnet 47).

The above, however, does not yet answer the question "What makes close cousins within our capacities of images and passions, imagination and affect?" Why isn't will closest to imagination in our cognitive and affective psychic household?

The will is classically understood as desirous reason or rational desire; Thomas Aquinas, citing Aristotle, is a main reference (primarily *Summa Theologica* I, Q. 80, 82). Thus the will is not an executive agency for decision-making (as in much current writing) but our power of being intelligently impassioned or passionately thoughtful—meaning, either way round, the will has some good in mind. In other words, the will is not confined by practicality but completed in finality: it looks to good ends. In sum, the will is close to, in fact, *is* the intellect, and though it may employ images, be they vivid (pictures) or spare (diagrams), it is not led, informed, instructed by them; they are conveniences.*

> Will and intellect are traditionally understood as mutually inclusive: Will is greater than intellect by having appetite, intellect is greater than will by having insight; so they're extensionally coincident. Some people find this paradoxical gobbledegook, some of us find it deeply illuminating.

Why is it not? Why is the will-intellect not image-prone? The question presents itself: What is the capability of an image with respect to truth-telling and truth-revealing? As for the former, since an external image is spatial in both field and figure and not verbal, it can't *tell* anything, where "tell" means not only "give a description" but "tell true" or "tell false," and "false" refers to a lie or a mistake. It can *show* a situation but not whether it's for real, or whether it's deceitful or erroneous. Only the painters, or mapmakers, or draftsmen know, and sometimes not they, so the truth might be said to lie in the maker, not the image. The same goes for a mental image.

As for truth-revealing, that's far more tricky. Candid cameras and naturalistic painting are pretty good testimonials as to, say, who was where or looked how. It's mental imagery that poses problems and questions. Summoned and compared mental images will have pretty much the same range of truth values as external pictures. But what about self-presenting imagery, above all dreams but also waking apparitions. Do they reveal truth, that is, *do they show us something we didn't know before?* Here problems (resoluble) and questions (perennial) abound.

I've had dreams from which I awoke now knowing whom I loved. I've dreamed of one dead and come awake now knowing where I thought he was and what it was like—and that I was expected and willing.*

I count the revelation of me to myself as new knowledge.

Waking, self-presenting images also seem to impart something akin to learning.* But here my doubts thicken, even

I mean spontaneous, unprovoked internal imagery, not the technique of imaginative writers whose verbal descriptions, when attentively visualized, do often show more than the author tells. One more example: In Paul Scott's *Raj Quartet*, there is a climactic episode when Ronald Merrick, a British functionary, a man environed by the pathos of poignantly hopeless perversion involving sex with power, has a culminating meeting with the socially slighted and internally potent churchwoman Barbie Batchelor. She storms away from it riding an out-of-control tonga, gone permanently mad. Read it and see it: Scott tells no name, but Merrick assumes, in detail, the looks, aspects, and locutions traditionally attributed to Satan, for example, from Blake's depiction. In fact, Barbie recognizes him. She says: "I have seen the devil." But the reader already knows it (Book III, *The Towers of Silence*, Pt. V, Ch. 5).

more than about dreams. Am I not, finally, the impresario of the show? Am I not displaying my truth to me? Had I, soberly, collected myself and thought it out—wouldn't I have known?

Aren't these images illustrations rather than revelations? And
yet—there's an element of ultimate not-me-ness in such apparitions. Bluntly put: I don't have much productive imagination; I couldn't devise a plot, produce characters, in short,
write a novel for the life of me. And it isn't for want of words.
So I'm ambivalent about the solution. It remains a question.*

> *Ambivalence,* "valuing opposites equally," seems to me a respectable
> retreat from a false choice; *ambiguity,* "wandering round-about" is
> pusillanimous.

I have written myself way past a phrase, "psychic territory," at which I meant to insert a complement: the facial
landscape. So I'll play catch-up now. After all, our mirrored
carcass, clothed or nude, is, I guess, the image most attended
to, and our face is the most minutely inspected part of the
whole. Moreover in a world in which all fellow citizens who
move in a social setting are masked, the significance assumed
by that small facade of a globe on a stalk, now unhandsomely
occulted, is almost a provocation. Thus:

E. Self-Regard

I took my casebook's advice, in part:

> Look in thy glass and tell the face thou viewest— (Sonnet 3)

and here's what I saw and said: Why should that frontage in
the silvered glass be me? It doesn't seem to fit, particularly.
Well, here's a blessing: it's good enough for practical purposes—not spectacular enough to become an attractive nui-
sance, not repulsive enough to be an unsheddable grief. I
haven't any complaint against my mortal sheath, per se. It's
just so very *particular,* when I'm a sinkhole of *indeterminacy,*
and yet so *ordinary* when I'm so terminally *peculiar.*

It's a strange alienation, but quite well-founded. Why, for
instance, have looks at all, at my age? Does a person, in fact,
have looks? It doesn't seem to me that I own mine to begin

with. I was accorded them, didn't have much say. Then, others might happen to look at me (not now, I'm in COVID-19 lockdown), and I can't make or prevent them from doing it—unless I want to make myself inconspicuous and thereby become the more conspicuous.

Next, do my "looks" literally "regard," face them, these others?—for instance when I'm not looking? Then why am I made (mostly, as I said, by nature—I could effect some limited alterations) to present myself in the world in so inadequate an investment?

And what, really, is that inadequacy? I'll put it this way: outside I'm a person; inside I'm a territory.*

> Person: false but delicious etymology: per-sona from Latin *personare*, to make a continuous, pervasive noise. Same verb, interpreted as "to send sound" (*sonus*) "through" (*per*), in other words, a mask. So I'm a being who sends noises through a mask.
>
> The territorial view of internality I found, to my delight, fully imagined in Augustine's *Confessions*. In the book on memory (X) he speaks of the landscape within, an enormous venue (Ch. 8). In my beautiful Elizabethan translation (William Watts), it is "an infinite roomthiness," in which, along with much scenery, "There also meet I with myself." It's really too splendid for technical terminology, but one might say it's the grandest ever "phenomenology of internal consciousness" (Husserl).

F. Housekeeping

When you're, for the time being, living in your books, you should keep house, have a schedule, some regulations to go by—especially when it's a personal, or as a devoted Kantian may say without shame, a subjective book, one that releases internality.*

> Otherwise, we mostly *should* be ashamed of subjectivity. I mean, of not even trying to do otherness, the object, the justice of interest. I had a *very* good upbringing: I was bidden whenever I said in German "I and Wölfchen [my little brother] . . ." to reverse that, to say "Wölfchen and I . . .".
>
> Objectivity has a bad name as a demand (so does every demand for virtue; it makes people goodness-aversive). If you think some-

thing is good to do, just do it. "Actions speak louder than words."
Yet, oddly enough, sayings are quite often said because they're wisdom (albeit, canned). And here I've talked virtue myself! Oh dear!

Necessary afterthought: If preaching without certification isn't
so good (I'm only saying that a Rabbi or a Reverend has a venue
avoidable—or seekable—by their congregation), asking from
wanting to know "What is Virtue?" is itself virtuous. (Where I was
born it was obligatory to end every screed with an obeisance to
the "Poet-Prince," *Dichterfürst*, Goethe. I go instead with a grateful
salute to that Greek Goblin, Socrates.)

Rules of the House—

1. Since Aristotle's description of mentation, particularly
of thinking, as "[being fully engaged] in a work" (*energeia*),
as distinct from doing a deed (*praxis*) or making a thing (*poi-
esis*), really appeals to me, I should keep some concomitant
thoughts in mind both as suppositions and as enigmas:

a. I will sometimes think, or even write, something like:
"It came to my mind. . . ." That a thought came *first*, and *then*
the words to immatter it (in order of time) I do not doubt, but
"whence came it?" is a perplexity (a serious puzzle) or even a
mystery (a sacred enigma). It came spontaneously, though not
quite—I was in attendance. Spontaneity is a mode of occurrence in which the event eventuates *as if* by its own will rather
than mine.* I'm not totally out of it, though: I have to be

It is distinct from "contingency," which qualifies a happening that
would be likely if certain conditions were to come about.

receptively expectant, whether I am on explicit standby or
not.

The ever-present enigma here is: Whence? The English term of resolution is: inspiration; the German term, less
high-flown, more concrete, is *Eingebung*, "putting into." But
whether the spirit breathes it into me or a giver puts it there—
the question remains: Who, whence?

b. Activity (*energeia*) is describable in the paradoxical
phrase "immaterial motion." To be sure, my subservient brain
is flashing about wildly (I believe what I've read), yet think-

ing is not motion, which requires a mobile, be it mass-like or force-like.

Consequently, or so it seems to me, thinking is not exhaustible, but its brain is, and so is the brain's body.

It follows: *move.**

> Leave the phone on its base in the other room, first to recharge it after these long COVID-19 conversations, and second to induce the fast motion needed to get there before the caller hangs up, thus avoiding the answering machine. Talking to a device is demeaning.

2. Maintain faith in reality. That's not so hard after ninety-plus years among the souls, things and settings of a sometimes handy, sometimes recalcitrant, but usually quite real world. It's more problematic with the beings I'm closest to these days, the ones in books.* There the following

> I watch TV but not for reality. Self-contradiction has become the dragging anchors' m.o. (When I sailed with my skipper and colleague Bert Thoms, he taught me to set the anchor so it *wouldn't* drag: disaster-avoidance.) Example of paradox: Preach against divisiveness but incessantly badmouth the president whom nearly half of my fellow citizens elected! (Not me. I'm editing this page on June 16, 2021; still no word whether we're done with him.)

hypothesis—not dogma—is helpful. I learned it through years of translating Platonic dialogues—decades with many a discussion and ne'er a quarrel with my colleagues Peter and Eric: There's a preexistent Greek text and an English text-to-be, and standby German, French, and earlier English ones. But outside, beyond these, there's *the* meaning, and that's to be the transvestite, so to speak, to be reclothed in a new language-vestment, to be "carried across," *translated* from Greek to English, as safely as we're able.

So the lesson was, is: extract memory from beings that utter and beings that don't.* And then the residual perplexity

> Here I mean by "meaning" not that something is *signified* but the *something* that is signified, that is, not the intention, but its object. So, for example, not indirectly, "That *was* my meaning," but forth-

rightly, "*Get lost.*" (I've said this often in silent speech, but I've never uttered it. Too late now.)

is: Is this meaning-extract *the* essence or *my* take?*

> Hegel, in the *Phenomenology* (I), relying, I think, on a false ety-
> mology, identifies the *mein* in *Meinung*, "opinion," with *mein*, "my."
> So an opinion is *ipso verbo*, in its very word, mine, or, as we say,
> "subjective."

3. Here's a hard lesson to learn: punctiliousness, which means proofreading, from sensible punctuation to lucid structure. Why care, from the period to the volume? For your own satisfaction, once the thing is a book. Because if trifling solecisms annoy you, you'll go ballistic over large mess-making; for you know perfectly well that, where the matter itself is opaque, the logic must be extra-lucid.* Besides, you don't

> I mean informal logic. Symbolic formalism doesn't seem
> to pertain, because symbols don't have the center-tethered
> meaning-variance of words, and propositions don't have the mean-
> ing-plenitude of sentences.

want the meticulous readers to get hung up on these splinters of unhoned writing.*

> And they will. Give your most looked-to readers an offprint of your
> last, best-loved offspring, your long-awaited brainchild, and the first
> gleeful words will be: "There's a misprint right on the first page."

4. How to read? No approach should turn into a routine, a sort of critical protocol, yet I should look at these aspects of a fiction I'm immersed in before too long:

a. Negatively: Do themes displace people? For example, is ideology overwhelming character (except if it's characteristic that it did)? Is symbolism quashing figures of speech, so that the imaginative double-visions of metaphors and simile are appropriated by jigged look-it-up, stand-for, relations? Is the writer's ideation occluding my intimacy with his human beings?

b. Positively: Does the first sentence contain the course of the story and the last its resonance beyond it? Take *War* *and Peace*: It begins in 1805 with a soiree, an elegant chattering evening entertainment in St. Petersburg, the court's city, at the beginning of Napoleon's campaign. It ends in peace at Bald Hills in the country, where the whole extended family now lives, with a youngster in bed thinking of his dead father and promising to live well for him. The whole story, mostly of the war years, from that social evening to that longing night, is an arc, from triviality to gravity.*

> *War and Peace* encompasses seven years of war and seven of peace, twenty-four times as many pages for war as for peace. But that's not because Tolstoy doesn't know how to make peace interesting, to wit, *Anna Karenina*. I'm still wondering why.

c. By genre: Do the epics, dramas, novels I'm reading display a rhythm characteristic of their kind? Do epics peter—suggestively—out? The ones I venerate seem to. Here's Homer's Odysseus (with his father and son) about to go into battle with the fathers of Ithaca whose sons he's lost on his way home; he's only stopped by divine intervention. Here are Milton's Adam and Eve, ejected from Paradise, who in the last line, "Through Eden took their solitary way"—solitary? after that first night of wanton rather than natural congress? Surely there was Cain in the offing. Do the tragedies generically and properly end catastrophically, as Hamlet ends with a stage full of corpses? Do novels conclude with all the knots tied, particularly with the marriage knot, to wit, Jane Austen who ends *Pride and Prejudice* with *three* marriages, two desired, one forced?

5. Don't shy away from, don't lose sight of, those odd questions and problems, between jejune and extravagant, homely and suspect, that present themselves. For example:

a. Do fictions have cognitive force? When I've clued out that Natasha will marry Pierre,* have I gained cognitive value?

> If you've attended a certain dinner party on p. 64, you'll know a wedding will occur, as is told late in the book.

Have I learned something?

b. There is nostalgia for things that never were. *Nostalgia*, "homesickness" is the ache for a "return" (Greek *nostos*) home, to a bygone time, place, person. But sometimes nothing so longed for has gone by; it's an ache for a nonexistent. If nonexistence can be invested with the pathos of pain, does it begin to exist? Can imagined lost loves acquire a sort of reality, a quasi-reality? Of course, but how?

c. Are we entitled, nay, required, to query some very generally accepted notions? For example, must I assign a part of myself to an Unconscious? On the contrary: common notions, ordinary beliefs, should be treated with reverence, but expert, technical terms with skepticism.*

> Christian Sabella, a quondam freshman of mine, once said in class that "the Unconscious" was the soul-expert's device for not ceding control over *anything, in or out of* their clients' consciousness.

d. It will lead to a deeper apprehension of certain terms to look at them through their antitheses.* For example, consider

> Aristotle is always a good guide to how thinking works. Some things, he says, like privations, are "somehow cognized" by their opposites (*On the Soul* III iv). And images become intelligible first as what they are not. It is, however, sadly the case that Aristotle belongs among those positivists who deny, under many rubrics (*ibid* III iii), images their inherent, ultimate indeterminacy.

fiction through the nature of fact and imaginariness through beingness, Greek *ousia*. *Ousia* is a notion hard to live without. It denotes both ideal essence, but *also* this very thing here, tangible, visible, graspable by sense and thought. Thus a mental image differs dramatically from an essence-fraught, thingly *ousia*—how? That frames the problem approachably.

Or, on a more global level: It is plausible to me that there is a transrational kind of knowledge which is not linear. I mean a mentation that is not a thinking-out, reasoning, extended in time and sequential, proceeding from suppositional conjecture to mind-settling conclusion, but thinking which is beyond the temporal labor of rationality and its ultimate satisfaction, which is immediate; I mean intellecting, "seeing," leaping from intimations to more complete apprehensions of essence.*

> Sometimes the pair of terms "understanding" (*logos*) vs. "reason" (*nous*) is used synonymously. Reason is, confusingly, used for either level of mentation by different authors.

Then I might ask: Are the same levels evident in images and so in the imagination? Is there, beyond the sense-related, worldly imagination of mental imagery, a *non-sensory imagery*, a sort of invisible visibility, such as Plato calls "form," *eidos*, or better, "look," since *eidos* is derived from the verb for "seeing" (*idein*)? Aristotle says just that: "So then the intellecting power intellects the forms in images" (*On the Soul* 401 b).*

> Plato's *Phaedo* (81 c) hints at a clever use of myth to exemplify invisible visibility: Hades, in Greek Aides, is etymologized as A-eides, "In-visible," and is yet spectacular, as Hell ever is, from Homer through Dante to Milton.
>
> If philosophical terms that stick are apt to have a dual origin in thinking (of course) but also in soul-experience, might such notions as forms, genera, universals have their "psychological" origin in the experience of mental imagery—which would show, once more, the cluelessness of calling such a notion an "abstraction"; they're just the opposite: a "substantialization."
>
> I leave the question of psychological, as opposed to intellectual, origins of philosophical notions hanging in the air; they are less innocent than they might seem, even risqué: Does it confirm or devalue an idea that it arises from psychic affect rather than from mental activity? Surely neither—this psychic origin is simply a strong manifestation of a possibility, but it is not yet an affirmative assertion.

CHAPTER TWO

Evasions and Nullifications

This chapter will, perforce, be largely aversive—so the shorter the better. Of the many possible, but to my mind non-operational, answers to the question: "What are and whence come the originals of the imaginary images of the imagination?" I've chosen three, since the exposition of inutility gets boring quickly.*

> Perhaps even sooner to the expositor than to a first-time reader, unless he/she is a devoted caviler.

These three are the claims: 1. Imaginary images are explicable *as imaginary* by originating as a brain activity, as *emerged* from the brain. 2. Human beings are capable of "creating" what Shakespeare calls the poet's "airy nothing" as a divinity creates *ex nihilo*, "from nothing." And 3. Language is not to be looked to for meaning since it is not meaning-communicative but behavior-producing.

A. Mind Emergence

The literature concerning these claims is vast, and that small part of it which I once knew is not current.* But, as I can't say

> "Literature" has the most curious double-meaning. It denotes the very venue of the fictional images I'm thinking of—for example, it includes, *very* iffily, the Bible and, very definitely, *Mansfield Park*.

On the other hand, "literature" is applied to, say, scholarly articles, of which imaginative vividness is not, usually, a prime characteristic, and to instructions-for-use, where fictionality would be much at fault.

Let me take this occasion to confess to a prejudice—a pre-judice because I tend to bring along that frame of mind: Having done my share of it, I'm no great believer in scholarly research. It has, on occasion, made a savvy idiot of me (my adaptation of the pathology called *idiot savant*). But if any fellow teachers read this, I would beg to be held harmless for saying it. For I've noticed that, while people are praised for their courage in speaking truth to power, it's almost as dangerous to speak truth to impotence.

often enough: this is a personal, amateurish, un-researched musing.

Emergence is a wonderfully double-faced word. It is used as the term of a solution when it is equally the name of a problem. In both meanings it applies to the relation of brain to mind.* The word itself tells that the relation is unilateral—

Which makes it as consequence-laden a term as I can think of. I can't resist ranging Hobbes's fiercely pithy deflationary take on the imagination under emergence theories. He says, in *Leviathan* (Pt. 1, Ch. 2), referring to Newton's first law of motion, on inertia, that "IMAGINATION . . . is nothing but *decaying* sense." So images emerge as sensation persists but loses force; they are merely inertial sensations.

mind emerges from brain activity, but no reciprocity is contemplated. Let me begin with a very formal definition of the adjective "emergent" and walk it back to a more casual one. So here, unpeeling the thought kernel contained in the logistic formalism, is what an emergent feature is:

2. "If P is a property of w, then P is emergent if and only if P supervenes with nomological necessity, but not with logical necessity, on the properties of the parts of w." (*Emergence*, 2008, eds. M. Bedau and P. Humphreys)

1. A [P]roperty of a [w]hole is called emergent if it reflects exactly the features of a primary whole, not, however,

as a logical relation [logically] but as structured by a
fact-related general law [nomologically].

0. "Emergence" means that a complex has issued from a
   primary whole that is similarly constituted but belongs
   to a different realm of being. Prime example: The
   material brain has given rise to the non-material mind,
   which is, consequently, the reflection of the former in
   structure and function but in a different universe.

To prove this we would need a complete description of
the faculties and functions of the mind plus proof that these
align with the modules and circuits of the brain. My amateur's guess is that the brain's structure will have been well
explored several millennia before the mind's depths have been
plumbed.

The emergence theory of mind seems to be thought of as
consistent with the reduction of mind to matter, of materialism; indeed it is not obvious what is mental about an emergent mind. In any case, the theory does not respond to my
question. For if all that is in consciousness is brain-based and
thus—what else could it be?—brain-like, then somewhere in
my awareness little warm, wet figurines of sulky Achilles and
sweet Billy Budd should appear, an absurdity of which even I
am incapable.

Still, an objection might be made that the above rejection
of reductionism is too general, too little focused on mental imagery, to take hold. Here's a pertinent line: "Since I
left you, mine eye is in my mind." (Sonnet 113). "Since I left
you"—that's absence.*

> So absence does not only make the heart grow fonder; it also
> makes the imagination work harder. Nonetheless, I do not believe
> the claim found in mental imagery literature that such imagery
> cannot be simultaneous with sensory presence. On the contrary,
> their co-presence can be poignant.

Most mental images, however, and, *ipso facto*, all imaginary images, occur under conditions of *absence*; material reality, which reaches us as perception, requires de-fleshing, dis-carnation, to eventuate in the imagination. I shall go into the logic of images, which requires philosophizing, in the next chapter, but it bears calling on here: Perceptions, although they've sloughed off their matter, yet carry into our experience a message of their physical origin.* And it is unclear how

> At times, indeed, mental images can be hyper-graphic and super-sensible: say a sylvan road, a style to be climbed, a walker's *type*, yet completely *itself*, in detail. I'll attempt more description of mental imagery as an *experience* below.

the brain as a physical organ can be by itself responsible for this mysterious double capacity: *receiving* the world as immattered and *retaining* the world in mental imagery as a discarnate afterlife in its material absence.

The second forfending of engagement with my question is the now-current locution of "creativity." People wish to be called and are called creative, in analogy to, or even in competition with, the God of the Bible.*

> I learned to regard this accolade as suspect from Jacob Klein, Dean of my college in the fifties. I received this teaching (which sometimes appeared like a speech tic) with thoughtless avidity, because it could be applied ironically to some local artists whose paintings seemed pretty bad to me—and because it fit in with a serious question (this was just a decade after the European events of World War II): whether the Divinity would have been wiser for once to forego His creativity, that is, with respect to the sixth day's creation (when God made man, for my abiblical fellow citizens).

What, really, is wrong with the attribution of creativity to so-called "artists," makers of works whose primary properties are practical inutility (usually) and sensory delight (sometimes)? I hope it will come clear when I lay out the ontology of images, external and internal, that figurative art, at least, is incompatible with *ex nihilo* creativity but closely tied to copying "something," "somehow" different from the real thing—that something, that somehow, being precisely what engages me.

All in all, I go with the verse my father had frequent occasion to quote at me when he left his string beans and I had to eat mine. (Recall that Jupiter = *Jovis Pater*, "Father Jove.") He would say:

Quod licet Jovi, non licet bovi.
"What Jupiter has license to do,
My little calf, it's not for you."

or, more bluntly:

"What's licit for me is not so for thee."

or, generalizing:

"God 'creates,' humans 'make.'"

I'll say a little more on making, especially on image-making in the next chapter, but briefly here: "making" *requires* that some material and a model be given—not so "creating."

The final unhelpful notion I want to present is that words don't have a meaning except as they are used.* I want to claim

> "... [T]he meaning of a word is its use in the language," Wittgenstein, *Philosophical Investigations*, no. 43. The meaning of this sentence has attracted much comment in my own copy of the book. I found, in my handwriting, seven meanings of "meaning" I'd collected or composed. So I'm reluctant even to reference it. The approach I eschew is just a version of Wittgenstein's thought.

that it is sometimes precisely in their common use that words *lose* their meaning, generally because we're just not thinking, or in particular because their etymology, their root-meaning from way back, is occluded. That holds very blatantly for the early senses of "image," "fiction," and their cognates.

Here's a way I see the meaning issue: There seem to be two speech modes, call them invention-language and musing-language, corresponding to two opposed mental modes, call them concept-concoction and being-reflection. In the former, thinking goes "creative" in the way delineated above. It, or rather I (because my will is in it), "come on" or "move in on" an inchoate notion, tweak it to my own taste, and qualify it into the cachet of novelty. In short, I make something up in my mind and then give it a name, as did the first human. Whatsoever he "called every living creature, that was the name thereof" (Genesis 2:19). This still holds not only for natural but also for intellectual beings. We're the appointed name-givers, in some cases of objects that we've made.

The latter mode, reflection, is not inventive but receptive, and the thinking mind does not *make up* but is *made up* by the object; the mind mirrors, reflects on and from the object so as, on reflection, to articulate its truth as truly as possible. And is correspondingly suspicious of neologisms.

This is the juncture, however, at which language contributes meaning, at which speech speaks and words are not bare labels but "illations," conclusions come to. These outcomes that are included in the word itself, are (I think it's fair to say) usually occluded in the daily use of the word.* And so words

> To repeat myself: These encapsulated word histories should give us to think, not cause us to conclude.

in use do lose something of their meaning. That's why the previous chapter was heavy on etymology—as meaning-remembrance.

I've left to last what might seem to be first, the nullifying question: Do mental images exist by any respectable standard of "being there"? You'll see why I so left it: As a problem, there are plausible impossibility proofs of it having a resolution (primarily: you can't get the critters to hold still for a data collection). As a question it has *all the aspects* of a perennial: The more you think the more engaging gets the perplexity. So here it is:

B. THE EXISTENCE PROBLEM

The ever-simmering human problem, whether images are people-friendly (bringing The Book to analphabetics), or idol-atrous (diverting people from worship to art), grew bloody in the early Middles Ages. A problem of more intellectual cast, whether mental images actually exist, became a much-debated issue in the later twentieth century. It, however, remained bloodless, a little bit in both senses, especially since the term existence was hard to fix for these pseudo-beings.*

> In all fairness, it was not a term in the debate, but only in my way of thinking, which is not in the vocabulary of cognitive science but of philosophy. In fact, in retrospect it looks to me as if this controversy was an artifact of *the* postulate of cognitive science—see below.

The central book for the issue was Stephen Kosslyn's *Image and Mind* (1980) on the pre-imagery side and Zenon Pylyshyn's paper on the anti-imagery arguments (1973). A very brief presentation of the two sides, taken from Kosslyn, will do here. When I thought I understood the principal anti-image arguments, I effectively backed out (though I read quite a bit of the debate and reported on it in Part Two of *The World of the Imagination: Sum and Substance*, 1991, 25th Anniversary Issue, 2017, pp. 207–383).

What disqualified me from engagement was, first, that my experience was, of course, mostly introspective and thus not laboratory-amenable and, second, that it might have to be largely discounted because though quite vivid it was yet merely "epiphenomenal," a mere add-on appearance without much cognitive causality. In other words, you might enjoy such imagery, but you could not reliably consult it to learn anything new. To me it seemed that no impressive human experience is discountable, and that unless self-knowledge is not cognition, I surely learned news about myself.* The

> I'm astounded that for the sake of argument I would write this last clause: *No* piece of self-knowledge is ever utterly new—but this bit

of wisdom is not in the epistemological armory of the knowledge sciences—as far as I know.

positive anti-image argument was, in sum, that imagery "is best characterized as using propositional representation." I thought to myself: "and sometimes the converse."

The pro- argument, cleverly framed as laboratory science and "the quantification of introspection," was initiated, at least for me, by R. N. Shepard's experiments with mental rotation, which showed that subjects appeared to be *watching* mental figures rotate because they reported different times for rotations of different length and complexity. Kosslyn reported numerous really neat designs for outing introspection in controlled settings. I think the general conclusion was that this problem was not definitively resoluble, but that even without rational proof, seeing supported believing.

Nonetheless, I don't want to neglect one much earlier anti-imagist whom I greatly admire, William James.* More accurately,

> In his abbreviated *Psychology* of 1892, Ch. XIX, "Imagination." But, probably before him, Karl Marx (my admiration for whom is not so great) says in *Capital* (1867–94, I've lost the reference) that an architect needs a mental image to build. Incidentally, the chapter on the fetishism of commodities is an imaginative masterpiece (a forked-tongue compliment to give a political economist). Note, not so incidentally that, counterarguments not withstanding, it is quite possible on occasion to reject the opinion of him we love and approve the view of him we mislike.

James does not deny that people have mental images. In fact, as the great American philosopher he is, he speaks very positively about "individual differences." He thinks that people's power of visualization differs (as, I think, American individualism requires) quite substantially. What he does energetically deny—more energetically even than does Hume, is that "any mental copy . . . can arise in the mind, of any kind of sensation which has never been excited in the mind." In other words, all mental imagery is recollection from memory, either simple or composite.

This seems commonsensical—too commonsensical. It's not, of course, empirically *provable* (but what human matter is?). My doubt, however, is experiential. I really can't tell whether any color or shape I've never before seen has ever appeared in dreaming or waking imagery, but I know that there are sensations of never-seen, never-heard experiences. I think that is because images are not only composite occurrences of atomic sensations—this color, that shape, this time, that place—but wholistic presentations with strong unique atmospheres and occasional novel, *revelatory* elements—entities and environments. Moreover, images are often, probably always, feeling-imbued. There is, as I've described, a sober, flat, affectless, gray Sunday-afternoon look of things, and we might think "that's them," naked, bare, *for real*. But I think that even these sensory impressions are made to be passion-absorbent, and so they will come alive on their own. There is no feeling-stripped reality, or not for long.*

One determinant reason for admiring William James for even more than his lucid style (the like I've never read in a scientific paper): He says that there is not yet a science of psychology, only a hope of one. But when the discoverers do come, "the necessities of the case will make them 'metaphysical'" (penultimate sentence of *Psychology*). John Sarkissian, renegade biologist and long-ago colleague, used to refer to a type he knew as "boor scientist." Catch such a one saying *that*!

The discovery James is expecting concerns the relation, the translation of brain states to "sciousness," of brain to awareness. That was 1892; now it's 2021. No one doubts *that* the relation exists and is discoverable; no one knows *how* the translation is completed.

The Question is to be: Do imaginary, *feigning* images have *originals*? This, if anything, is clear to me: It's not approachable without a serious consideration of their *Being*, that is to say, of the deeper aspects of the meaning of the term "image"; of the behavior of the thing, an image; and of the nature of the image itself, its *imaginity*, so to speak. I'll begin the third chapter with the last, the deepest inquiry.

CHAPTER THREE

An Analysis of Image Being

A. ULTIMATE IMAGES

These two approaches are clear to me: *One*, the inquiry will have to pursue *ultimate* images. By "ultimate," I mean final, extreme, beyond—with respect to so-called reality. By "final," I mean the last resort; by "extreme," as far as I can reach, by "beyond," what transcends the world I live in. Thus "ultimate" also means what is *ultra*, on the far side of my thinking.*

> One way to think of the ultimate image: Most pre-ultimate images are Janus-like. Janus was the Roman god of gates, with a face both in front and in back of his head. So most images are in turn models and copies, originals and imitations. Not so the final image; it is single-faced, in fact, the origin of images. "Image" is here used from my point of view; I'm imagining an original.

What is humanly ultimate in the image way? Take an angel, or rather his portrait.* It's intended to be the picture of a

> Angels are indeterminate in gender though nominally male.

supra-human being, that is, it is, except for the wings, human in appearance but not in essence. Who is its original? I imagine that the painter would not refer us to a photograph but to a mental image. The painting is a realization, a "turning-into-a-thing," of that image. What this external image has in

67

common with its internal original is what I want to call a dis-
carnation, a dis-embodiment of the picturable shape. What it
has in common with a snapshot, were there one, is the material underlay, the supporting material plane.* The first point

Mutatis mutandis for moving and sounding images on screens.

made, then, is that the mental image seems to be the accessible
ultimate image, the original which renders perceptions as factual memories and underlies artifacts as imagined images. But
the question "of what are these first copy-spawning images
the images?"—that question is not asked.* Which does not,

That's true of my reading around, which acquired the curious accolade "research." I *was* an ardent participant.

however, mean that it isn't spectacularly well answered—
though in places that are ignored by the very fact of their prom-
inence, Homer, *Iliad*: "The wrath—sing, Goddess, of Achilles
Peleusson,/ the fatal wrath . . ."; "The man—speak of him
to me, Muse, the multifarious man . . ."* These beginnings

"Peleusson"—the patronymic Peleiades; "multifarious"—*polytro-
pos*, of many turns, versatile. "Multifarious" literally means
"many-speak": Odysseus is an Olympic-class liar.

are intoned and passed over, but they answer the question
"Whence come the mental images from which the poet, in
turn, forms his song and his tale?" The Muse brings it from
Olympus. I've been to Olympus up in Thessaly and the Muses
have vacated their home, so the question needs revival.*

Truth check: It's 9,600 feet high. I was only on the slopes, but it
felt deserted. All of Greece feels that way; whenever the archaeologists, the "accountants of antiquity," take over, moist nostalgia morphs into dry-eyed debris-cataloguing, the possessor-ghosts
watch at a distance. I should know, I've done it (*Agora* VII).

Two, the question "What makes an image an image?" will
have to be asked. Question One, "What is the ultimate imagery accessible to human beings?," I regard as satisfactorily

answered to go on with, but real work is required to be done, or redone, for the second inquiry. I say "redone" not in the sense of repairing work already done, but because I'm only rethinking a text that seems to me grandly satisfying: Plato's *Sophist.**

> There is no article in the Greek title. That *may* betoken that *Sophistes* is treated almost like a name—or as something at once well-known and unique, a type and an individual.

It is a dialogue of many facets. The conversationalists, the interlocutors, are wonderful in both their absence and presence. Socrates, who incites the conversation, will be absent as a participant, though present as a listener. Participating as his re-presentative is Theaetetus, an adolescent too deeply intelligent to be smart, who is as ugly—and ugly in the same way—as Socrates: his visual and intellectual image. The leader of the inquiry is a stranger-and-guest (*xenos*) from Elea in Italy. That town is the place where Parmenides functioned both as statesman and as founder of what is thereafter called "philosophy," "the loving [pursuit] of wisdom."

There are people who call themselves "wise-*ists*," soph*ists*; they are traveling salesmen of wisdoms.* Some of the people

> My colleagues Peter Kalkavage and Eric Salem and I decided to translate *Sophistes* as "Professor of Wisdom."

conversing today had decided yesterday to discover what makes a sophist a sophist. They have agreed that sophists as a class are doubly involved in images: First, they are images *themselves*, not real lovers of wisdom (philosophers) but look-alike plyers of wisdoms (sophists). Second, they make and vend images, pseudo-philosophical propositions.*

> The attack is really on sophistry, not on sophists, toward whom Socrates is mostly respectful.

So now it is incumbent on the participants of the dialogue to say what an image is—not by giving an *analysis* of its elements, or a *description* of its function (such as I'll try my hand at later in this chapter) but by revealing an *ontology*, that is, by proposing metaphysical categories, those that go beyond the world of nature and of artifacts to transcend (go way beyond) or penetrate (go deep into) the appearances among which we move.

It seems to me that the intention to approach imagery ontologically assumes at least two prior beliefs that appear to me plausible simply because they permit us to get down to work.

The first assumption is: it is possible to give a verbal account of a visual item. Surely mental images are—to sweep all the problems up in a prefix—*quasi*-visual. So leaving aside the quasi-ness of this enterprise, to think about the being of these images is, since thinking becomes concrete and communicable in words, to articulate visuality. To say succinctly what kind of articulation ontology requires: it is explanation.* But

> The *logos* that appears in ontology occupies five columns and ten headings with many subheadings in Liddell-Scott, the great Greek lexicon (until this year, when Cambridge issued a new one). The third of these is "Explanation." The word means "[setting] *out plane*-wise," and so *plainly*. Hence the very term, referring to a didactic narrative, bears in it a reference to visibility—as mystifying as the problems about to be set out in the text.

while we seem to be able to produce descriptions and explanations, not a soul has told, as far as I know, how sights, in which occur things, and environments, views that are infinitely expansible and infinitesimally reducible, are expressible in words that have definite denotations and limited connotations, or how words that intend kinds are able to spawn different images without number. Who can doubt that we do these two-way conversions between spatial and verbal modes readily and can learn to do them better and better.*

> Yet here's a desirable externalization we don't seem to have in our power. I've never seen a depiction of a mental image *as a mental* image—as an *image*, yes, numberless—all of fiction and poetry.

> But what does not seem conveyable is the peculiar mentality of internal images—which I'll work at below; for example, how persistent in experience and fugitive in contemplation they generally are, and how paradoxical they tend to be. (The waffle-word "tend," which I usually take pride in abrogating, is here fitting.)

The second assumption can be put more succinctly. The account, the explanation is to be given in terms of *Being*.*

> Greek *on*: nominative neuter participle; *ontos*: genitive. The verb is *einai*, "to be."

Being is one of the higher categories of metaphysics, the one in which Thinking and Plenitude coincide.*

> *Existence*: "Being here-or-there in place and now-or-then in time"; I take it as a sub-class, a specification of Being.

These ultimate images, then, seem to me to be describable as follows. 1. They stand beyond most artifact-images as models pressing to be realized in drawings, paintings, sculptures, and mundane artifacts (in rising degree of material presence). 2. They are the residues, laid up in memory, of perceptual deliveries from the world. 3. Thus when the senses are deliberately shut down or fail on their own, they salvage the real world in mental form. 4. Not all mental images, however, are attributable to perceptual "input," not all are holistically apprehended or mosaically composed of perceptual residues; some mental images are merely imagined, "imaginary." By whom or by what, according to what model or original, functioning in what venue, is precisely my question. 5. These imaginative images seem to bear a special relation to the past. 6. They can provide satisfaction and produce pleasure of a sort comparable to, but also utterly different in feel from, those of so-called reality; they are capable of giving pain, which betokens their ability to slip out of our control and therewith show a certain independence.* 7. That means

> Assuming that not all mental pain is self-hurt, masochism.

that our imaginative imagination turns into a problem set; it is necessary to deal with a varied inventory of mental imagery: unsummonable dreams, intrusive hallucinations, effortful recollection, *etc.*, *etc.*

Mental images, then, belong to a larger imagery class, whose two other major sub-classes are these: One, there are the natural and semi-natural images that appear on natural mirrors such as still water and on artificial mirrors such as our ubiquitous "silvered mirrors.* Two, there are the artifacts,

> In Milton's *Paradise Lost,* a still lake, a "liquid plain," plays such a role, fatal to humankind. Immediately after being shaped from Adam's rib, Eve awakes, sees herself in its water—and falls in love (IV 455 ff.). It's a wonderfully complex image-moment: Milton's verbal image of the image of a Biblical figure confronting her own image.
>
> Here's a remarkable fact: In dry, mirrorless places, no human being has ever fully seen its own face or back. And with the advent of moving and auditory imaging on screens—what a, not altogether happy, surprise was in store for us: So that's how I look to my world!
>
> More, once again, for later: Who, being (as we each are) the only one somehow acquainted with our own soul, has not upon looking into a looking-glass asked herself: Why should this small particular mask be the fitting front gate for as large a territory as my soul?

the works of art, that are attempts to realize, to reify, "make into a thing," the images of the mind.*

> I say "attempts" because, as I've said, poets and painters talk that way: "I'm trying to capture what I had in mind." And often: "It's eluding me." This propensity of mental life to become evasive under attention needs inquiry: Is it due to the technical fact of standing in one's own light or to the ethical fact of shame at going public? See below.

Yet, for all their experiential elusiveness, mental images are surely determinable and definable—have in fact already been delimited and designated. My search now is not for what is *general* to mental images as mental phenomena, but what is *essential* in them as logical beings—not what my senses tell me but what human thinking can discern.*

> People who can't believe that sense-transcendence is possible (the most acute of whom tend to be Anglo-Saxon in birth or soul) have determined that what I'm about to set out is nonsense. I agree that the philosophical buck stops right here: sense or nonsense. You can't go behind those thought-attitudes, where psychology decides ontology.

Here's another way to put the general/essential distinction. It seems to me that there are two approaches to a subject: outside-in and inside-out. The outside-in approach assembles our appearances and/or experiences we have with them: phenomenology. The inside-out approach engages in musings and collects categories: ontology.*

> Both are worthwhile and, indeed, necessary. They stand to each other, once more, as description to concept-formation; the former without the latter is head-less.
> For the categories of Being, see any philosophical dictionary. "Category" is from Greek *kategoria*, literally something "said of" someone, an accusation. Thus a category accuses its content of being what it is; it arraigns it, *de*-nominates it.

Since it is the Being of images I'm after, being has to come into focus. As it was for the approaches I might make to a subject, so, it seems, it is for the object that I'm making my subject here, Being: It can be studied from the inside out, the attempt to reveal, unveil, its very selfhood or from the outside in, the effort of delimiting it by looking at what wraps itself around (so to speak) and so bestows on it, *as* object, a shape.

There is a pathos, a poignancy in this constitution of all we live with, in, by: It is, as said above, often first, even best, revealed to us by what it is not.* What moves us here might

> Again: the pervasiveness of not- and non-, of negation as a verbal activity and of negativity as an ontological condition, seems to me one of the prime mysteries.

be—I'm conjecturing—an analogy to our peculiarly human situation: we know each other, that is to say, we know each others' soul, only by what it is not, by our body; our looks must tell us of our invisibilities.

Be it Latin- or Greek-derived, opposition or antithesis, this universal duality offers, once more, what is often our best way into an object of inquiry.

Nonbeing is what is outside of Being and circumscribes it. But Nonbeing immediately proves to be duplicitous, two-faced. It has a curt, simple meaning: nothing, zilch, nada—white-out, *absolute* Nonbeing. But there is also a *relative* Nonbeing. This category is not starkly opposed to Being as a whole, but shows itself in speech, as when I say: "I do not mean this particular being here but that *other one*, which *is not* this one."

B. Being-and-Nonbeing

What I've said so far about Being (with its implied monism) and Nonbeing (with its duplicity) comes out of Plato's deepest dialogue *Sophist*, introduced above. Although the pair Being and Nonbeing is presented in order to provide images with an ontology, the participants are much more interested in these categories than in the images in which they are to be found.*

> The human element that underwrites the gravity of the Being/Nonbeing exposition is that it involves a philosophical assassination, a patricide. The Elean stranger commits it on his *"Father"* Parmenides. He shows that the denial at the heart of Parmenides' poem (which sets out the founding of our West's intellectual way, philosophy), the claim that Nonbeing is not speakable or thinkable, that *not* is not usable speech, is mistaken (249d): that Nonbeing *is*—as Otherness, Difference, Diversity. Note that Parmenides' claim is self-contradictory at its origin, since it *speaks* of Nonbeing—and its negation to boot.
>
> Note, too, that Nonbeing, given vitality as Otherness and Diversity, also supplies the ontological foundation of America's principal present political concern: the diversity of human "identity"—tribal sameness/national difference.

So assume that a sophist is not only himself an image, the mere copy of a philosopher, but also a maker and purveyor for money, of images (268).* Then the task of the participants,

Socrates was never paid, though he was invited to dinner, e.g. *Symposium* (174a). Apparently he had a job as stone-mason, perhaps as sculptor (*Diogenes Laertius*, II 19). In the latter case, he had lived experience with image-making, hence was a very engaged silent presence in the *Sophist*; visualize his byplay!

led by the stranger, is to say what an image is essentially—if they are to hunt down the sophist, who has fled into the thicket of imitating and image-making (235 ff.). But first, what is he an image of? He imitates, images, a philosopher; he is a wisdom-monger, a *soph-istes*; the philosopher is a wisdom-lover, *philo-sophos*. Plato employs a sort of blatant subtlety—it is blatant because it is quite explicit, subtle because it is laboriously cumulative—to define the Sophist.* The Sophist

The stranger employs a *method*, "a way pursued," called "division and collection," by which the universe of discourse is successively subdivided into a discarded not-class (call it left-hand) and a saved positive class (call it right-hand). When all the right-hand subclasses are collected, the result is a very precise definition.

This result is clearly dependent on the belief that the world as thought about and spoken of has that pervasive yes/no structure.

turns out (last paragraph, 268d) to be a human producer of likenesses in speech. And these images-in-speech are understood to be *similar* to truthful speech (240a).

This result may seem less than spectacular, except that on the way similarity, likeness, has been ontologically explicated. What is similar to something is not truly the original, it is the contrary of true; it is un-true. Here Theaetetus (the student we pray for) says the crucial three sentences:

Theaetetus: "Yet somehow it is, after all."
Stranger: "But not truly, as you say."
Theaetetus: "No, I admit, except it's genuinely a
    likeness."

Stranger: "Then what we call a likeness that genuinely is [a likeness], is not genuinely?"

Theaetetus: "Nonbeing does risk being intertwined in some such interweaving with Being and a very absurd one too" (240b-c).

The Stranger now enunciates the grandly consequential conclusion: Our querying of the "many-headed" Sophist has compelled us to agree "that Nonbeing somehow is." For Plato's philosophy the important outcome is that the major forms must be entwined, related in a tapestry-like interweaving. And the important next task, soon taken up, is to identify this relative Nonbeing as Otherness (254e ff.).

Meanwhile we have an image-ontology: What I'm about to say is not said explicitly this way in the dialogue, but I think it is exactly what Plato, through the Stranger, intends: If images are to be understood through similarity, it is a non-reciprocal similarity. An image is similar to its original, but the original is not properly said to be similar to the copy; the sameness is eclipsed by difference. For the copy is a fall-off, a decline from, the original.* But what is similarity? It is the phenomenal

> Example. We say: "He's the spitting image of his father," but not normally "he's the spitting image of his son." Shakespeare loves this kind of image-musing. Sonnet 3 plays with the contemporaneous image a person casts on a mirror, an image that is co-mortal with the original: "Die single, and thine image dies with thee," and the image from procreation that renews and outlasts the father and the mother: "Look in the glass and tell the face thou viewest / Now is the time that face should form another, . . ." And "Thou art thy mother's glass, and she in thee / Calls back the lovely April of her prime."

consequence of the interweaving of Forms, in fact, of two of the greatest ones, Being and Nonbeing.

Thus: *Being intertwined with Nonbeing* is the ground of images—though this had seemed impossible (241b). Images are what they are not and are therefore founded on the togetherness of Being and Nonbeing. Even common sense may say yes to this analysis: The image of any item is *like* that item, that means it both is the same, that is to say, is identical with, *is* that item, but then again it *is not* that item in being constitutionally and hopelessly secondary, dependent: often less in dimension, later in time, lacking in vitality.*

> In Katharine Weber's poignant novel *Still Life With Monkey* (2018), an inspired English teacher assigns this homework: Write sentences illustrating the distinctions among "same," "identical," and "similar." I've been tempted to try right here.

But there are difficulties. First, Theaetetus's reminder that the problem of the interweaving of Being and Nonbeing, insofar as it had seemed impossible, has not been addressed. What is this relation of interweaving, or intertwining of forms? How do we de-figuralize this physical metaphor for the invisible form?*

> My mental image of this interweaving is the genetic double helix.

Second, if this definition is to work, it has to be convertible. It's not enough for images to be such an interweaving; it must also be true that all such intertwinings are images.

Plato, I believe, would attribute, if not to the speaking stranger, at least to Socrates listening, agreement with the proposition that "all imagery and only imagery is an amalgam of Being and Nonbeing."* Socrates would find this assertion

> The original proposition plus its converse.

to be true—for the odd reason that there are no items in his cosmos that are not images. The world and all that is in and beyond it, up to, but excluding, the absolute origin, the Good, has, on every level and kind of being, an imaged character. I am here supposing that the universe set out in the four divisions of the so-called Divided Line of Plato's *Republic* (509) is Socrates' universe—a pretty hardy claim, to be sure. Again: all the contents assigned to the four divisions of the line, starting with the shadows of the bottom segment to the forms at the top, are produced by imaging the next higher segment; even the forms are images emanating from the Good, which is itself beyond this ascent, as the Origin. Or in reverse, as a descent, the cosmos is a system of cascading images, thus pervaded by beings-and-nonbeings and their ontology.

The next effort has to be to work out terms of the language and discern the visualizations of consciousness pertinent to my inquiry.

C. Table of Terms

At some point I must ask how to talk about imagery in terms of (logical) *class*. I mean, more precisely, the following pair of pairs:

universal/general // individual/particular.

The antonym (word-opposite) of "universal" is (probably) "individual," of "general" it is (by the dictionary) "particular."

"Universal" means worldwide (whatever that world or universe might be), and its determinable least constituents are the ultimate "un-dividables," namely individuals. We use the term (not exclusively) of human beings to mean persons, beings that have the dignity of selfhood. "General" is more fuzzy, not hard-edged, mostly but not strictly defined by a genus; its opposite is "particular," which pertains to a particle, equally indefinite in size or gender.*

> Confirming usage: "More unique" is in logical no man's land, while "more general" is perfectly fine in its indeterminacy.
>
> Aristotle brings forward a meaning for *ousia*, "substance, such as real estate." The word is derived from the feminine participle of the verb "to be" (*ousa*) with a quality-bestowing ending, *ia*. Thus it means: the quality of being a being. Aristotle (*Metaphysics* VII) uses it for the kind of entity you can point to and say "*this*." It is his opposition to Plato compacted into a word, since the latter regards such sensory "thises" as precisely *in*substantial.

So disregard general/particular as too vague. Then the problem is: Are mental images individuals? (Not: Are they depictions of individuals?) They often are, indeed very vividly so, though often, too, they are vaporously atmospheric. The query is: Are they *as images* individuals, as are paintings on canvas—"Wrap each individually," we say.

Well, images can be, in Vico's term, imaginative universals. But I think they're *not* individuals. They are ontological glitter, whose deficiency in either metaphysical being or physical substance (e.g., the flatness of paintings) is very precisely their strength: They have the ability to be specifically secondary, derivative—and so to fill our world with recognizable lookalikes in quantitative plenitude. If it wasn't so filled, we would be swamped in the aforementioned chaos of pervasive, radical individual difference and the ultimate indigence of universal uniqueness, the chaos of pervasively discrete distinction.

For mental images the same holds, but more so. *What* they represent, certainly often has individuality, the feature of being the last, most specified reaches of the universal. *How* they represent as images, however, leaves them unsuitable, certainly to be individuals but even particulars. They are, once more, *sui generis*, that is, in a genus of their own, the betwixt-and-between class, composed of Being and Nonbeing, the class called Images, Copies, Representations.*

> Image: imitation; Copy: copiousness; Representation: again-presencing—just to remind myself of these illuminating etymologies.

There are words I find myself writing a lot because they are apt to the thoughts in my mind. I've tabulated them on the next page so that the denotations and connotations will be as clear to the reader as to me—which is not very.* My heading

> Denotation is the direct relation words have to an object, connotation is the very subjective and variable peripheral significance they carry.

says "terms"; terms tend to be more technical than words. These terms, however, are fairly homey words to me.

Table of Terms

Object	Being:	Vital presence (opposed to mere appearances), Categories (definite properties).
	Nonbeing:	Relative antithesis (diversity, otherness), Absolute opposition (nothing).
Function	Actuality:	At work in mind or on matter.
	Potentiality:	Able to develop into actuality; "real" possibility.
Nature	Existence:	Being here and there (in space), Being now and then (in time).
	Inexistence:	Not in the world.
Thing	Reality:	Thinghood, thingliness, class of definitely discernible objects, graspable by mind or hand.
	Irreality:	Fugitive to sense and thought, vaporous both metaphysically and metaphorically.
Negation	Contradiction:	If A is T, B, the opposite, is F. (If he's good [true], he's bad [false].)
	Contrariety:	If A is F, B, the other, is not necessarily T. (If he's not good, he's not necessarily bad.) He might be a third thing. (Tertium datur, a third is feasible—he might be mediocre.) Contrariety is less definitive, more subjective than contradiction, as prefixes not- and non- are synonymous, but non- sounds softer, so better for contraries.
Veracity	Truth:	What is so, rendered in speech. (Honesty, the desire to be truthful, is no guarantee of truth-speaking.)
	Falsity:	Falsity means both misapprehension and deceit. Thus it implies ignorance in respect to the former and canniness for the latter.

D. Intending Speech

"Words can also be used to talk about things that don't exist."
Language "is the engine of our imagination."
—David Adger, *Language Unlimited* (2019)

It seems to me that these two crucial sentences may be conjoined as follows: "Language has the capability of moving the imagination, because words can also be *intended* to *intend* nonexistent objects."

I've used the verb "to intend" twice here but in really interesting different significations. The first use signifies "putting to a purpose." For example, mother in a reproachful voice to a teenager: "I intended those meatballs for dinner." So we have uses for words besides ordinary jabber; I can think of these:

1. To bring things into being: *creating*—uttering a new sentence never said before as well as naming items never named before. Example: "In my previous life I will have invented an imaginograph that records my mind's imagery, carefully edited." Here I am, god-like, being active "in the beginning" of a scrambled time, intending to create radically novel entities, though often they turn out to be only minimal variations on current existents. That imaginograph is actually already freely available under the brand name of Memory.

2. To relieve the pressure of privacy: *expression*—permitting the "pushing out" of passion and feeling and so inviting sympathy and fellow feeling.

3. To publish our views: *communication*—bringing about commonality of information, often in hopes of support. There is an odd notion that language is essentially for communicating in this etymologically basic sense, but I doubt it, because of 4. and 5. below.

These next three items involve not only intention/purpose
but also a second use: intentionality/aboutness.

4. To *utter*, "outer," ourselves to ourselves internally:
    "self-address"—speaking silently within, not only to
    quasi-hear ourselves be, but to give quasi-sensory con-
    creteness to our mentation. It is, as the locution of
    "uttering . . . internally" with its externalizing etymol-
    ogy intimates, a many-faceted paradox that we have
    to face: Our thinking is originally wordless mind-
    work, mere meaning, pregnant inwardness, word-
    less significance waiting to be externalized. Utterance,
    "outerance," is then effected by means of that mirac-
    ulous capability of language called "intentionality,"
    the ability of words to stretch themselves toward and
    about thoughts and things, so as to make mentation
    externally presentable and objects communicable.
    And immediately, before even getting out, it devel-
    ops another duality, a self-separation: We talk to our-
    selves, orate to the inner hall, albeit empty, ask, answer
    ourselves—sometimes in our own or a friend's person,
    sometimes in an invented interlocutor's. In these inner
    conversations, even debates, are we one or two? Do we
    run from behind one lectern to another, or are we each
    other in turn (parse that!).

5. To *impose* our will: "command"—the ultimate intend-
    ing, the origin of all purpose and finality. Here, too,
    are slews of questions. Chief to me: How are intellect
    and will related? Are they one, *both* intellectual desire
    and appetitive intellect, as used to be thought (obviat-
    ing a question a reader must—if rarely—ask herself:
    Which is more to be blamed in me, perversity or stu-
    pidity?). Or is the will an independent faculty that can
    grow mighty, even—or especially—in the intellectually
    underendowed? And the grandest question: Is it liberal

to believe that badness results from weakness? Could the reactionaries have a point? Is badness, if it has a grand format, evil rather than base, to be admired? (Of course, I'm thinking of Nietzsche, *Beyond Good and Evil*, 260.)

As for the intentionality of volitional language it seems to me very interesting, because here rhetoric enters with especial force. As the art of persuasion, it is bound not only to aid *intention* (purpose), but to affect *intentionality* (aboutness), not only to shape the order given, the *object* of the intention, but, by its intentionality, to lay itself about the *subject*'s will so as to bend it.

6. And so, to *grasp* entities: "aboutness"—the most potent power of words, as I've said, technically called *intentionality*. I am repeating, but it's crucial: This is *the totally mysterious but indubitable* capacity of individual words to "tend yonder" (Latin: *intendere*), to tend toward entities, thoughts, things, or settings and to lay themselves about them, to be about them; I like to think of "being about" as preserving some of the significance of physical grasp: snaffling. The nice thing is the prefix *in*, yon, which signifies what is crucial: Words and their objects have no common space; a word is a realm apart from its object, even if the object is itself a word. We signify this by quotation marks: "Explain the word 'intentionality' to me"; I've just done that, and it's quite different from explaining intentionality; anyhow, you don't quote a concept, but its terms.

These are the uses that I can think of for words and the more fundamental, non-purposive functions of words.* Then

---

To me it follows that to speak of language as a tool is overstating a truth; unless every human activity is instrumental. It's not so,

some are their own ends, as is speaking, on occasion. Sometimes
that's not even so good: rattling on. But I'm thinking in particular of one of the preoccupations of this inquiry: fictional narrative,
word-renditions of the imagination's images.

to the point: How do words serve the imagination?

Well, first, the case already discussed, *description*. This is
a deliberate use of language; it is intended to elicit imagery—
I'm persuaded. It's hard to imagine what people blind from
birth or lacking the imaging capacity make of it, unless it includes auditory and tactile elements, or these readers man-
age to translate visual elements into the other senses. Recall
". . . that which we call a rose, / By any other name would smell
as sweet" (*Romeo and Juliet* II ii 93), which manages to talk of
aroma as visible (red), odorous (smell), and gustatory (sweet).*

> This so-called synesthesia, in which different senses are activated
> together, must play a large part in descriptive writing, when the
> author, having vividly imagined in one sensory mode, knows with
> great clarity that other senses participate, as when the gentle touch
> of vernal winds evokes the beguiling fragrance of opened buds.
>   That there are mental images of all the senses and that they have
> potency is certain: imagine on a Sunday at brunch time a bagel with
> lox on cream cheese and what the mere image does to the appe-
> tite—not to speak of more soul-involving passions. In this inquiry,
> however, visual imagery, to the detriment of the other modes,
> especially music, is the topic. Music—I'll say it again—is the lan-
> guage of Paradise, where a sonata will be a three-part essay as well.

So much for language as instrumental. What is even more
problematic in the sentence that is guiding me is the claim
that words drive the imagination. It is certainly well-observed
that one of the purposes which words can be used to fulfill is
the summoning of images: "Where on the wall of my study
did I hang that etching of Plato's Cave (*Republic* 514 a ff.) that
I've had forever?" And I begin downstairs to do a quasi-visual
walk-about of my study upstairs until I see it. Here memory-
images rather than imagination-images are involved.*

> Memory images were a great preoccupation in the Middles Ages and
> the Renaissance. There is a scholarly literature (especially Frances

A. Yates, *The Art of Memory*, 1966), but the study seems to have gone out of fashion. So has an inquiry of greater depth, that concerning the existence of mental imagery, which I touch on in this book.

But, by and large, experience seems to teach that, while words purposefully invoke mental images, imaginative images also and often arise spontaneously when they will and independently of language.* But the more pointed problem,

There is some evidence that animals have mental images.

whether language is needed to arouse, energize, not random imagery but *the* imagination, meaning the cohesive, organized, in short, the *productive* imagination, which is manifested in linguistic or material compositions—that is not so easily soluble.

We might, for example, wonder whether it's not often the other way around. That is: mental images arouse language. Do infants (which means literally "the non-speakers") dream? They certainly make sucking sounds, as if they saw a breast. Little kids, too, seem to have pre-story images. I was reading to my (nominal) godchild, four-year-old Chris, from a dinosaur book I'd given him. I looked ahead and said: "Chrissy, I'm sorry but something terrible will happen." He said joyfully, "Go on." I told him that a star would fall on them, and they'd all be gone. He said: "No, they won't." I asked how he knew. He said: "I was there." He was utterly serious, and, of course, somehow he had been.

There's adult testimonial, too. Paul Scott in his book of essays, *On Writing and the Novel* (1987), starts off the piece "Imagination in the Novel" like this: "You begin with an image . . . ," and his *The Jewel in the Crown* like this: "Imagine, then, a flat landscape . . . conveying to a girl running . . . an idea of immensity."* So mental images can certainly drive

Scott's *Raj Quartet* (of which *The Jewel* is the first novel, 1966) is, in my reading, the greatest novel of its century, which is why his testimony counts.

Re mental images as novel-start-ups: "The creation of a novel
starts with a sort of explosion: images appear and coalesce, people
and landscapes come into focus, . . ." Rosamond Lehmann inter-
view in *The Art of Fiction*, No. 88 (1985).

verbal composition.

Don Adger, recall, has the following reasons for putting
words in front of images (a selection):

1. Words can talk about things that don't exist: "At Hog-
warts, Harry Potter flew on a 'hippogriff.'" Preliminary
objection: a word doesn't "talk about" but "intend" a thing.
Query: Does the thing that doesn't exist exist, or doesn't it?
If it doesn't, what were you talking about before when you
told me what kind of thing it is that words do and don't bring
into being? I say that I understand what the author means,
but not if he's allowed to talk like that, namely, to mention
an entity and then to assert positively that it doesn't exist.
Not anywhere? Nonexistence is ontologically swampy and
whether or not you can talk about it at all is the oldest established philosophical question—by Parmenides. Established,
but afflicted congenitally with "begging" itself—it pretends
to inquire into the existence of that which it has mentioned as
its given object.

In any case, images can certainly show things that don't
exist, for example, that "hippogriff."

2. Syntax is fundamentally creative; I can, by mere colloca-
tion bring things into being. "Flying cat." Objection: Imagery
can do that too—it can attach wings to a cat.

3. Words, syntax (he means phrases), now sentences: "A
purple hippo just licked my toe." I suppose that's the nick-
name of the hippogriff above, now empurpled. Here a new
concept and a fictional world is said to have been "created."
Objection: Well, it's an imaginable world of shoeless Joes
and friendly hippos, but a poor analogue to the Creation. I
think that there is a permissible comparison—perhaps even

intended—between the Biblical, the paradigm-Creation of a real world by God's verbal command, and the use of language to effect the creation of a secondary, nay, tertiary imaginary world.*

> If it is at all plausible that, as I tried to show, the Creator Himself was working from a mental image, so that the human creator is working from the image of an image.

Here's the point: the first Creation was confirmed by its Creator as good (Genesis 1:31). Human images, however, can be both good and bad. In contemporary use "creative" sometimes means "made up, fabricated." Some images are just thrown together, not attentively externalized from a robust mental image, but concocted as-you-go; some are forcibly, laboriously composed to some external specifications. Some are even spontaneous spillovers from some internal cesspool. But most smell of the mental glue with which they were pasted together, charmlessly serviceable: that toe-licking purple hippo.

Here is a, to me summary, observation: Words intend, "tend away from us toward the entities" they enunciate. But these entities, including images, do not in turn stretch toward words to be "about" them. So images have a kind of self-sufficiency, literal *self-evidence*. Words incline to images, not the other way around.* It's probably because images are rooted in

> There is a big exception formally acknowledged in the prosodic term *ekphrasis*, "speaking out." It signifies the verbalization of a sight, usually a visual artifact like a picture, so it is a description. To my knowledge, the two most famous such *ekphraseis* are the Shield of Achilles (*Iliad* XVIII) and Keats's "Ode on a Grecian Urn," where the vase itself begins to speak. Here's the way I see *ekphrasis*. It's the *inverse* of my inquiry, which is: What original is a fictional expression the description *of*? How do we turn *words into sights*? Ekphrastic passages raise the problem: What guides us in turning a vision into a paragraph? How do we turn *sights into words*?
> I imagine that if you've answered one question you've probably not answered its inverse; the way from vision to words is not quite the reverse of that from words to visions.

both realms, the world and the mind. But for words it's Cato the Elder's *Res tene, verba sequentur*, "Mind the matter, words will *follow*." (My italics.)

E. Diagrams of Consciousness

1. Venues

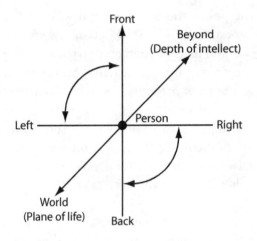

2. Times

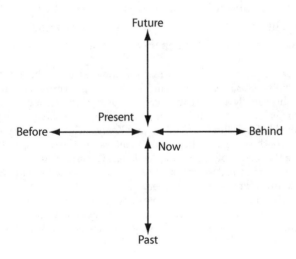

3. Reasons

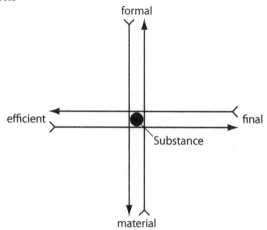

1. *Venues* diagrams a human being, person, individual, situated in a spatial plane (in nature, plain), facing front, turning his back to it and projecting himself intellectually into a factually present World on the one hand and into a transcendent Beyond on the other.
2. *Times* diagrams the two time phases, Past and Future, centered on the Now, and their aspects, their appearances, to a human being's Present as Coming and Receding.
3. *Reasons* diagrams the Reasons and Causes imputed to objects and demanded by the human intellect, taken from Aristotle's *Physics* II.

And now to collect the kinds.

F. KINDS OF IMAGES

I might say, preliminarily, that imagination works antithetically to an algorithm: receptive variability vs. jigged formalism. So some expansiveness, overlapping, diffuseness might be forgiven—not so amusing as, but perhaps ancillary to, image-inquiries.

1. Natural images: shadows, images on natural mirrors like still water, interpretable rock formations.
2. Artificial images: silhouettes, paintings, sculptures.
3. Mental images: spontaneous and unbidden, such as dreams; hallucinations, random, stray, passing mental pictures; briefly perceptual afterimages.
4. Mental images: summoned, such as perceptual memories; daydreams; orienting environments; pictorializations of music.* But above all,

   Egregious example: *Fantasia* (Disney, Stokowski).

   disciplined fictive and exuberantly fantastic imaginary images.
5. Spatial thinking: diagrams; tables; formatted writing.
6. Imaged passions: mood-, feeling-, emotion-images.
7. Verbal fictions: visualizable narrations, in turn derived from mental images and fantasies.
8. Descriptive scenes: writing intent on rendering a mental vision, perceived or imagined, with precise detail.
9. Emergent sights: "aspect seeing," seeing alternative or unintended patterns or figures in designs.
10. Impassive staring: flat facts, like an office parking lot on a Sunday afternoon.

I've not obtained this list of kinds of images from research but from experience, not from study but from reading around, and it may be incomplete.* There may well be phenomenal

That is why I say "kinds" rather than "*the* kinds." There are numerous subkinds, for example, of dreams: "hypnagogic" and "hypnopompic."

image-sorts I've never heard of. There may, for instance, be parallel- or counter-worlds, though they may be so indiscernibly identical that the problem "which is the image, which the model?" may be undecidable.

So this is the beginning of a beginning, necessary but insufficient. Of course, collecting and classifying is not the point, but concept-forming as a phase of essence-seeking is. More clearly: I need to work out some understanding of the peculiar dependence relation of various kinds of images so as to get closer to the substance they share in some diminished form with their originals.

In trying to survey this field of inquiry, imagery, I've come on many an odd truth. There are many kinds of images—that's not odd—but this is: Among all these sorts there is one that seems to me more predominant, multifarious, common, and familiar. I am presupposing here that my fellow humans live, as I do, largely in their heads.* I mean that whatever we're

> Bad locution, though better than "brains," it should be "minds" or "imaginations."

up to, mental images (nos. 3 and 4), holistic or fragmented, persistent or fleeting, are with us, not unconsciously but subconsciously.* I don't mean that we are visualizing memorially

> *Unconscious*: an in-significant term. "Un-" means "not," with a touch of reversing, undoing, something established. If you're not conscious you're not differently conscious; you're just unaware. The term is helpful in keeping a certain therapeutic trade in business: it alone has the access. *Subconscious* ideas make sense to me. There are types of consciousness that are—retrievably—below awareness, for example, most of memory, which provides the rationale for habits and tastes and for the histories of our sensibilities.
> I now recall that many years ago, on a hike with a close friend, we discovered simultaneously that neither of us has an unconscious. No one knew us as we knew ourselves and certainly not through a part not within our awareness. I still think that if I address my mirror it will know better "who's the fairest of them all" than my (notional) psychologist.

or imaginatively every moment, but perceptual after-images and incipient mental images do seem pretty much ever-present. So it is odd that these so up-front and up-close phenomena are not always the first or even the last ones mentioned in enumerations of images. Hence I think that they're occulted by reason of familiarity—that, and, in academic writers, because some much trusted philosophers denied their power of existence.*

For example, William James and Ludwig Wittgenstein, of whom more below.

Let me now expand a little on the history of five pairs of image kinds. I shall take the existence of mental images, of the eye of the mind, for granted as of now, preferring the testimony of the poet to the arguments of the philosopher. Not only does he own up to having a mind's eye, but he tells the deepest condition for its arousal: absence.

Since I left you, mine eye is in my mind, . . . (Sonnet 113).

The absence is dual; it is not only in the element of Nonbeing that partly constitutes an image and thus makes imagery a possible substitute for physical presence, but also in the human original's absence, which raises the longing, the desire, that in turn incites the image in the mind's eye. Absence, human non-presence, will be the ghost haunting this inquiry.

So, then:

1. Natural images: When, as told before, Eve in *Paradise Lost* (IV 465) awakes from her parentless birth, and bends over a still lake to fall in love with herself, she is afflicted twice by ignorance. She has never seen and can't recognize herself, and she has no notion of the existence-deficiencies of images. So our insuperable, if partial, self-ignorance as physical beings and her unfamiliarity with the secondary world of images nearly wreaks havoc with the conjugal prospects of our first parents. She's in love, but not with an other.

Black shadows have been, from way back, less beguiling than colorful water-pictures, but more helpful. The moving shadow thrown by the *gnomon*, the "knower," the index of the sundial, was the rotating pointer, the hand, of (probably) the first all-day clock.* Whether figures in accidentally shaped

> The clepsydra, the water clock, measured short periods, say, time allowed for a speech, the *gnomon* functioned throughout a sun-lit day, but a day-and-night mechanical clock didn't appear until the fourteenth century, first weight-driven and very large, then spring-driven and portable, finally wearable.

natural conformations can be called natural images is not clear to me; perhaps they should rather have their own sub-kind: extra-intentional images.

2. Artificial images: They are classed as fine arts. They come in the second or third dimension (paintings, sculptures) and in various degrees of attempted naturalism and realism. The shelves are loaded with books about them. In those I've read, reference is often made to "the way the artist sees" things, but whether that implies that this artistic view is mediated by a mental image or whence the view originated—that's not usually the question.*

> The verbal imagery of fine poetry seems to me to beto-ken how acutely the true poet *thinks*; however, my free-verse friends claim it's how poignantly artists expose their own internalities—"*self*-expression."

3. Unbidden mental images: Of these, dreams are the most copious and most studied kind. The classic is Freud's *Interpretation of Dreams* (1900), which sets out his theory of dreams as disguised imaginary wish fulfillments. For me, dreams are rather to be understood through their god, Morpheus, whose name means the Shaper, Former, Molder, FEIGNER in Greek; awake we may be bureaucrats, asleep we're artists all.

Hallucinations differ experientially from dreams in having a characteristic of intrusive, often scary, presence; the faces and voices have the perceptual dimensionality of perceptions rather than of images.

Two conditions of dreams stand out for me. Not only do they come unbidden, they appear positively recalcitrant, they are will-resistant and desire-aversive. Thus an ardent longing to see someone in one's dream is practically a guarantee of being abandoned.* Second (and this is a condition particularly

"Good night, Irene . . . I'll see you in my dreams!" a feckless promise in a convention-bound song.

evident in Freud's book), truthful dream reportage is *ipso facto* impossible. In my experience, what constitutes the dreaminess of a dream is atmospheric, holistic. The telling of it is tailored to the request; the content in words gains the clarity of a narration: dream-transmogrification turns into fantasy-transformation. But dreams are not fantasies, imaginative extravaganzas—they are deregulated dailiness, waking life among realities carried on in sleep among imagery—in my experience.*

I came across a medieval dream classification in a footnote to Christine de Pizan's *The Book of the City of Ladies* (1405, Penguin, [1999] Pt. II, n. 5): enigmatic, prophetic, oracular, nightmarish, apparitional. I can't believe that even the Scholastics dreamed in categories.

4. Summoned mental images: judging, again, from my own experience, the "free time" of the day, and all too often the time on the job as well, is kept humming by a background of mild arousal from daydreams, or is more strenuously tensed by the deliberate rehearsal of perceptual or verbal memories, say of things learned.

Hypnopompic, "sleep-conducting" images, seem to me to be a summoned imagery that negates the notion of relaxation as the prelude to sleep—it seems rather to be the aforesaid sub-acute arousal. No doubt this topic is very much subject to the dogma-destroying fact of "individual differences."

Whether the mental images that are then externalized by the arts, be they productive, serviceable, fine, or liberal, are summoned or come self-presented, is too deep as a question, too diffuse as a study, for this classification exercise.*

> Alice Walker, for example, ends her novel, *The Color Purple*, with a brief epilogue. "I thank everybody in this book for coming. A.W., author and medium." "Research" on this matter would begin by reading a multitude of fine novels and determining what the authors themselves thought—if they said.

One more observation: Both adventitious dreams and deliberate daydreaming can be an opportunity for the untalented, the amateurs of the imagination to go "creative." Dreams seem to me, as I said, though intensely ours, not subject to our will, even recalcitrant to it. Thus they are one more type of testimonial to our very limited (and so to be the more cherished) autonomy.

Daydreaming, on the other hand, is up to us. Though waking dreams are mostly devoted to the production of pleasure (but also to self-torture, the perverse pain-pleasure of masochism), they can be shallow, disordered, and fanciful or serious, coherent, and realistic. The latter, inner story-telling, is actually a prelude to worldly activity: "In Dreams Begin Responsibilities" is the title of a pertinent story by Delmore Schwartz.*

> 1937; to be sure, the story is presented as a dream, but it feels more like one of those 'twixt sleep and 'wake dawn dreams that are nearly daydreams. In this enigmatic story, the dreamer, a young man, is watching his parents' courtship and trying to interfere with it in contradictory ways. He wakes up and, this being a story whose title is essential to its interpretation, we know that he now knows that he has an—unspecified—obligation to fulfill.

5. Spatial thought: I am thinking especially of geometric diagrams. When students demonstrate a proposition of geometry on the board, they seem to do it, so to speak, in two spirits. Some students are clearly copying a memorized mental image. When they've got it out onto the board, they inspect

it, add auxiliary lines, and point to it: "Behold," and we're to think out the verbal proof they should be telling us. Or the reverse, while they're reciting the proof, they're drawing the lines. It's never quite clear whether in either case it's a work of reproductive memory or of actual thinking.*

> Well over half a century ago I had in my class a young saffron-garbed monk on leave from his monastery in Tibet. He had mastered, with my help, an early Euclidean proposition: The base angles of an isosceles triangle are equal (I 5). It is known as the Asses' Bridge—either because fools can't make it across or because any fool can. But it was a lost cause to persuade him that, knowing this proposition, he didn't know "geometry"—and I began to see his point: having mastered a paradigm, why did he need further instances? Because, I came to see, the proof is *both* a certification and an exposition of the matter, and thus an invitation to proceed further with secured *and* material learning (Greek *mathematika*, "what's learnable")—or, assured of its possibility, to leave it to its own devices after sampling it to or through I 5. Just so did Vico, who, in his *Life*, tells how he "penetrated as far as" I 5. Vico invented a science of the imagination based on a gripping concept (a rare occurrence), the notion of the *imaginative universal*; he will show up later in this inquiry.

The deepest explanation of diagrammatic imagery is to be found in Kant's *Critique of Pure Reason* (B 33 ff.). In brief: The conditions of possibility for our dwelling in a world of which we may have a science are built into our cognitive constitution. It is dual, consisting of a field receptive to the manifold deliveries of sense and a set of concepts, activities of the understanding. The field, although receptive, is not passive; it has two *a priori* capacities, that is, aboriginal "intuitions," that shape all its matter. Whatever we experience is both *spatial*—its parts *are simultaneously there and outside each other, and we* face *them, as outside of us*, as our other, and *temporal*—its parts are *internal to each other, and we are them, as framing our self-consciousness, as our self*.* The

> Of course, this, though probably not incorrect, is too curt for comfort. Don't snicker: Kant is a lucid and accessible writer; see for yourself.

paragraphs, however, that are to my point are also arguably the center of Kant's first *Critique*. They are called "Concerning the Schematism of the Pure Concepts of the Understanding" (B 176–187). They have a simple but crucial task. There are two very diverse cognitive capacities, sensing and understanding. They must be got together to produce a cognition.

The schematism named above is "a hidden art in the depths of the human soul . . ." (B 181). As a picture is the product of the sensory imagination, so the schema is the analogous product (Kant calls it a "monogram") of the pure, pre-experiential imaginative power, that hidden art in our deepest soul. This "transcendental" imagination has the—unexplained—ability to meld sensing and thinking. The actual schematism is a table-like setting out of the involvement of the receptive intuitions of time and space with the conceptual categories of the understanding in the pure realm of the deep imagination.

One example will suffice, since it bears immediately on the question of how mathematical diagrams that illustrate thinking, the apprehension of spatiality, are possible.*

> Oddly: Kant carries out the melding of time and concepts in some detail but refers only in passing to the spatialization of thought (or the conceptualization of space—it is a symmetrical relation). In Heidegger's *Being and Time* this primacy of time comes to its culmination.

So Kant points out that no sensory picture can be adequate to the concept of a triangle (B 180).* The schematic, the quasi-sensory,

> Because 1. every diagrammatic triangle is not *any* triangle but *this* triangle, and 2. every diagram consists of lines that are not geometric lines; for "A line is breadthless length" (Euclid I, Def. 2).

the true diagrammatic triangle, exists only in thought and becomes quasi-visual by reason of the transcendental (cognitively primal) imagination and its magic.

This is spectacular. Something terminally inexplicable comes about all the time—words generate congruous images, mental or material, and pictures invoke concordant words.

And the philosopher who knows how we construct our en-
vironing and our inner world doesn't know how *that* is
done—*and says so.** He does, however, supply some enabling

> I think I know of several fatal dissonances in Kantian philosophy,
> but I can't think of a more personally trustworthy thinker since
> Socrates.

conditions. The enabling field for geometry, transcendental
space, is not, as I said, a supine extension; instead it has inherent receptivities. It allows inscription; the understanding may
draw on it as on a tablet. Moreover it imposes inherent positive characteristics on these inscriptions. For example, it is
Euclidean with respect to parallelism: there are equidistant
straight lines that thus run to infinity without diverging or
crossing—and infinity itself is such an inherent feature.*

> I think that when Kant, now surely among the angels, learned, a
> little more than a score of years after his death, that a Noneuclid-
> ean, consistent geometry lacking parallelism had just been discov-
> ered, he would even then have grieved for a great loss: that of the
> human imagination—for a straightforward image (same shape,
> different size; in sum, similarity) depends on the Euclidean Par-
> allel Postulate (Euclid I, Post. 5; VI). And mental images, however
> elusive, do seem to preserve shape. How else would we recognize
> them, or say to ourselves "I can't get it right, it won't come into
> focus," and "Grow large! Now diminish!"

A final thought about diagrams that issues in a really interesting problem: trying to understand areas. If diagrammatic
lines give a (closed) figure its form, its area (or volume) might
be said to give it its matter. The reason this way of speaking
makes sense is that area, just like the stuff, the material out of
which things are made, is fungible. I mean that you can trans-
form it into different shapes, separate or aggregate it, while
preserving its amount, just as with rolled-out dough. Probably the best known geometric example is the Pythagorean
Theorem (Euclid I 47) which shows that (and how) you can
meld the squares built on the sides of a right triangle into one
sum-square on the hypotenuse (the long side, subtending the

right angle). And you can do the same thing for circles; you can "square" them—if you're satisfied with just approaching area equality very closely, as closely as you (or your calculator) have patience for reiteration.

A next—I'd call it a question now—would be: Is the area delineated in a closed figure somehow different from the field of all figures? Although naive beholders (like children, who tend to cover the inside of figures they draw with back-and-forth scribbles) may have a feeling that it must be so, yet it can't be. The name of the field, without and within the figure, is *space*, or more descriptively *extension*, "what tends out, away from itself"—within which space, *places* (Greek *topoi*) containing locations, precise positions, are seated, the contents of which can be matter of a different sort, physical material. The diagram below displays my subdivisions of a spatiality for present purposes. It is a lay topology (a "study of a place").

And that raises a third issue: Kant's understanding of a cognitive constitution that makes geometry possible required the introduction of a productive imagination, which inscribed its

A Topology for the Imagination

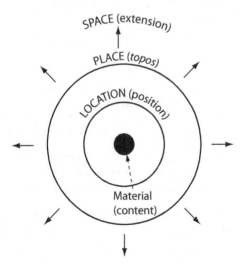

figures in an experience-yielding field that has some intrinsic
active characteristics of its own. Chief among them would be a
capacity for similarity, for imaging (usually called "Euclidean
geometry"). The relevance of this situation to my exposition is
that this inherent activity of the field is probably attributable
to the same strange quasi-matter that explains, no, *is*, area.

To my delight, I found myself anticipated by Proclus who,
in latest antiquity (mid-fifth century C.E.), wrote a *Commentary on Euclid's Elements*. In his philosophical prologue
(he is an ardent Neoplatonist) he brings together, by way of
explaining the nature of geometric objects, practically all the
terms with which I am concerned in this inquiry. To my mind,
he solves the problem here, namely how area can have several attributes of materiality when geometry is thought of as
abstracted from body: he brings in *a specifically mathematical matter, an imagistic matter* (¶ 50–56).

Because Proclus wants to stay in the wake of Plato, he tries
to move human effort from imagination (*phantasia*) to intellect (*nous*), from images to forms (¶ 55).* Proclus introduces

> For Plato this means *superseding mathematics* and its images and
> formulas to rise to the notion of forms, from *eikones*, "likenesses"
> to *eide*, invisible "looks" (*Republic* 510b, third to fourth part of the
> Divided Line, Socrates counting upward).
>
> Aristotle has a way of circumventing the imagination as well: by
> *renaming*, according to Proclus, who claims that the much debated
> *nous pathetikos*, "affectable intellect," mentioned only once (in *On
> the Soul*, 430 a 24), is really the imagination. Proclus points out that
> the very phrase is a contradiction in Aristotelian terms, since the
> intellect is in no way "pathetic," affected, "suffering" in the sense
> of having things happen to it. On the contrary, it is through and
> through active; indeed, it is activity itself, and as such, the cosmos's
> divinity, its final *unmoved* mover. For full activity is, for him, non-
> material motion. It is an inherently paradoxical thought, which is
> necessary to salvage common sense. I'm bordering on the oracular
> here, but given time, time, time, I'd try to make it plausible.

a new notion to supplement the matter of sensory things, that
imagistic matter: *hyle phantaston*, "matter of imaged objects."
He describes it thus:

[T]he other is imaginary, as existing in the plurality of pictures in the imagination. For imagination, both by virtue of its formative activity and because it has existence in and with the body, always produces individual pictures that have divisible extension and shape, and everything that it knows has this kind of existence (*Proclus: A Commentary on the First Book of Euclid's Elements*, Translated with Introduction and Notes by Glenn R. Morrow, Princeton University, 1992, p. 41).

Proclus explains that the imagination has these features because it has a *central position* in cognition, between the senses that draw in an incoming outside and the intellect that reaches for what is beyond the physical world. Accordingly, its objects come from life and have spatial features: division (sectability), extension (spatiality), and figure (shapeliness). Particularly in the multitude and magnitude of each kind it expresses its reference to the sense-world, except that all its pictures are *free of bodily matter*. But since its kind of cognition, its thought, is pictorial, it does require matter, an intelligible yet imagination-affectable matter of its own—that the imagination itself provides—the *hyle phantaston*, "matter of imaged objects."

The particular figures of and on this image-receptive stuff are, *ipso facto*, sometimes similar; the same in shape but possibly different in size: imagine a set of concentric circles.

This long report on a very thoughtful mathematician has its justification in the appealing invention? discovery? of *imagistic matter*. Since I'm about to turn to images in passion, here's a transitional observation. The image-receptive matter seems to me to play a role in accounting for a wonderful, life-augmenting, tedium-dissolving capability we have: that of experiencing distance-, absence-, non-existence-overcoming, in a word, imagined love. For the passion of love, like all passions, requires matter in which to invest itself. If no embodiment were available, it would flutter around as does the soul of an unburied dead person about its unreceptive resting place.

So the imagined matter confirms the imagination in its centrality—between Being and Nonbeing, as they show up concretely as presence and absence and join as absent presence or present absence—as life lived imaginatively.

6. Imaged Passions: As diagrams exhibit a de-fleshed, barebones austerity, passions—they too can be imaged—appear as the very opposite of these linear whited sepulchers.* Aristotle,

> I may seem just to have countermanded what I so positively set out just above—that diagrams too have their matter, their flesh, so to speak. My excuse: I'm here reverting to what we commonly think and say.

in *On the Soul*, says something at once mystifying and very much to my purpose. He speaks of the passions (*pathe*) as "reasons immattered" (*logoi enhyloi*, 403 a 25).* I think that

> The whole sentence bears 1. a damping and 2. a fascinating translation. 1. "The affections [of the soul] are immattered laws." Here Aristotle is saying that psychic properties have physical explanations. And 2. "The passions are immattered thoughts." Here Aristotle would be explaining why we can apply speech to our feelings. It's a real question because, on the face of it, our feelings, so ultimately our "ownmost" (as the Germans say, *eigenlichste*), so unutterably particular, so terminally private, are very defectively communicable—the more intense, the less lucid.
>   Pascal says in his *Pensées*: "The heart has its reasons, which reason does not know" (277). To me that seems a close parallel to "immattered reasons," albeit in a Christian context.

he means that our passions, our concentrated feelings, are, far from being irrational (*aloga*), thought-imbued. The poet, embroiled in love, might regard thinking passion as a contrary-to-fact condition: "*If* the dull substance of my flesh were thought, . . ." (Sonnet 44). But suppose the philosopher, for once, knew better, what would follow? Our passionate attachments would have the staying power, the stability, would evince the purposefulness, the finality, would show the cause-clarity and reason-fraughtness that belong to the involved intellect.

Suppose then, that reason not only can move, even control,

passion; indeed, it is unintelligible that it shouldn't. That's what I believe—not so much because Aristotle seems to have it right when he says that human beings are thoughtful animals and that even our desires and, in general, our appetites somehow have reason (*Nicomachean Ethics* 1102 b 31). For he is speaking ethically, in terms of controlling our conduct. But I am thinking of what he himself has encapsulated in his phrase for human affect, "immattered reason"—that our passions, feelings, emotions are shot through with rational intention, purposefulness, calculation, judgement, and wit. To this, Shakespeare's Sonnets, which I've had recourse to so often, bear best witness. In them, subtle intellect and helpless love are fused. Thus Fulke Greville, too, rightly addresses Love, the Divinity, on having "married Reason with Affection" ("You Little Stars").

So thinking may impute thought to passion. There is an inverse imposition that is commonly regarded as fallacious, the so-called "Pathetic Fallacy." This is the name—"pathetic" here means "concerned with passion"—given to a propensity people have for investing the natural environment with a pathos of which it is not capable, by reason of lacking personhood and its cognitive constitution. Thus it is a term of critique, mostly applied to poetical expressions.

I don't, however, follow this self-confident condemnation of phrases, such as a "lowering sky," which implies that the sky had a surly, ominous look. I would agree that the sky probably is not in fact threatening us, meaning that it is not itself angry. At least I suppose not. I am inclined to think it is not incarnate enough to have a soul such as harbors *pathe*, feelings.

Yet it seems to me a fact that it can have that look, and it seems far more interesting to explain how it can appear irate than to zap a locution.* There must be something about a

---

A recent experience—a thunderstorm, rumbling and grumbling way off, then overhead, now clattering at me: "Now really listen. I'm trying to tell you something."

darkling sky or, for that matter, the plain beneath it, in a
world that has no light, "nor certitude, nor peace, nor help
for pain;/And we are here as on a darkling plain" (Matthew
Arnold, "Dover Beach")—there must be some capability this
sky has for lowering at me, or the plain for keeping armies on
it uninformed: "Where ignorant armies clash by night." So it
is, to my mind, more interesting to ask what beings that are
capable of articulate immattering (those *logoi enhyloi*) have
in common with beings like skies and plains than to mask the
strangeness of it by false falsification.* There is help: defense

> To me, it is a rule: Where several accounts are given of a phenom-
> enon, try to prefer the one which leaves the subject with the most
> inviting depths to be penetrated, that is, which bestows on it the
> most interest. For apathetic boredom, a sense of universal in-sig-
> nificance, is the most dangerous, and intense interest is the most
> salvific of all passions—an insight dear to me and to be pursued
> below.
>   *The* attractor of interest is penetrable depth, that spatial third-
> dimensional metaphor for what is surely non-spatial and a-dimen-
> sional. Here is a telling and apt experience with my usually so
> trusty and measured Roget's *Thesaurus* (Greek: "treasure-house"),
> when thought outpaces language and I need the word for my
> shaped notion. Look up "depth": You will find reference to physical
> depth, the kind divers leap into, in dark type and to mental depth,
> the kind human minds penetrate, in light type. But there's no ref-
> erence for object-depth, for the profundity of *things*—which must
> surely sometimes exist if minds are to work their way into them.
> Which brings me back to the text—to the problems and the ques-
> tion associated with the investment of apparently soulless nature.

for pathetic imputation from the best of sources, Alexander
von Humboldt, the explorer and naturalist.* Humboldt, in the

> My quotations and paraphrases come from Sarah Dry's *Waters of
> the World* (2019, pp. 73–76).

face of effects I, too, cherish in memory, asks exactly my question: "What was it that gave scenes like these [he is recall-
ing the Cordilleras, the mountain range stretching down the
western Americas, and of Tenerife, one of the Atlantic Canary
Islands] the ability to move a man's heart, to spark the 'cre-

ative powers of a man's imagination'"? Especially the varying motions of nature gave him "the eerie sense that nature was imbued with emotion—his own emotion." Humboldt himself writes:

> Impressions change with the varying movements of the mind, and we are led by a happy illusion to believe that we receive from the external world that with which we have ourselves invested it.

Humboldt has mitigated "fallacy" to "happy illusion," and so bypasses the problem of our pathos and our willing collusion and leaves the question of nature's capacity for rousing feeling simply unregarded. Is it an askable question and should it be asked? Yes and yes.

So the question is not about our psychological capability for being touched by that which is not itself responsive to feeling. Not that it isn't a deeply engaging question—why we, in fact, have thing-love.* But my present question is rather what

> Perhaps it shouldn't be that surprising. Don't we torture ourselves with that peculiarly adherent love for those that are constitutionally unresponsive: "They that have pow'r to hurt and will do none, / That do not do the thing they most do show" (Sonnet 94)?

features in nature or things makes them lovable, such that our arousal is not a bad fallacy or even a happy illusion.

I must be looking for a feeling-analogue, for something that models responsiveness without being responsive. Or, perhaps, something that pagan Aristotle and Christian theologians know all about: that ultimate object of love that attracts us precisely because of its self-completeness and consequent unresponsiveness *in kind*.*

> Aristotle: "unmoved mover" (*Metaphysics* XII 7) and Thomas Aquinas: God's "love without passion" (*Summa Theologica* Q. 20, Art. 1, Reply to Obj. 1).

7. Verbal fiction: This is the kind central to my inquiry, because epics, and their modern successors, novels, are page-

by-page incitements to visualizing that, in turn, generates mental imagery, and it is its origin I'm asking about.*

> The immediate reply is: I've already answered the question when I say that the words in sentences and paragraphs "generate" the images. Careful attention to the words, for us usually written, is, of course, the condition of images eventuating. But that the words are not a sufficient condition is shown by the fact that each single instance of language can spawn indefinitely many recognizable depictions in any one or in many people.

It is famously said (I can't recall by whom and about what, but I'll supply my own subject) that fictions require "the willing suspension of disbelief." That demand shows them to be antithetical to philosophy. For fictions are make-belief while philosophy is warrant-belief. The condition of making a reader believe a story is surely precisely that he should give up doubt and give himself over to trust in the tale.*

> That trust isn't, of course, blind faith in its worldly factuality. It is more the willing induction into a made-up realm.

Warrant-belief, as required in philosophizing (in my understanding, of course) is the sustaining activity, opposed to novel "making up," of undergirding, grounding the opinions we held in the beginning. For I am persuaded that where we start, there we end—with this invigorating difference: When our baseless opinions are grounded, planted, rooted, they acquire ramifications and (metaphorical) footings, and, without losing the vigor of the experienced instances, acquire the depth of intellectual insight.*

> This vision is an amplification of Socrates' view that philosophizing is the trans-formation of baseless opinion into well-founded knowledge. Here's an example from the Platonic dialogue *Laches*: Good soldiers may be of the opinion that courage is fearless steadfastness in the face of danger; thoughtful warriors will know that it is knowing what is truly to be feared, namely doing wrong, and that fleeing before it nimbly is actually true courage.

A reader might well wonder: Philosophizing concerns itself

with imaging. Is imaging, and especially imagining, ever, in turn, about thinking? The more illuminating hypothesis says *no*. These two capacities, of course, have relations, but they're not reciprocal. First there is the one/many relation of word to picture, thinking to seeing, just mentioned.* Then pictures

> To be sure, one image, be it mental or material, could cause several verbal descriptions, if the describer produced imaginative add-ons. But if he stuck strictly to the reportable facts, his account would be pretty nearly anyone else's. For example, on being shown the picture of a certain memorable tea party (there is such a picture) every competent person asked to describe it would say early on: "There were four characters at the table, two animals and two humans, a hare, a dormouse, a hat-wearer, and a girl, Alice."

differ from thoughts in having no positive way of being negative, of directly expressing denial and absence; they certainly cannot *show* Nothing. A picture could *imply* absence; it might be *interpreted* as negating; it might even *intimate* Nothing—but it cannot *display* Nothing.*

> In the tea party picture there are five unoccupied place settings (no chairs). That might imply expected yet absent guests, but you would have to use conjectural language, not description, to claim it.
>
> The picture seems to negate the rude tea party's cry to late-coming Alice: "No room"—but that's only because its figures are said to speak; moreover, there actually is room for five more—the picture asserting its positivity.
>
> Finally, the picture, one might argue, does show a nothing: It shows nothing of all the world that's beyond the picture. But then, we—not the picture—might argue that that's precisely what it really hasn't got room for: Nothing! Makes your head spin, does Lewis Carroll.

But above all, pictures are not, as are words, *about* a matter: A sentence, as I've said, can lay itself about, seize hold of, *intend* a matter; it has the feel of an activity, particularly when the matter is (as they used to say) proposing itself to the word to be snaffled.* We do say that pictures show their subject

> Would-be guests at English country houses were said to "propose themselves" for the weekend—and stay through Tuesday.

or even announce it in an engraved bronze tag: Rembrandt van Rijn, "Aristotle Patting Homer on the Head." But surely "shows" is figurative here, since "to show" is an action verb. A picture doesn't show anything; it doesn't display anything any more than a showroom can have an intentional target except as a manner of speaking. The picture *is* the show. Words, however, are essentially intentional; they intend a matter that they are about.

There is a particular kind of speech that tries hard to *be* a picture. Novels often contain long passages trying to convey a dawn in all its magical sensory modes: breezy, fragrant, sonorous, and above all, variably tinted with the rising sun.* I am

> You can tell their writers have put much effort into these scene-evoking words, more perhaps than into the bravura high points of their story. They thicken the effect with copious similes, sometimes piled on by threes. The most flagrant example I know takes up the first page-and-a-half of Virginia Woolf's *The Waves*, a description of the sea, beginning just before sunrise, printed in italics. Sample: "Gradually the dark bar on the horizon became clear as if the sediment in an old wine bottle had sunk and left the glass green. Behind it, too, the sky cleared as if the white sediment there had sunk, or as if the arm of a woman couched beneath the horizon had raised a lamp and flat bars of white, green and yellow spread across the sky like the blades of a fan. Then she raised her lamp higher and the air seemed to become fibrous and to tear away from the green surface flickering and flaming in red and yellow fibres like the smoky fire that roars from a bonfire."
> Oh my!

making a point of these descriptive efforts because, as I said, in them the word is trying to become view, to become sight not in the sense of acquiring vision but of gaining visibility.

I cannot say that this may never be—because it ever was: the production of mental images according to a verbal script. Also I need to remind myself that visualization is the minor mystery, perhaps resoluble into a set of problems. The real question, in these pages, is: Visualizing is summoning images deliberately: Whence?

When these images eventuate at my bidding, it is in accordance with a script, but scripts are sightless; they are prompts but from a sightless realm, that of language.*

> Someone might interject: "Don't we *see* the words on the page?" Yes, but written language is a *prompt* for spoken speech; it is rarely a picture. In fact, the only word I can think of that is a picture is the "O" that expresses surprise.
>
> Recall that in antiquity written texts were read aloud by servants. Augustine reports, evidently intrigued, how Bishop Ambrose read to himself silently (*Confessions* VI 3). Many of us, unless we're reading bumf (*i.e.*, bureaucratic prose), still vocalize silently—certainly if it's poetry.

I've made two categories of mental images: spontaneous, self-appearing and summoned, deliberate.* As ever, these classes

> "Self-appearing" should be a dictionary word (it's not among the many "self-..." in the Oxford English Dictionary). It is analogous to the thought-provoking term "self-evident," which seems to claim that something is so, simply by being outstandingly see-able. So, if something projects itself all by itself into appearance, it must be somehow dynamic, have vitality. And that seems to be true of mental images. They can, as Alice Walker's are, be thanked for coming: "figures of delight" (Sonnet 98).
>
> *Manifest*, "hand-struck," palpable, does a similar job for touch. Why isn't such self-exposure attributable to beings: "He is always (or never) self-evidently self-evident, that ...."? I know people and things of both sorts.

get tangled and melded, particularly so in the case of mental images, in general and in particular.*

> I feel impelled to explain myself, to say something (though it's probably obvious anyhow) about my continual checking and countermanding of categorical claims. Far from being the consequence of indeterminacy, skepticism or any other sort of mental waffling is, I think, the shadow of doubt that should go along with all assertions so as to keep open the possibility of further truth-seeking. The "shadow of a doubt" rule, in preventing a guilty verdict on a charge that is, at that moment, undecidable, implies that it is possible, in better conditions, to do better. So that's what terminal relativists foreclose.

In general there are writers who have a sort of dual genius—for vividly detailed visions and adequate descriptive words. Arguments against the precedence of imagery (often part of a claim that it doesn't exist to begin with) assert that there are writers of a second sort. They simply produce verbiage, unguided by any envisioned idea, any preceding mental shape, hence by any images—thus obviating the distinction between "summoned" and "spontaneous"—neither.*

> This "verbiage" would turn into ultimate pure *logos*, that is, terminally rational speech, if a fiction could be written that had no sensory reference in it. Not even Hegel's *Phenomenology of Spirit* (which tries hard) can achieve that. On its penultimate page, it turns out that the work exhibited, to achieve absolute knowledge, "a gallery of pictures."

I think both types exist, the twice-talented and the totally condition-liberated, talent- and training-free writers. Their products tell on them, and it would make for a lovely conversation to ascertain the indices for discerning their debility.

In particular, I've got a prime exemplar of the dually talented writer, whose every page offers examples: Thomas Mann. I'll cite a case from his first novel, *Buddenbrooks*. Here comes Herr Grünlich ("Greenish") seeking the hand of Tony Buddenbrook, whose family, purblind for all their worldly wisdom, thinks he's suitable:

> Through the garden there came, hat and walking-stick in the same hand, with rather short steps, and head somewhat stretched forward, a man of middle height, of about thirty-two years, in a greenish-yellow suit with long coat-tails and gray cotton gloves. His face, beneath his light-blond head of hair, was rosy and smiled; besides his nose, however, there was a conspicuous wart. . . . His favoris [French: side-whiskers] were of pronounced golden-yellow color.—Even from afar he executed, with his large, light-gray hat, a gesture of devotion (Vol. I, Pt. III, Ch. 1).

This is, as the Germans say, Herr Grünlich *"wie er leibt und lebt,"* "in body and soul." And the persistent problem is: When was he alive in his body and where—so that Mann could thus describe him, that is, first see him and then verbalize this vision?

Could he have done it the other way around—first write him down, then see him? I can't think how. Moreover, is Mann's depiction spontaneous or summoned? Probably both: Herr Grünlich appeared to him, the Lord knows whence. But then, he'd been imagining and reading fiction, so he was replete and receptive. And he'd been telling stories to himself and others forever and gotten a good German *gymnasium* ("high-school") education, so that he had the vocabulary and the locutions.

And now to scenery in words.

8. Descriptive scenes: the writing intent on rendering a visible scene, from Lilliputian miniaturization with its own strange charm to grand panoramas such as Tolstoy's battles in *War and Peace*, offers interesting specific problems.*

The strangeness of miniature charm is its ambivalence. On the one hand, tiny things—gnats, midges, ants, in short, vermin—are psychically off-putting and physically irritating. On the other hand, miniatures do have a kind of magic about them: of all the enchantments in *Gulliver's Travels*, I would bet that both children (there are expurgated, defanged versions) and adults (who read as much for the critique of humanity as for the fantasy) recall the tiny "small-thinkers," the Lilliputians, best.

I find this charm mystifying. The facile and current solution is that we, the folks of the right size, have absolute power over the tiny ones. (Not so; in fact, in Swift's book the Lilliputians are in control.) But that's not really charming. Another possibility is that down-sizing is an exercise in Euclidean similarity (our specifically human spatial mode) and an engrossing question that it raises— *Gulliver* answers it—whether size, which is inherently *not* qualitative, hence merely quantitative, has nonetheless an influence on the ethnic character of a species. The Lilliputians have punctilious souls.

But it may be something even more odd: Babies in their littleness are cute; perhaps adults, when they are generically, that is, tribally, tiny, are even cuter. But then what makes babies so you want to hold them? (General helplessness in the face of the cuteness question—better, problem—shows up in the word history:

from "acute," which is just what "cute" isn't; such wide meaning
swings betoken irresolution.)

One old theory, that infants evolved into cuteness as a care-
soliciting behavior doesn't really explain why the appeal works;
after all, people don't hug babies only *because* they need to be
changed—and sometimes they cuddle them when the kids *really*
want their bottle.

Perhaps the attraction is that they are in the speediest *status
mutandi* human beings are ever in, and so fascinating in their cuteness. Or perhaps because they're like pillows.

Here's a problem: Why do readers have a tendency to skip
descriptive passages, especially of nature, with an inner expression of irritation? "Cut to the chase, why don't you!"
Some canny authors, as Virginia Woolf above, open their
novel with a long description because most readers just can't
bring themselves to start on p. 3.

I think the solution is that description, especially of scenery, requires really meticulous visualization, real, if lovely,
work, though without the spice of plotted action. In reading good writers, it's a mistake to skip, because besides missing the views themselves, the self-blinded reader misses the
mood-setting for which an artful author uses scenery.*

Most memorable: a dual scene from *War and Peace*: In early spring,
Prince Andrei Bolkonsky is driving, inattentive and disengaged,
through a forest. Suddenly he notices a huge old oak, rigid, mis-
shapen, and grim. It speaks to him (that is, it makes him articulate
his mood to himself): ". . . There is no spring, no sun, no happiness . . ." (Bk. II, Pt. III 1). Later that spring, on his return journey,
he looks for but cannot find his old oak. But then he sees it. Trans-
figured with dark-green foliage, it stands "rapt and slightly trem-
bling in the rays of the evening sun." He is seized with joy and all
the best moments of his life—a battle, a death, a friend, a girl, a
night—come into his memory. Then he knows that "life is not over
at thirty-one," and resolves to show what is in him. It's a culmina-
tion for the character and the book, both.

One more observation: Descriptive writing seems to me to
require unforgiving focus. One way it can go wrong is to run
away with itself and become its own end. Since, I've found,
my aversions exert a perverse urgency, I anticipated myself

in citing my prime exhibit, the opening pages of *The Waves* above, when it belongs here.

Another, a worse way is symbolism, a very crude mode of signifying. A fiction full of symbolism should, to save readers trouble and put critics out of business, be prefaced with a sort of glossary: "Whenever you see A, associate it with B, or C or D or all three." The artful writers do not, in my experience, degrade figures of speech into symbols. For example, there is Robert Frost's "Silken Tent."

> She is as in a field a silken tent
> At midday when a sunny summer breeze
> Has dried the dew and all its ropes relent,
> So that in guys it gently sways at ease,
> And its supporting central cedar pole,
> That is its pinnacle to heavenward
> And signifies the sureness of the soul,
>
> . . .

This marvel of an American sonnet is all one sentence. Its central line (the last one I copied out) is also its interpretation. The grand simile of the tent does not "symbolize" or "represent" this woman; it *signifies* a property of her soul, its subjective sovereignty, its internal authority.* "Signifying" is much

> A way of being, not necessarily of doing, though it will color actions.

subtler than symbolizing. Rather than the singular, hard and fast, though opaque, relation of "stands for" or "jibes with," there are multifarious signals involved in signifying.* These

> "Jibes with" renders the Greek etymology of *symbolon*, "something joining together." A contract was completed when a strip of pottery was broken and each party received a piece which fitted into the other's, proving that, say, a deposit had in fact been made.

range from gestures to exclamations, intimations to assertions, fraught silences to watering eyes.

9. Emergent sights: This is the phenomenon of seeing the same picture in alternative ways. I think this appearance does pertain mostly to human, two-dimensional designs. After all, there's nothing remarkable in getting different views from different perspectives, in moving around the real, solid furniture in the world. (Well, in the present respect; of course, the fact that most entities have backsides, backyards, back entrances, backstairs, is remarkable. For example, why are these back-positions often regarded as somehow indecent or at least demeaning: "Go 'round the back, please!")

The phenomenon of aspect-seeing has its *locus classicus*, its standard reference, in Ludwig Wittgenstein's *Philosophical Investigations* (II xi). There you'll find a drawing he calls a D-R-head, a duck-rabbit head. The veiled reason for dwelling on the appearance I'm about to describe is, I think, that it can be ammunition in an attack on so-called foundationalism or essentialism, the claim that fugitive appearances are underlain by stable principles and that some kinds of things have a way of being, an essence, that articulates what they are and ever were meant to be. For if appearances are ever-changing, then, with one additional disavowal, nothing remains that is stably just what it is. That last repudiation is of the existence of mental images. For internal imagery would make "aspect-seeing," the flipping of one design into several meanings, quite explicable: we have alternative mental perspectives on one and the same picture; one internal view sees a rabbit in its meadow, the other a duck in its pond.

Here's a description of the very simple D-R-drawing. It's an outline of a head shape on a longish neck, facing left. On the back of the head there's a little nick; it will be the rabbit's mouth. Facing left, there are two long protrusions, the mandibles of a duck's bill or the laid-back ears of a rabbit.

Now here are oddities. Wittgenstein refers to this drawing as if it were predominantly a rabbit. But it looks, on the page, like a duck, and if it quacked like a duck *it would be a duck*.

To become a rabbit, to have the bill or beak turn into rabbity ears, you have to rotate the picture, to give it a quarter turn to the right (the direction of reading and page turning) so that the ears stand up and the nick becomes a mouth. Now it's a long-necked rabbit-head.

Here's the main oddity (I really mean my problem with the whole big deal about aspect-seeing): the drawing is actually a *deliberate design* to produce a double aspect. It's really a diagram; compare Tenniel's entrancing drawing of the rabbit that runs across Alice's drowsy vision on a hot English summer's day (in *The Annotated Alice*, ed. Martin Gardner, 1960), and whom she follows down the rabbit hole into Wonderland. This rabbit is fully equipped to live and breathe, with whiskers, a stand-up collar, bowtie and checkered coat; he's looking anxiously at his pocket watch, and he's just an un-duplicitous rabbit who's late. Here's my point: the more you fill in the depiction, the less aspect-seeing occurs; it's an artifact of design.

So I look around my study from my writing chair and everything has just one aspect, its own look. No, there's a little black-lacquered box with golden leaves and apples in gilded repoussé. And behold, four of these ornamentations have come together to form a man's face: deep-sunk eyes and golden side-whiskers (like Herr Grünlich's favoris). It occurs to me: Words are much more copiously aspectual. My favorite: German *Gift*, "poison"/English gift, "present." —Snow White's poisoned apple is the bad queen's gift.

10. Finally flat-fact staring—the a-pathetic, non-affective mood (yes, a self-contradictory sentiment!) of that office building's parking lot on a Sunday afternoon. It puts me in mind of a French children's song that Frenchie (Irma Sangiamo) taught me: *Les enfants s'ennuient le dimanche*, "Children are bored on Sundays."

Seeing "French" and "Sunday" together recalls to me that Jean-Paul Sartre's *Nausea* (1939, trans. Lloyd Alexander)

gives the apathetic feeling that I am trying for an elevated significance, a curiously readable story and a name.* The book,

> "Curiously readable" because it is so unpleasantly impenetrable to
> a reader who has only the most evanescent experience of *its* titu-
> lar feeling. "Nausea, timid as dawn. . . . I was morose and calm. All
> the things around me were made of the same material as I, a sort of
> messy suffering. The world was so ugly, outside of me, these dirty
> glasses on the table were so ugly . . . the very existence of the world
> so ugly that I felt comfortable, at home." (Five pages before the end.)

whose structure is a dated diary, emphasizes two Sundays,
one as the day when the expected fails to eventuate, the other
as a day missing from the week's entries. Nausea here is not
a physical sickness but a metaphysical one, "existential" to
be precise. The anti-hero's problem is that this existence,
being here and now, is filled with existents, layer upon layer
of them, like those proverbial truths: existents all the way
down, obstructing any possible Beyond. And the Sundays are
blankly—and bloodily—bleak.*

> The fictional editor gives 1932 as the date of *Nausea*'s first diary
> entry. Recall that the Nazis seized power in 1933, and the anxiety
> *of* existence turned into fear *for* existence.

An attribute of imagery to which I've not done justice so
far should now be considered. Readers would probably agree
that mental imagery is closely connected to every sort of psychic affect: feeling (all-overish), emotion (expressed), passion
(undergone). That relation brings to the fore one deep difference in the imagery family: Does it come up on its own or is
it called up? and the attendant problem: Does imagery, and
especially mental imagery, arouse affect, or do affective per-
turbations arouse images? So three more sections, and first:

G. SPONTANEITY AND SUMMONING

We—I, at least—get better at self-observation and—what
counts as much—at its description. So a revised self-report on

image-seeing is in order for this penultimate chapter. The self-isolation of COVID-19 has—others report the same—induced more vivid dreams and, of course, the propensity of old age for much sleeping has given more opportunity. But mental imagery has also, so to speak, benefitted. There is some revision.

A strong and significant distinction has emerged. Let me stop myself in my tracks to say: Mental imagery must be at times, as our most intimate and expressive cognitive product, terminally individual. But I'm convinced that this idiosyncrasy stays within the bounds of the generic; better said: such imagery is a kind and has specific properties.

Here is the distinction. There are occasional, unsummoned and unbidden (that is, neither deliberately called forth nor particularly desired, though by no means hallucinatory in feeling quality), strongly enunciated pictures (if I may speak so of visuality), deeply molded into the field, vividly colored, and somewhat resistant to evanescence: faces, strange but not hostile; scenes of nature, familiar but not identifiable—humanity and donegality (see K). Chief identifiers: spontaneity and vividness.

Then there is the second type, attempted recollections of memorial material and effortful coagulations of desired presences. These are neither spontaneous nor visually easy, but rather laboriously expressive and effortfully composed. They are—and here it gets interesting—almost-thoughts, close to verbal articulation, as if sensory visibility had just emerged from linguistic thinking. Were I asked: Are you seeing or thinking?, I couldn't rightly say; I'm experiencing an incarnation. One tenacious feature: desirous feigning is *never* successful; the field's matter is recalcitrant.* To re-asseverate the

---

And of course it is subject to the "white elephant" obstruction: You're promised a pot of gold if you *refrain from* thinking of a white elephant for an hour—not the way to wealth. Here is its inverse: You expect to behold your heart's desire if you *undertake to* bring it to visibility—count on being stood up.

interest: a certain type of mental imaging is the very scene of
sight-summoning language, that is, description, words staying around, so to speak, to see through their own transmogrification into sights.

And next:

H. Worldmaking Places

It seems to me possible to see the whole, the world, and to see
it in a variety of ways.* Let me list them—as is also my way.

> I say this here with perfectly unwarranted confidence. Actually it
> should be impossible, since I can never get out of it so as to sur-
> vey it. For wherever I step, there's a bit of the universe. Rely on it:
> it takes imagination, in particular, model-making. So more of that
> elsewhere.

As so often, this primal meaning of "world" is illuminating. It seems wonderful that, although I wasn't, and I'm sure
most of us aren't, aware of this aboriginal meaning, it ghosts
through my sense of the word: "World" has two components,
wor, earlier *wer*, is cognate with Latin *vir*, "man." The second element *rld*, earlier *ald*, is cognate with "old" and signifies "age" or "life." Thus *world* means "life of man," and this
jibes with the feeling most of us have, I imagine, that there is
some humanity embedded in "world" that "universe" doesn't
have. "World" means "where I'm meant to live."

This isn't a bad place to consider two words in the same
meaning-sphere. Both are more immediately Latinate and
thus more bureaucratic.* So, I'll start with another list; the

> Understand: I regard "bureaucratic" as a cuss word. "Universe"
> and "environment" are not etymologically but semantically
> related. *Universe* is from Latin *vertere*, "turn" and "into one," in
> other words, the heavens viewed as a physical system. The *vir* in
> "environment" is cognate, *not* with "man," but with *veer*, "change
> course," and betokens what "veers round about" and "encom-
> passes." The former is the subject of space science, the latter is apt,
> besides real science, to spawn ideological zealotry, right and left.

words will come in handy for the list and the list will help to discern in what world my question-sphere is at home. So here are the ways I can discern in which to see "the whole":

0. Or not to see it, that is, to be terminally local. I don't think this parochialism goes with a developmental stage, say a primitivism. I think it's purely personal. Some fellow-humans are so engrossed, enmeshed, enchanted, that they dwell entirely in the Here (though not necessarily in the Now; they might be devoted local historians or ancestor worshippers). I'm imagining a woman with babies or a man with a career—or if you like, exchange the objects of the preposition.

1. As a place of places. A place (Greek *topos*) is a dedicated container, the physical realization of a psychically engirdling receptacle, as in olden days the city or town had a wall, a circumvallation.* The town, though, is not the least, the most

> "Town" is a cognate with German *Zaun*, "fence." My own town, Annapolis, Maryland, founded in 1650 and given its present name in 1694, had town gates, but more to keep out the cattle than foes; it had no wall, being largely surrounded by water. So I navigated it, in my little sloop.
>   Apropos etymology, it's suddenly come to me again that to think of the language that way is to hear it speak on its own and to be always saying more than I'm uttering; it's purely wonderful—a benignly retracted forked tongue.

contracted, *topos*, nor the home—but perhaps that's the bed.

This *topos*, this enfolding "there" can be perceived; I think from two ends: *ante* or *post*, before or after.* For example, the

> Someone (I think it was Gertrude Stein) said of some city (I think it was Oakland): "There's no there there." She meant most precisely that it's not a place. She's half-right: as a city, large swaths are featureless (perfect flatness is antithetical to placeness), but then you get to your friends' house, and you realize that the whole grid is filled with places.

accepted ancient cosmology was *ante*. The place preceded the content. The earth was at the stable center, its preordained, proper place, and, with it, humanity's (geography); the sky above was full of disorder; clouds, thunder and lightning, fallen stars (meteorology); above came the planets, the "wanderers" in the heavens, disorderly to observation but regularizable by a clever mathematics of epicenters and epicycles (astronomy); and finally, the place-determining spherical container, the crystalline shell studded with stars (cosmology)— movement everywhere but at the center, every mobile placed in its prescribed trajectory, its orbit, and the whole a *kosmos*, an "ornament," and a place of places. And beyond it, a placeless, bodiless divinity, an unmoved mover, who causes all inner cosmic motions not by swiping the sphere or pulling at souls but by motivating through the attraction of his being. Thus geometry precedes astronomy. Plato's *Timaeus* images this kind of world-making: a Divine Craftsman *makes* the world in accordance with a model; it has a huge cognitive consequence for human beings: We can, in turn, make geometric models of the world.

The *post* procedure has as its book *the* Book, the Bible; not a craftsman, a maker, but an invisible (though audible) God, a Creator, creates, freely and not according to a plan or model, a world in which he places his creatures in what zone or element he chooses, contingently, to engage our conscience—not mathematically for our apprehension.*

> There is a literature on this first kind of world: *Topophilia*, "Place-love." It deals with a modern sort of sensibility, a special sensitivity to the atmosphere of places: donegality, soon to be expounded.
> A serious inquiry into "place" (mine is a mere mention) would immediately come on this problem: What is the field void of places, the complementary "in between," to be called? There is one empirical aspect to this query: Is the real world dense with places or are there interstices? Aristotle calls such emptiness just that: void or vacancy (*kenon*, *Physics* IV 6–9); "vacuum" is misleading since it is the term for an artifact, the pumped-out and sealed-off matterlessness of modern physics. All this is beyond the loose specificity necessary to my inquiry.

2. As a space of spaces. Space is the very antithesis of place; it is featureless, mere extendedness, extension, "stretching out," not very elegantly but so much the more adequately formulated as everywhere-getting-out-of-itself, elongating-itself-hood. Left to itself, a heap of atoms wouldn't know what to do with itself, since there is no direction toward a place to be.*

> Lucretius, in his poem *On the Nature of Things* (first half of the first century B.C.E.), seems to present a notion of space based on Epicurus's materialism. But he spoils it by filling the space-void with a downward rain of atoms endowed with weight, which, in swerving into each other, form the configurations of the world (Bk. II 216 ff.). For how would each atom discern in which direction to assert its gravity? Space, as mere extension, has no inherent directionality—or it is something more than mere flat space. The notion that space does have intrinsic potencies expressible geometrically is a next step, in physics.

The space I am describing is navigable because it can be overspread by a web of discernible *locations*. An arbitrary origin, assigned the non-number 0, is introduced and around it is drawn an orthogonal set of two or three axes, a paper image of our ego-centered plane or solid world.* Immediately

> I am putting it that way because when we draw the axes we have chosen a location in space for the origin, and, having fixed it, we, humanly speaking, tend to think of ourselves as located at the origin—though that's extraneous to the notional arbitrariness of the origin.

the space is strewn with locatable loci, each of which has a unique numerical address projected from the numbered axes, usually positive numbers to the drawer's proper right, negative numbers to the left. As the world of places has a primary reference in Plato's *Timaeus*, so the space of locations goes under the name Cartesian. It's worth knowing about as antithetical to the world-pictures I'm concerned with—seriously antithetical, even inimical, be it a blank or a potent spatiality.

3. As a space, infinite and even exponentially infinite, infused with force and filled with ever-divisible infinitesimals, namely atoms, randomly heaped or self-organized and essentially unsupervised—in short, material, scientific, and a-theological.

Here's an expanding addendum on the stripped-down, despoiled-of-places, filled-with-forces spaces of nos. 2 and 3, the space of science, our would-be dominant space.*

> As a teacher at my college, I believe that mathematics (the science of pure spaces and pure numbers) and physics (the science of nature, of bodies in motion) are liberal arts and, consequently, parts of any higher education that is for real. So I am far from denigrating this bare space which is receptive of its own beauties. It looks that way only in the context of making room for picture-imagery.

4. And, flipping back from bleak, void-underlain materialism, albeit illuminated by being mathematizable, to a world of imaginative plenitude, both a universe of locations and an environment of places, venue of human understanding and also human imagining:

I. Space Stripped Down

In accord with my belief that you can sometimes apprehend a term's content best by considering its extreme opposite, here is an understanding of space that is as terminally devoid of donegality (see K.), as non-, un-, in-donegalitan as can be. It is Hegel's, set out in the *Philosophy of Nature*.* To use an inept

> The middle part of the *Encyclopedia of the Philosophical Sciences in Epitome* (1830).

figure, his is as rock-bottom an approach as can be. It is ultimately thought-out, and it presents space as the terminal worldly *nothing*.

It is one with Plotinian space in centering on the prefix *ex* with its "out of and away from" signification. But it differs in not attributing some internal life, some activity of capturing a beyond that "extending" intimates; this space is self-extend*ed* but not self-extend*ing*. Instead it is completely *abstract*, "stripped of quality," and *immediate*, "devoid of relation." Here are Hegel's words. But first, since Space is in the thought-sphere of Nature, here is, in epitome, Hegel's understanding of nature: "*Externality* is the very condition in which nature as nature exists" (¶247).

Then he says:

> . . . Nature is the abstract *generality of its being-outside-itself* (*Aussersichseins*)—whose mediationless indifference is *Space*. It is the wholly ideal side-by-sideness (*Nebeneinander*) because it is the being-outside-itself, and it is absolutely continuous, because this "being-outside-one-another" (*Auseinandersein*) is as yet completely abstract and has no determinate distinction in itself (¶254).

Abstract, qualityless self-externality ("being-outside-itself"), featureless distance—that is space, except for one characteristic that falls directly out of its asunderness ("being-outside-one-another"): continuity. Why is this Hegelian, this ultimate space, continuous and therefore, I suppose, infinite? Why, to ask in another way, is it the very antithesis of place, which is continu*al*, that is, recurring,* but not at all continu*ous*,

That is, recurring in their placehood, but not at all in their qualities. Each place has its own character and atmosphere.

that is, uninterrupted. On the contrary, places are, if anything, interruptions of continuous space* and in their very

It is an intriguing question, whether places are indeed interposers *into* space, displacements, or absorbers *of* space, advantage-takers.

being, as containers and enclosures, finite. I suppose that the spatial continuum follows from the very lack of vitality of space as an abstract self-externality; it just doesn't have it in it to effect self-definition, self-delimitation—or just to stop.

The reason this most general space seems to me to have an element of excitement in it for the imagination is this. Images, more than most items, require a ground, a field. To think out the ground of all grounds, this final space, is to face a scarily thrilling fact: It—whatever—all "takes place" on? in? an insipid wilderness of abstractions that wants nothing but to capture a nothingness in which to get away from itself.

I'll end this exposition of the abstraction-littered desert that thinking has assigned as our ultimate field with a lovely example of how it becomes a place:

> It came now to him as an audible hum. The whole community of the great house was humming at its work. . . . Sebastian heard the music and saw the vision. It was a tapestry he saw, and heard the strains of a wind orchestra, coming from some invisible players concealed behind the trees. . . .
>
> All was warmth and security, leisure and continuity. An order of things which appeared unchangeable to the mind of nineteen hundred and five (Vita Sackville-West, *The Edwardians*, 1930, Ch. 2).

If you like a location that is also a place, your twenty-twenty (2020 C.E.) mind will recognize this event as one of those "moments of being," a phrase coined by Vita Sackville-West's friend Virginia Woolf for those very epiphantic episodes; the rest of the time is non-being: cotton wool. "Moments of being" is wonderful, "cotton wool" is time-snobbery. Mundanity, dailiness, is the grazing-ground for extraordinary eventuations. It's not a desert but a world.

I figure that world to myself in this, by no means the only, conceivable way: There are settings, scenes, environments and in them figures fixed and moving, and furniture stable and mobile. Now let me remind myself of the question motivating this inquiry: What are the originals of those images that originate in mental vision and are sometimes expressed in physical products?

J. AGAINST FANTASY

That inquiry threatens from the very get-go to be involved in confusion. On the face of it, it might be dismissed as being "merely semantic."* There is, however, a difficulty more real

> In my youth, that was the prime put-down of the innocents by those in the know. As so often, the innocents were deep and the sophisticates only smart. "Semantic" means "pertaining to meaning," and what is more consequential than meaning?

than linguistic equivocation.

The Greek word for imagination is *phantasia*. Behind it stands *phos*, "light," hence the verb *phainesthai*, "to come to light, to appear." This word has, as for us, two moral flavors. The negative one is "seems but is not," the positive one is "shines out." That's the first problem. The second is that a philosopher, Plato, who is deeply interested in the nature and worth of images (*Republic*, *Sophist*), is the proponent of a denigrating view of our world. He says it is the scene of Appearance as opposed to Being, of which it is a mere image. While Being betokens substance (presence), reality (thinghood), genuineness (truth), Appearance is evanescent, infirm, and disingenuous.* Consequently, as I pointed out, all the

> Of course, this ontological denigration is complemented by an extra-high epistemic valuation, since for us humans the way *to* Being is *through* appearances. Socrates himself is consummately this-worldly. He gets old before he is executed.

images I'm concerned with, as re-presentations of visible (standing here for all sensory) objects, are secondary images, images of images, by the very constitution of the world.

Of course, the two perplexities collapse into one; the dual signification of "appear," be it in Greek or English, renders the duplicity of our world as veil and as re-velation.

The *phos*-words, however, enter our language directly as a diminution of *phantasia*-imagination, as fancy, fantasy, fantastic; these signify imagination-lite, imagination unbridled, imagination banalized.

All that was prelude to a repudiating consideration of fantasy literature. I do it regretfully, because it is the very genre that engages most joyfully in worldmaking. My chief example in this exercise is from one of the seven books of the *Chronicles of Narnia*. Narnia must be one of the most extensive fantasy worlds ever published.* My negative example comes

> I say "published" because I imagine that, safely protected from disrespect, these worlds have lived internally through lifetimes—to come home to, as it were, anytime. Confession: Actually I can't get through others' fantasy accounts, including *Narnia*.

from the fourth Chronicle, *The Silver Chair*, Chapter XII. In it the wicked witch, Queen of Underland, Hell, of course, turns into a serpent on the reversed pattern of Satan in Paradise.* She is slain after she attempts to persuade the human

> Who is a snake to begin with and quite glorious (Genesis 3:1 and II Corinthians 11:14).

children by rational argument that neither Narnia nor Overworld—ours—exists, and that (she tells the primary child): "You shalt be king of many imagined lands in thy fancies."*

> Note the careful distinction between Under*land* and Over*world*. Hell is worldly as hell, but it is not a World.

Under her magic, her enchantment, the children nearly succumb to her preachment that there is no world but hers. They fight to retain their memories of the sun and the stars of Overworld, and, above all, its lion-divinity, Aslan.* And they take on

> Two-score years ago I found a nicely detailed, slightly battered little lion in the street. I took him home, painted him gold and he is even now sitting on top of my Phenomenology shelf, fawning on a green-patinaed statuette of my goddess Athena, who is fitted out with armor for war and an owl for wisdom.

her rationalistic arguments, along these lines: She claims that their sun is but a magnified lamp and their Lion but a cat writ large. One of the children's group, a non-human, claims not to know what she means by a world, and, giving himself pain, which is said (contrary to my experience) to clear the head, he stamps out the fire from which the queen's enchantment emanates. Then this creature, called Puddleglum, speaks for the company. He admits that she may be right, and that they may all have dreamed up the "real" world overlying hell, which latter is all the world there is. "But four babies playing a game can make a play-world which licks your real world hollow."

It's the climax, and the Queen of Underland turns, as I said, into a serpent, which is killed by the prince and company.

Here's the point. The argument mounted by the good side for reality over fantasy is simply a surrender. It's a terminally unserious last word: Dream-play wins out over worldly reality. Narnia is existentially, meaning in degree of thereness, to be rated higher than Earth. Disenchantment is more existence-remote than fantasy.*

> Miguel de Cervantes's Don Quixote demonstrates a similar inversion in the windmill adventure of his second expedition (Pt. I 8). He *sees* windmills but *knows* that they are giants, turned into windmills by enchanters. Normally we would call that a disenchantment, but here it's made to do the work of enchantment. Implied is a denigration of the normal world. That makes perfect sense. Fantasy was once a special preoccupation of Christians, who met in a literary group, the Inklings. To these Englishmen, fantasy was otherworldly—one might say, otherworldly in sensory costume: fantasy is the imagination usurping spirituality—to its detriment.

I am trying to show the inferiority of fantasy, which is named for illumination, to imagination, which is so called from copying.* The reason why the latter mode of mentation

> Help from Hobbes: "Judgment . . . without fancy is wit . . ." (*Leviathan*, Pt. 1, Ch. 8). Hobbes is the most unabatingly witty author I've read, but he uses the term "wit" to mean "discernment."

and genre of production seems to me more respectable can be put this way: discipline versus license.

Here's an example of fantasy's very clever, yet somehow ill-begotten spawn: Luigi Pirandello's *Six Characters in Search of an Author* (1921). The title of Pirandello's play, which I had never read, came suddenly into my head. It seemed highly pertinent to my inquiry, which may, after all, be formulated in this way: Do viable figures of fiction have some aboriginal selfhood, some existence from way back, *independent of* and *antecedent to their author.** Moreover, the capacity of the author

The Italian title does not speak of characters but of *personaggi,* "personages." I do not know if the second meaning that the term carries in English, a "person of distinction," comes through in Italian; if so, it might have given Pirandello the idea of partly autonomous "characters."

That English term "character" is of Greek origin and is onomatopoeic; it imitates the scratching of a stylus on pottery as it in*scribes* (same sound) a sketch. A little book by the Peripatetic philosopher Theophrastus, *Characters* (c. 319 B.C.E.), is a human typology from "Jabbering" to "Shysterism." Such "characters," types, caricatures, were visually realized in terracotta figurines—post-classically.

that brings these figures out is specifically called "fantasy."

Pirandello wrote a preface to *Six Characters* (1925). It turns out that the characters were born in the author's fantasy, a "mystery of artistic creation which is the same as that of birth." Pirandello says that he hates symbolic art, in which the characters are allegorical machines, and that his personages have a life of their own. However, he decides to reject these six, who, because they are unnatural, that is, artistic creations, suffer the torments of orphans. They, having been born, are beyond the author's control, while he is also detached from them. They are to live on their own in their own world, the stage, where they engage in desperate struggles amongst themselves, against the Manager, and against other actors. They are in this perpetual torment because they must mirror that of the author's spirit.* Their play is never

There is this notion in post-romantic (of any age) writers that suffering confers significance. The romance-resistant soul says: "Pull yourself together"—and has more regard for silent suffering. Jane

> Austen is the mistress of this mode: it is, I think, because of her
> heroines' reticence that, without knowing them intimately, we
> come to know them well.

presented because the author rejects them. On their own,
they suffer because they are at once scripted, fixed forms,
and alive. Of one figure, Pirandello says that "not knowing
that she is a character does not prevent her from being one."
The dramatic scene can be endlessly repeated, "unaltered and
unalterable in its form" . . . "yet not heard as a mechanical
repetition but . . . alive every time . . . embalmed alive in its
incorruptible form." The six embody the lesson: "Conflict
between life-in-movement and form is the inexorable condition not only of the mental but also of the physical order."

It is not determinable whether this lesson is a curse or a
blessing. The author, be it the writer-of-the-essay, author-
who-rejects-his-six-that-seek-him, or actor-who-plays-author-
of-his-drama-onstage, declares himself in torment, and the
elaboration of the living fiction's complexities reaches terminal confusion.

Yet the issue had to be broached at some point: What is this
life that fixed-form fictions seem to live? Had the author not
put himself so much at the center of the exploration, namely as
birth-giving, rejecting, creating Father, the essay would have
been an acute attempt to explain what we could mean when we
so easily speak of characters, image-figures, as "having life."

As for the question concerning the originals of images,
Pirandello can't help. For his six personages were brought to
him fully made by Fantasy, *his* fantasy, and given birth by
him. (Though that's a muddle: she brought them ready-made.
Well, perhaps it was a cephalogeniture, like Athena's, who
sprang, fully formed, from Zeus's cleaved head.)

In other words, the six (man, widow-woman, little girl,
older boy, sexy still older girl, young fellow) are post-partum
posterity not ante-eventuation beings.

By way of bibliography, I want to include an addendum

that is revealing for the distinction between fantasy and imagination. Both the books here mentioned are really inventories more than inquiries.

The smaller, by a well-known fantasist, Jorge Luis Borges's, *The Book of Imaginary Beings*, is a short-entry collection of fantastic inventions, mostly beasts (whose illustrations, by Peter Sis, are somewhat more cuddly than the word-descriptions warrant). Their number lacks a few of ten dozen; fantasy creatures come in crowds (not so beings of the imagination), indeed Borges calls the task of cataloguing them "infinite."

Two of these have appeared in this book, the hippogriff, precisely described in Ludovico Ariosto's *Orlando Furioso* (1532; Borges is meticulous about his creatures' origins), and the chimera (whose dubious identity I will grapple with) is explicated. I cannot resist reporting Borges's confident demand that the centaur, albeit "the most harmonious creature in fantastic zoology," be not accorded a Platonic essence—as indeed, I will claim, should no fantasy-being. It's a point worth making, since exactly the possibility that figures of the imagination have their origin in Platonic forms must be a serious possibility.* Borges and his collaborators use imagination and

> There is a complexly wonderful fact, known to me as an ardent admirer of William Prescott for his histories both of the conquest of Mexico (1843) and of Peru (1847). In the latter he describes how the Inca warriors, who had thought that the Spanish cavalry were centaurs, were filled with consternation when one fell off his horse—and consequently gave way to the Spaniards in confusion.

fantasy interchangeably and believe that a monster spawned by these powers "is nothing but a combination of elements taken from real creatures," and that is why "the combinatory possibilities border on the infinite."* I would say that this may

> An interesting reflection on their view of the imagination: They seem to imply that it is more fecund as a factual mosaic than as an originating wholism.

define the way of fantasy, but not of imagination.

The second book, by Alberto Manguel and Gianni Gua-dalupi, *The Dictionary of Imaginary Places* (1980), is a very large and long book that the authors call a "gazetteer," a geo-graphic index, and fear will become endless. In fact, a little over a thousand entries are included. Excluded are, among other types, places of the future because they are not among the "places that a traveler could expect to visit." (They must have had this clever criterion for being visitable: have an imaginary place locatable in the real world and in real time— a logical hybrid, a thought monster to match a fantasy beast, say a chimera.)

The entries are researched, sourced and richly illustrated with maps (city grids: preferably rectangular; countries: largely islands; continents: somewhere in a real ocean) and pictures (classical vedutas and Potala-lookalikes).*

> Potala Palace in Lhasa, Tibet, is the traditional residence of the Dalai Lamas. It is the go-to picture for fantasy-places.

The fantasy plans and maps, like the place descriptions, have, to my apprehension, a strange element of willfulness to them. I mean that they are constructions of desire, often meticulous executions of incidental appetites—conceptions of impulse willfully realized. The beings of the imagination come, on the other hand, in some part, spontaneously and call not on the will that enforces the demands of our wish, but on the care that attends to the needs of the work in hand. The creations of fantasy are fabrications, sometimes pro-duced with that narrowed-eye concentration you see on peo-ple producing doodles on notepads during meetings. In brief: imagination brings forth spontaneities shaped by art, fantasy creates by craft.*

> The imagination I'm thinking of is emphatically not the one I found defined in a book on the imagination recently published (2017). It has two virtues. 1. It makes you laugh. 2. It is certainly *not* fantasy: "The *imagination* is an embodied voluntary simulation

system that draws on perceptual, affective, and memory elements for the purpose of creating works that adaptively investigate external and internal resources."

Some difficulties: 1. "Simulation" is the key word but also, as my attempts to understand "similarity" have convinced me, a problem rather than an explanation. 2. How embodied? 3. How creative? 4. What are these investigatory works? 5. Adaptive to what?

Finally, a missing genre: I haven't listed any fairy tales. They seem to have elements of fantasy: anything might happen. Well, for that matter, the logic of fictions does not evince itself in predictability. On the contrary, that's where the author's originality proves itself: the totally unexpected happens, *but* the moment you read it, it's the *only* thing that could have happened.* No, fairy tales are not fantastic, first

> Query: Isn't that like Life? Answer. 1. Good fiction *is*, in certain aspects, lifelike, and 2. in life you're entitled to ask for assuringly mundane reasons; in fiction the causes might be even more magical than the event.

because they're intended for children, and children welcome—as is known to anyone who's ever been one—reasonable restraints. And second, fairy tales are tinted (or tainted) by moral intention. G. K. Chesterton's essay "The Ethics of Elfland" (in *Orthodoxy*, 1908) sets out, engagingly and idiosyncratically, what that morality might be. As I understand it, it lies in the treatment of facts as disembarrassed of the laws that involve them in a structure amenable to scientific explanation. In fairy tales, facts, as atomic and isolated, have the aspect of miracles, God's individual creations, and as such they sanctify the world.*

> This is purely Humean. The enlightened David Hume, to be sure, writes against miracles (in *An Enquiry Concerning Human Understanding*, 1751, X "Of Miracles"). But he denies any "necessary connection," that is, lawful causation between events, in favor of "constant conjunction," that is, contingent but expected sequence (*Enquiry* VII, Pts. 1, 2). Thus he turns, in effect, *every* discernible event into a miracle, a stand-alone fact that might surprise us, a novel eventuation.

Fairyland is lawless because it is directly under the supervision of God.

Here's another notion with more charm than logic:

K. DONEGALITY: ATMOSPHERIC ESSENCE

Puddleglum, who above claimed ignorance, needs to be told what a "world" is in the imaginative sense. Michael Ward has devised an answering word: *donegality*, a welcome notion with an odd name.*

> In *Planet Narnia: The Seven Heavens in the Imagination of C. S. Lewis* (Oxford Press, 2008), *passim*. Given to me, providentially, by Ryan Shinkel, a St. John's Graduate Institute alumnus. Here's the place to mention a helpful book of essays: *The Chronicles of Narnia and Philosophy* (Open Court, 2005, ed. Gregory Bassham and Jerry L. Walls).

Donegal is a peninsular county of northwestern Ireland, evidently with a beautiful coastline. Donegality is Ward's word-invention.* It betokens what I think of as a *tertium quid*,

> In its restricted use it applies to "a subtle and sophisticated technique," that of assigning the *genius loci* of a place to one of the planetary deities (42, 251), such as "Jovial spirit," "Mercurial powers," "Saturnine qualities." The technique reminds me of the astrological assignment of "temperaments," dispositions, to the planetary deity under which their possessors were born. Thus a "Jovial spirit" implies jollity.

a "certain third thing," clearly forced into unity with naturally acceptable, well-apprehended terms.*

> A chimera is *one* triple beast: "In front a lion, in back a serpent, in the middle a ?" (*Iliad* VI 181). The name of the central head is "chimera," but whether that means "she-goat" or is a monster-name is unclear. Is the whole beast a monster composed of three natural parts or of two animals with a myth as center? It's beautifully pertinent to "donegality." I think there are two natural animals and one, central, hopeless monster.

To clarify a notion it sometimes helps to view it front and back, from different aspects. Now donegality is presented as

at once an essence, a quiddity (whatness, 75, 116)—an ontological take, and also as atmosphere, a mood gone sensory—
an affective view.

So, upfront this donegality sports *essence*, commonly
thought of as the intrinsic nature of an actual entity. The
back of the fantasy creature is "atmosphere," which, sensi-
bility recalls, is a mood-infused air wafting through a place.*

> Perhaps it even defines the place *as* a place.

Now try conglomerating the two notions into one fantasy-
beast by means of a unifying "third something." That will
be a very monstrous chimera. An atmospheric essence or an
essence-fraught atmosphere is a nonesuch.* Donegality is

> Except when essence means perfume. Indeed, what is wanted is
> diffusible essence and inspissated atmosphere.

chimeric, a notion-monster.

And yet! Just by reason of being a thought-monster, it
points the way. Essence, again, is the firm, inherent nucleus
of what a thing is truly meant to be. Atmosphere is an evanescent projection upon a scene of subjectivity in its imaginative mode. Whoever has read even a little philosophy, or
heard of it, will see that essence, on the other hand, must have
a ready home in the intellect and its transcendence. And such
a one will also see that essence and atmosphere must be nonetheless kept together if the question of originals is to have an
answer. It is a way of saying that places and spaces, the venues in which sights and feelings come together, so that visions
vibrate with emotion and passions imbue shapes—that these
venues must have some supersensory *ground* (as ever, a metaphor: an uncircumventable short-circuit!). Otherwise put:
The -ity suffix of donegal-ity must be metaphysically findable,
the genius of location, the spirit of places, must be discernible
in ontology—or theology. Why? Let me remind myself: Mental images are figure-and-setting preserving. Settings some-

times (places more than spaces) display donegality, which is preeminently image-spawning.* But since donegality is also

> I am here, not inappropriately, I think, expanding the term to serve not only as a technique for literature but as a practice for reality.

itself a work of the imagination, as anyone who has ever traveled with an imagination-challenged companion will attest,*

> Example. Scene: the Acropolis of Athens, walking around the peristyle (inside the columns) of the Parthenon, where on the blocks above the columns, the architrave, there is a frieze depicting the cavalcade making ready for the Panathenaic Procession, a great festival. Person I: "What if, as we are looking, the architrave went slowly blank and the procession appeared wending its way through the Propylaea, that entrance-building there?" Person U: "You need a cool limonada!"

the task is a little more defined: to find—not fabricate—a way to think of feeling-affected spatiality and the power that functions there, a transcendent impregnation.*

> Either by myself or in someone's philosophy—possibly the Neoplatonists? Get reading Plotinus.
>   Kant's notion of a transcendental productive imagination, already considered above, is emphatically not a candidate. It is, to be sure, a great productive power (*Critique of Pure Reason*, B 181), but its works are *not transcendent*, beyond experience, while it itself, albeit a deep power, is merely *transcendental*, which means that it belongs to a human person, a thinking subject, and is specifically responsible for experiential, this-worldly, cognition only.

Let me reframe the question in a problematic way, so that I can attack it.* I'll begin with a raised but unfulfilled expectation.

> Attacking a question is like battling a benefit.

In *On the Soul*—where else?—Aristotle has a lot to say about the imagination.* Most pertinent to this inquiry are two connected

> And is the more to be attended to, although there are tons of more current publications on the subject, because his observation of his own internality is the less obstructed by therapeutic and cognitive expertise.

passages. The first goes to the apprehension of the forms by the intellect: "The intellectual [function] intellects the forms in images" (431 b 3).*

> "Intellectual function" (*noetikon*) is probably not a part of the soul but a capability. Here's a confusing phrase: Aristotle refers approvingly to the intellect as the "place of forms" (*topos eidon*, 429 a 28). Does this imply that the intellect has parts, is extended?
>
> Intellect, as distinct from linear thinking, is direct thought, insight. As for the forms being apprehended in images (*phantasmasi*), that may be a dig at Plato—and this is a really interesting issue. There is, as far as I know, nothing in the *Dialogues* that tells explicitly what people at the Academy, in various stages of initiation, actually experienced when bidden to think of? contemplate? find ingress to? the forms. It's possible that these acolytes, perhaps encouraged by Socrates' myth-making, had their own, very private mental pictures (quasi-sensory imagery) as distinct from the intellectual insights (non-sensory envisioning) that the masters had in mind. In the dialogues we are told of Socrates' contemplative immersions (*Symposium*, 175 a, 220 c). Could we see into his soul, would we find it functioning intellectually or imaginatively—or could he do both at once? Would we see clearly defined figures or atmospheric panoramas or, perhaps, a blank screen?

And then, as an afterthought, this crucial Aristotelian passage:

> But whether or not it is admissible for the intellect to intellect [an O.E.D. verb, though obsolete], something that belongs among things extended (*kechorismenon*), when it is itself not extended in size, must be looked into later (431 b 17).

The Greek word translated as "extended," *kechorismenon*, means literally "room having been made."* I saw it translated

> The lovely word "roomthiness" appears, as I've said, somewhere in my Elizabethan version of Augustine's *Confessions*. I'd like it back in use.

in this passage as "separable" (by translators who, as so often, couldn't believe their eyes). "Separable" is a metaphysical term for thought-objects that are not mere abstractions but have independent existence. The qualification "in size," however, countermands this rendering, while the similarity of room-making to *extending*, "stretching-out," speaks for this as well.

But above all, the *non-fulfillment of the promise* to consider later on the problem that Aristotle has discerned is significant. The problem is real, hard, and perhaps even insoluble, so it's swept under the rug—no more to be mooted about. It is precisely my question: How can thought, the unextended in the realm of ideas, dwell on space, extension in the world? If there were spatial-ity (be it as a universal abstracted from real things or the kind of separable thought-object referred to above), then space, since it has an essence, could become an object of thought, a kind of an-atmospheric donegality. I've written myself here into a recognition that seems compelling: Descartes thought that Extension was for Mind its only substantial other and its sole object,* but, *pace* Descartes, this

E.g. *Principles of Philosophy*, Part One (1644), ¶53, 63, 75. "Sole object": except for God, an "uncreated and independent thinking substance" (¶54).

substance-pair seems to me the ultimate incongruity, space being terminally inapprehensible apart from some minimalist mental imagery, moving images at that—something in itself nondescript, pushing continually out of and beyond itself: self-establishing by self-superseding.*

And yet—haven't I myself just confronted space in my mind?

So, donegality in sum: It effectively turns space into place, or perhaps, less drastically, describes "placeness" well. It denotes the figuring-forth in a quasi-sensory way, of the atmospheric essence of a place that *is* a place, a container that imbues its contents with containedness per se. Before it got a name (2008) people came on this notion and used its language.* It has presence.

Examples: *Texanity*, in Jan Morris's *Journeys* (1984), the essay "Trans-Texan." An odd variety: *tincture of green*; in a cemetery, "the darkness of a leafy place took on a cast, a tincture, of green. The air smelled green, of course, so the shading he thought he saw in the darkness might have been suggested by that wistfulness the breeze brought with it, earth so briefly not earth. All the people are grass. Q.E.D." (Marilynne Robinson, *Jack*, 2020). Green-Wood Cemetery in Brooklyn, close to where I lived in my teens, had lots of grave-park donegality: It was the most beautiful place within miles—and offered a course in miniaturized monumental architecture, Egyptian, lots of Classical, up to Brooklyn brownstone. Green-Wood's donegality, including the feel of sempiternity, participated in turning me into an archaeologist—just long enough to publish a book, on early Attic pottery.

L. IMPASSIONED IMAGERY

As love accretes time it loses its edge (except, of course, for those sudden re-florescences). So images are more casually envisioned, more relaxedly held. In compensation they become a permanent part of the interior furniture, part of a dowry, an endowment, as the Germans say, an *Ausstattung*, an outfit, a reliable recourse—a muted comfort. Could there be an imagery practice to refurbish its acuteness, as people do their daily yoga, though with an opposite aim? (I'm sure in fact there is, with how-to books.) Well, we come in different life moods. For some people, a daily routine spells dullness, diminution of poignancy, and for these an imagery-discipline might work. For others emotional homeyness, feeling-familiarity, welcomed habit, bring out the blessing of the ordinary, the usual. They are the chaos-preventives and boredom-forestallers, which underwrite the spontaneity of the imagination. What *am* I thinking of—sending our freest capacity into therapy?

Better to pursue the perplexity of burgeoning than attenuating love with respect to imagery. So here are some questions and answers:

1. Why in the absence of the entity loved (be it person, venue, thing) is a photo more eagerly pulled from a wallet or called up on an iPhone than an image is raised in the mind? Because a material, or, at least a sensory picture has exis-

tential thereness; in fact "to exist" means to be *there*, pointable-to, in a place at a time. In its dead stability it pledges reliable access. And in its more flaccid phases, love becomes dully rapacious; it wants reality, thinghood. The antithesis also holds: at its most robust, love can live off the mind's eye's sights and sensory evidence is less required.

2. When does passion rise to a pathology? Here's a case: When, self-enslaved by his own passion, the one indentures himself to the service of the other's passion, a hopeless involvement of passivities ensues:

> Being your slave, what should I do but tend
> Upon the hours and times of your desire? (Sonnet 57)

And what do you think this attending is filled with? Images. And they ensure that, "though waiting so be hell" (Sonnet 58), there is no escape short of oblivion.

3. How is that infection caught? Through the intake of the senses, first the distance senses—a voice, a vision; and only then (this used to be *the* hurdle, and my pity goes to the young or childish old who no longer have the inhibitions, the holdings-in, the self-forbiddings of our youth, those toners of the psychic fluid)—touch. But, to be sure, this holding-off would not work, were the mind not full of the absent figure. More: At ultimate moments, distance having been closed, the body's eye has lost its sights to touch, and the mind's eye takes over.

4. What, who, is the object of passion? A being at once made for me as nobody and nothing else could be *and* unintelligibly, randomly eventuated—both: completely pre-determined and utterly contingent. And here's a curious parallelism of passion and image. Images too are at our beck and call and then again not:

GLENDOWER
I can call spirits from the vasty deep.

HOTSPUR
Why, so can I, or so can any man,
But will they come when you do call for them?" (*Henry IV*,
    Pt. I, III i 52–55).

Finally:

M. AROUSING MUSIC

Duke Orsino is being hypothetical: "*If* music be the food of
love . . ." (*Twelfth Night* I i 1). It's thought-provoking. What
feeds love but its object? And if music does so, it's a beloved.
That's not sophistry; to me it's a real object of musing. Am I
in love, say, with the theme of the *Art of the Fugue*:

. . . it is not the tune
But the turns it takes you through, the winding ways
Where both sides and the roof, and floor are mirrors
With some device that will reflect in time
As mirrors do in space, . . .

So says Howard Nemerov in his poem, to be sure, about
the *Inventions* rather than the *Art*, but nonetheless apropos.
For that's not so unlike love, either—the person loved and
the gyrations you perform together. Yes, a piece of music can
be an object of love. But, of course, the Duke means something much simpler: Music can nourish love, even ignite it.
One evening there's a person, there's the music, and the latter
wreathes itself about the former and infuses its attraction. Or
alternatively: the same music overcomes the ordinary passion-
inertia of mundane existence and, for once, the beauty really
is in the eyes of the beholder.

In my kitchen a little old radio, from a dozen delivery systems back, has been reactivated. With much individual and

joint button-pushing, I've pried it out of its decadal rigor mortis and got it to play an old tape long lost inside, Bach concertos transcribed for two and three pianos. Evidently he didn't mind what instrument you played his music on: "universal music." Out came that music, with a naive clangor, an ancient sonority, a far cry from current engineered perfection—the musical analogy to womb food: pure nostalgia, yet the realest of real, that universal music.

Bach is my own love, who am musically ungifted, technically unreceptive, but hopelessly faithful—an outsider's, not a musician's, love. Ten, twenty years this tape was in hiding, in abeyance, and not a jot of its immediate address is gone.

It came to me: the same question that preoccupied me then—what's it saying? What's being revealed?—is the one I'm working at now. I am asking, What's behind the imagery?, because the enchantments of sounds and sights of music and images are *somehow* constitutionally linked to their derivative secondariness, to their dependency on an original, on a Beyond. And so, "somehow" isn't good enough; at least, if not answerable, the question must be specifiable.

Now to particular commentary on the role of an original, and first from Olympians and their epics and from the one God and his Bibles.

N. POLYTHEISM AND MONOTHEISM

The treatment below is almost brutely curt; it deserves a book. However, although it needs to come into focus, it is peripheral, or perhaps better, circumstantial rather than essential to my question concerning the ultimate originals of mental, and so also external, images.

Here is the present issue: What is the role played by, and the respect accorded to imagery under polytheism and monotheism, the religions of many gods and of one God? The Western pagans, or heathens of antiquity, who lived around the

Mediterranean, the Midland Sea (both land-locked and central) and further inland, were "rurals" (Latin, *pagans*) who dwelled on the heath; they were derogatorily so named not because they were boors or clod-hoppers, but because they were "civilians," not soldiers enrolled in the army of Christ. Those Romanized ancients were, of course, highly civilized, and they abounded in cults and ethnicities.

The Greeks were nonetheless the ones who named the issues over which images cross into history. Let me list them for later reference:

> *iconoclasm*: image-breaking
> *iconodulia*: image-service (of Saints)
> *iconolatria*: image-worship (of God, as opposed to *idolatry*, "idol-worship")
> *iconophilia*: image-love*

> "Icon" is from Greek *eikon*, "image." "Idol" is the really telling word. It is from *eidos*, "form" plus a reducing suffix "-lon." So an *eidolon* is a reduced *form* (a grand word in the Platonic tradition), a phantasm—and so it becomes the word for a *mental image*—a "lesser form," which has standing neither in reality nor in philosophy, neither in the world nor in thinking. This linguistic fact fits in with one aspect of Socratic-Platonic philosophy, the attack on image-making. The other aspect is the Platonic Socrates' understanding of the physical and metaphysical cosmos, up to the ultimate origin, the Good, as one great ontologically staged image-cascade (*Republic* 509d ff.).
>
> Here's fun: A correct translation for the phantasm-word *eidolon* is "formula," since the Latin suffix *-ula* signifies diminution. Language does have interesting opinions.

I'll begin this section on Pagan and Judeo-Christian divinity over again, with a listing of the ways of the bygone Pagan gods compared to those of the surviving God. It is preliminary to the problem: How do the differences get expressed in imagery?* I've discerned two spheres: depictions of divinity in

> I would be abashed to enter into the question why mosques, churches, and synagogues abound while temples are in no need of decommissioning, being ruinous study and tourist sites. But

I imagine this: The circumstance that for Christians the role of images became a life-and-death matter at one point, while the Jews took the Second Commandment forbidding image-making seriously from the very beginning, was of serious consequence to the survival of the Only God, before whom the dozen Olympians proved impotent.

the arts, in esthetic works and (once a far more acute issue) the relation of cultic images to worshippers in aiding faith—in sum: god-images as artistic and as devotional objects. Here is the list:

1. This appears to me to be the most telling difference between the two bibles (epics, "wordings") of the Greek Pagans and the two Bibles (beech, "books") of the Jews and Christians, the *Iliad/Odyssey* and the Old/New Testament respectively:* In the former, the pagan case, the *plural gods appear*

Beech trees provided the bark on which early writings were scratched. "Bible" is from *biblos,* Greek for the inner rind of the papyrus plant from which paper was made. There is food for thought in the namings of the Judeo-Christian scriptures by their material underpinnings: God's word in matter.

to humans in the images of men and women. The goddesses, great Olympians, sometimes behave like vulgar shrews, throwing the epithet "dog-fly" at each other (*Iliad* XXI 394, 421), or assume the guise of a polite little girl (*Odyssey* vii 22). The most poignant case of their possible close relation to a human being is Odysseus and his goddess, Athena (xiii 221–440). In the latter, the Judeo-Christian case, the *reverse relation* obtains: *all human beings are made in the image of one God* (Genesis 1:27).*

Thus the Bible sets the stage for modern egalitarianism.

2. Both religious groups have *dual Scriptures*; the Pagans have the above-named "wordings" (epics), one of war, the other of victory and the ensuing returns (*nostoi*) of the veterans to their heirs, the ancient *War and Peace*. The Christians have the word of God; the "Old" one is the history of his cho-

sen people, from whom will spring the Christ, the "Anointed." He is told of in the "New" Testament, which means "Will," the inheritance which is to supersede that of Moses (Hebrews 15:28)—much as individuals revise their wills and reallocate their benefactions.

3. The Pagan *poets* are the gods' *theologians*; the Bible is God's *own word*. The epics' exegetes are scholars; the Bibles' preachers.

4. The gods demand, besides *cultic observances, burnt offerings* to feed them, savory smoke being the analogue of their evanescent physicality. God wants *belief* in his existence (nothing I've ever read reports any Olympian being concerned with that) *and devotion* (ditto; the gods satisfy their lust without much interest in affection). In sum: gods want *objectivity*: gifts; God wants *subjectivity*: love.

5. The gods (usually) *forget* wrongs if compensated; God *forgives*—but probably remembers, as do human forgivers.

6. The gods like elegant *verse*; God hears *prayer.*

7. The gods rejoice in self-confidence and (probably) in *self-knowledge*. God requires humility and *con-science*, a sinner's self-knowledge.

8. The gods watch men's actions for their *entertainment*:

As flies to wanton boys are we to the gods;
They kill us for their sport . . . (*King Lear* IV i 39)

God sees into their hearts for *judgment.*

9. The gods revel in their multiform *visibility*; it's not so much incarnation, entering into flesh, as showing up, appearing, from dream apparitions that leave no material trace to potent bulls that engender offspring. God is in his very being *invisible* but sends a Son to be his incarnate self.

10. The gods stand to mankind as to yet another species and see men as having a *common nature*; from the

Olympian point of view their chief special feature is (probably) their fearful mortality. To God, human nature recedes before human *individuality*, which comes into play because God gave each person the freedom of a will and the ability to employ it perversely: to sin.*

> Oddly enough, this individuality does not end up producing more distinctive personalities than does species-attachment: You can wear whatever suits you, so everyone wears jeans.
>
> I see no evidence that the gods much value the intellect except perhaps Athena, who loves her Odysseus because he lies so cunningly; recall that the whole "Odyssey," as told to the Phaeacians, is his invention—unless you think that Calypsos and Circeses and Cyclopses really ever did exist, and so must now—which I don't. They are his imaginative take on the whores, brigands, and the other fine folk he met in the Mediterranean ports on his prolonged return to Ithaca.
>
> It is wonderful that Aristotle, the least poetic of the five great thinkers (Heraclitus, Parmenides, Socrates, Plato), thought to repair the intellectual defect of previous divinity by calling his god *Nous*, "Intellect." This confiscation, however, of theology from poetry by a more earnest, treatise-style philosophy naturally entailed the suppression of grand imagistic manifestations.

I don't mean to attribute philosophy to the gods, but, once more, they seem to me to regard humans, their lookalikes, whom they have not made, as species-beings, whose common essence, above all, their mortality, makes them what they are. God, who has created men or at least their "First Parents," the procreating pair, looks, as I've said, on men as individuals, his creatures, free to act but each utterly beholden to Him for his existence. In sum: The gods see it, a human being, more as a *what*, God regards him, man, as a *who*;* the gods as

> *Adam*, "Man," came to be regarded as the proper name of the first man.

vulnerable, God is ever *scatheless*; gods are *made* or born, God is *self-caused*; gods are *transparent*, God is *inscrutable*; gods are *limited*, God is *omnipotent*; gods did *not make* us, God *created* us; gods *can be ridiculed*, God *never*—etc., etc.

Now to apply these differences between polytheistic and monotheistic divinity to the image-inquiry—first the issue that entered imperial politics in the eighth century and became violent: iconoclasm.

I am the happy owner of a twenty-four volume *Historians' History of the World* (first published by the *Encyclopedia Britannica* in 1904). It is unabashedly opinionated and says, introducing Iconoclasm, that "the Byzantine nation had grown accustomed to superficiality in religion and, as a consequence, to a worship of images which reached a point at which Christianity seemed about to sink back into Hellenism." I don't immediately go for the relation of superficiality in religion to image-worship—perhaps, as the iconophiles thought, images were in fact the analphabetic's way to faith (see below), perhaps visible images are even inherently closer to whole-hearted faith than sightless theology (an interesting inquiry but not now mine).*

> Still, here's a thought. Icons are immattered images—literally, because icons are usually painted on wood, for which the Greek word *hyle* is the same as that employed by Aristotle for "matter." So an icon evidences a relation similar to that which obtains in an incarnation. Insofar as an icon is an appearance, it's the embodiment of the human shape in no longer organic matter—a visual imprint on suitable stuff. Again, according to Aristotle, the matter is answerable for the particularity of each human being. Thus an incarnation, as distinct from a genesis, is an imposition of a figure on modifying flesh. Hence icons are artifacts that are (along with other depictions) somewhat analogous to incarnations. That is one way to see why icons both aid and endanger worship.

The passage's reference to image-worship as a return to Hellenism, that is, to Greek antiquity, seems to me to suggest a real insight: Greek paganism, with its Olympian gods, is deeply involved with the visualism, internal and external, commonly ascribed to the ancient Greeks.*

> Especially by the Germans. Thus Johann Winckelmann in his *History of the Art of Antiquity* (1764) speaks of the Greek propensity for picture-making and word-visualization (Ch. I).

Hegel, in his *Aesthetics* (1835) says that the Greeks brought themselves, in their gods, to a sensory visualizing, representational awareness of their own spirit: "Greek religion is the religion of art itself" (Sec. II 2).

Indeed, the Greeks are joyfully image-prone, while the Judeo-Christians might well be in moral confusion (that then breaks out into the excesses of iconoclasm) from the beginning. Didn't the God of the Bible himself engage in making us the image of images (Genesis 1:26–27) and not long after issue a Commandment, the Second of Ten, proscribing all image-making whatsoever (Exodus 20:4 and Deuteronomy 5:8)?*

The Ten Commandments of the Bible are divine injunctions. The great Greek attack on images and their poets is philosophic and occurs in Plato's *Republic*. Images are proscribed in Socrates' Beauty-city (*kallipolis*, 527c) because, first, poets devise them to produce stimulation rather than to tell truth, but second and more deeply, because by their very constitution they are defective in being—substance-deprived (Bks. II and X). Hence image-love is unethical insofar as the search for being is a human obligation. (But sin, rebellion against the divinity, isn't in it.)

But the Greeks live in easy proximity with the depictions of the gods. The iconography, the representational convention, is simple, so identifying a god is easy. Moreover, much of really fine Greek painting (and most of what survives) is on household objects, crockery like water pitchers and wine coolers, which though mostly plain, sometimes bore images.

Anthropomorphism, gods-in-human-shape, seems to have been a source of reverence rather than a bone of contention. This peaceableness about the relation of the gods to their cult-images is wonderfully displayed in Aeschylus's play, *The Eumenides* (*Furies*), where Athena appears onstage in the presence of her own old image: the staged imaging of the city's own goddess facing an image of her own image!* And she

On the hypothesis that the real cult object was not brought into the theater (best reference 439–440).

presided over a city whose very name—a plural in Greek (*Athenai*) as in English (Athens)—announced that the town was full of Athenas.*

> Euhemerus put forth in a novel (a very modern genre, scarcely invented in antiquity) a theory that the gods were actually kings and conquerors who had been elevated to divinities. It gathered no currency, from which I infer that there wasn't much worry about gods and their image-worship. The novel, a fabulous travelogue in which Euhemerus tells how he learned his theomorphic theory, was called the *hiera anagraphe*, translated by Philo, the Judeo-Greek philosopher, as the "Sacred Scripture." I think of it as elevating the imagistic anthropomorphism of Greek art into the realm of theology, an instantiation of Hegel's dictum that Greek religion is the religion of art itself.

To finish imagery's violent episode. The iconophiles adopted as a chief argument this formulation, alluded to above: "The churches are decorated with images so that those who do not know the alphabet may see represented on the wall that which they cannot read in Scripture." It prevailed. In the course of the early ninth century iconoclasm entered a period of practical oblivion. I am not saying this populist argument did it; a lot of favorable history went into the defeat of the image-breakers, but this people-friendly argument surely helped. However, it bears examination.

It sets aside the basic difficulty with images—that they are *not* the original, and in their existent presence may well displace *the* Original. The worshipper is then trapped in iconodulia or iconolatry as defined above, both being a kind of idolatry, idol-worship, the reverencing of a human-made object. The icon thus becomes an end at which worship stops rather than being the means of conducting the adoration through to the Original, Saint or God. Even in the icon's absence, it may have become fixed in memory and have captured the worshipper's intention *as* a memory.

But the problem goes deeper. What really does it mean to use the picture of a saint or of a sacred scene as an occasion for worship or, what is harder, to look at an anthropomorphic representation of an in-visible, triune Person—and pass through it? Surely it is no solution, then, to form a mental image of one's own, since it is the very notion of *re*-presentation that is inapplicable to God.*

> A lesser problem of the same sort appears on the sidelines: Why would most of us (I imagine) prefer a decent photograph to even a fairly vivid mental image of someone for whom we long in his absence? This may be the solution: When we really care, truth matters more than fraughtness, a photograph has more factuality than a fragile, fugitive-mental image—if less inner life.

A second problem is in the tacit assumption of this iconophile defense that, as it is possible to visualize descriptive text and get some agreement, so we can re-scripturalize a picture and produce an acceptable analogue to the original. To be sure, as with highly specific detailed text, it might happen, but scripture, theology, philosophy, will surely contain something not capturable in a picture, namely *thought*. For example, so-called syncategorematical terms—terms like "and," "if," or "because" that have no assignable significance until they are *syn*, "with" *categoremata*, that is, are with terms that are predicable, classifiable, *categorical*. For example, "if lightning, then thunder" means "see lightning, expect thunder," but "if" alone means nothing articulable.*

> William James, I now recall, disagrees; he claims that the syncategorematicals have a significance, a feeling-tone: "We ought to say a feeling of *and*, a feeling of *if*, a feeling of *but* . . ." (*Psychology*, Ch. XI). I think he's right; there is a feeling of iffiness (doubting the hypothesis), of butness (misgivings about a concession), and of andness (sensation of something more that belongs).

So images will miss the point; if not lead astray. Think of a picture—there are many—of, say, Matthew 2:11: the child with Mary, the wise men, worshipping and presenting their costly, aromatic gifts. But what wouldn't be there, would be the diapers drying out. Or, if they were, they'd look more like table than like baby napkins. And yet the absence speaks volumes, though it would take thinking to learn what it says. To me it may actually betoken a light pall over faith—if utter realism isn't all-poignant, if the sacred scene needs tidying up.*

> Are there diapers in any medieval crib scenes?

So now to authors.

First, Augustine, whose topology of the soul is sophisticatedly trinitarian.

O. Augustine's Trinity

In my colleague Ron Haflidson's lovely book *On Solitude, Conscience, Love and Our Inner and Outer Lives* (2019), I found a reminder that Augustine, in *On the Trinity* (c. 420 c.e.), engages, much in my spirit (but better, as I in his), with the mini-motions of the imagination.*

> I'd forgotten how concerned Augustine is with the ultimately logical perplexities of self-examination—not the problems of Christian conscience (that don't much concern me since I'm a merry pagan), but the problem of problems, that thinking itself quashes the more delicate capacities it aims to be "about," tries to envelop (*Trinity*, Bks. IX-XI). "What then can be the purport of that injunction 'Know Thyself'?" he asks (Bk. X, Ch. 2), having closely considered the daunting difficulties. Chief of them is our very image capacity, which brings it about that "the mind, supposing itself to resemble its own images, supposes itself to be a bodily thing" (Ch. 3).
>
> His solution is *very* subtle: The question how the mind can seek itself appears to involve it in a paradox. It is already more than with itself, it *is* itself. Yet bluntly put: It's a fact, we do try, and all but succeed, in knowing ourselves. The reason it isn't an absurd attempt is precisely the condition described above. There is something between us and ourselves: our quasi-sensory imagery. Remove these mental accretions and vestiges of outer things of the flesh, and you're already within yourself, distanced but not separated. A marvelous phenomenology of self-thinking is given in Bk. XIV, Ch. 8.

Augustine sees the human imagination as itself part of the imaging of the Divine Trinity, Father, Son, and Holy Ghost.

Indeed, the whole human cognitive constitution is diversified in the trinitarian image, which means that, as in the Trinity, each of the three mental functions is identical with, yet separable from, the others.*

> Augustine, of course, points out the deep differences between the divine and the human trinities, chief of which is that God *is* all three Persons, but the cognitive trinity is not me. It is *mine*, an ego intervenes. Not so with God and His Trinity (Bk. XV, Ch. 6).

The trinity that contains mental imagery, that is, the visions of the mind's eye (*acies animi*, "sights of the soul"), is the completely internal, inward trinity.* Its parts are the

> It corresponds to the preceding outgoing/incoming trinity: the visible look of the external object, the likeness received by the sense of sight, and the will or intention that fixes the eye's sight on the outer object (Bk. XI, Ch. 1).
> An earlier, more large-grained psychic trinity is memory, understanding, will (Bk. X, Ch. 4).

mental memory image (memory), the abovesaid mind's eye (imagination), and again the unifier (will) in an analogous but different capacity, that of keeping the mind's eye focused on the recalled memory-image (Bk. XI, Ch. 2).* Although

> The will, the psychic image of the Holy Ghost, is attention, love, relatedness. This is not the contracted, clenched-fist executive force of the modern will, of "willpower" or Nietzsche's "Will to Power." This will is identical with intelligent desire, perceptive inclination, thoughtful devotion, careful attention—in short, with the love that is not mere passion.

Augustine has no analysis of non-material images, his location of their organ, the vision of the soul, is helpful. As seated between memory and will, they have a source and an agent: recalled sensory material and a summoning power.*

> To complete the picture of the image ecology, I would propose that our memory does not only preserve sensory experiences but also non-external experiences. Both Hume and James think that we

are not capable of originating sensory events within ourselves, but to me that should get a lot of conversation—at the end of which neither would the problems have been solved nor the question answered, and yet we would know more, for instance how a *new* internal experience is to be identified. There is, moreover, an opposite suggestion in cognitive science, that no two acts of mentation ever are the same (D. Casasanto and G. Lupyan, "All Concepts are Ad Hoc Concepts," in *The Conceptual Mind*, 2015, sent to me by Amritpal Singh, one of our cherished alumni). That would obviate the inquiry, for sure. The influence of the will too, or better, the will as a constituent of mental imagery, is of consequence in giving it an intentionality peculiarly its own—its birth, not, to be sure, in sexual desire à la Freud but in thinking-desire.

There is, however, another way to see the cognitive trinitarian setting of the imagination. The will still holds the place analogous to the Holy Ghost in the Divine Trinity. The mission of the Holy Ghost has its mirror image in the will. The former is The Intercessor, the mediator between God and men; the will functions between memory and imagination to bring them together. The latter pair is something like the materials-supplier and the studio. The memorial/materials are more or less accurate reminiscences of a sensory experiences; the imagery-workshop is, of course, impersonated in a poet, who, once again,

Turns them to shapes and gives to airy nothing
A local habitation and a name (*A Midsummer Night's Dream*
    V i 15).

Since I'm with Augustine now, whose *Confessions* are my bible on the inner life of the territorial imagination and its works—

Intus haec ago, in aula ingenti memoriae meae.
Within I do this, in the immense court of my memory (X 8)—

this might be the place to discharge an obligation that I feel myself to have to this, perhaps my last, little book: to compose a forthright credo. So here it is:

The one most life-enhancing injunction I know of is the First Amendment (Article 1, 1791) of the Constitution of the United States (1787):

> Congress shall make no law respecting an establishment of religion, or prohibiting the free exercise thereof, or abridging the freedom of speech . . .

This part of our fundamental law seems to me to carry with it certain shadow-rights: the right to hear, respond, or be silent, to be agnostic or dogmatic, to be publicly active or stay privately passive—and certain shadow-obligations: to revere this country, be it by affirmation or through criticism, and to inquire, whether ruminatingly or reasoningly, into the "Divine Providence" on which the signers of the Declaration of Independence relied.

In sum, to date: The world that contains me shows signs that are believably interpretable as belonging to an artifact. Moreover, it is made of matter that I have intellect to understand; it supports my purposes, so that I am encouraged to function in it. So my world suggests, by analogy, that it has an author, whose existence and works I am bidden to ponder—now and then.

Here, then, is the sum total, unspectacular but soundly bread-and-butterish: in the face of acutely argued claims that the world is either a human construct or a self-originating automaton, I welcome wonder as my proper attitude to it.

I know myself neither to have been present at its creation nor involved in its making, so a certain modesty (never humility) is in order, together with a sense that, since theology is required of me, the competence must have been bestowed. In Paradise, if it exists, there will be yet another ability: music will articulate its meaning. Some have claimed it's a boring place. Not me.

And so back to business.

P. Plotinus the Neoplatonist

I'm in search of help, and, I suspect, a Neoplatonist, Plotinus in particular, with whom I have some acquaintance, might help. So I read through the fifty-four titles of his six *Enneads* ("Sets of Nine") and found the one that I'd hoped for: "On Intellectual Beauty" (V 8).

> *Peri tou Noetou Kallous* (fifth Ennead, eighth treatise). *Noetou* is usually translated "intelligible," but it means "pertaining to *nous*, intellect, mind." Of course, if it's intellectual it's *ipso facto* intelligible.

I'll say below why I looked to a Neoplatonist and what I found, but first, upfront: It brought no answers, yet it was helpful. It's a frequent experience: in working out why there's really no satisfaction here, I've gained a lot from having to clarify the parameters, the framing, of a possible answer.

Now, why go to a Neoplatonist? Plotinus is turning Plato's philosophizing into a system, an explicit, organized structure.* In this effort, he takes account of an absence felt by any

> And incidentally side-lining Socrates, whose way of philosophizing is to value inquiry over doctrine (*dogma*) and "perplexity" (*aporia*) over resolution. And yet, I'm persuaded that every Platonic dialogue contains, albeit *implicitly*, solutions to some of the technical problems *and* the answer to the preoccupying question. "Implicitly," however, means: work it out. In other words the dialogues are *ultimately* pedagogical, but not by a method of terminal teasing but by a positive promise of insight.

engaged reader. The soul, albeit tied to the body, is not physically apprehensible.* Yet, although it is ever-present in the

> Although that is exactly what the Greek *psyche* means: "a cool breath"; *psychros*, "cool" is cognate. Latin *spiritus* is also related to breath. Both words are onomatopoetic: you can hear the sibilation of breathing through your teeth and the popping sound of breathing through closed lips, as in "pant" and German *pusten*.

dialogues in passing conversation and myth-telling, there is no explicit account of its whatness, no dialogue subtitled "On the Soul" (*Peri Psyches*), and so much the less, one called "On the Imagination" (*Peri Phantasias*).

I think that is because for Plato's Socrates the soul is not topological (place-ordered); for instance, it isn't a "place of forms" (*topos eidon*).* It is, instead, diffused in location and

As it is for Aristotle, who did write such an essay, *On the Soul*.

versatile in capability—central but not pin-pointable. Hence the imagination, which is topologically central in the soul and cognitively central as the mediator between immattered and matterless sense objects, between touch-bound lust and sight-distanced love, has no place for Plotinus, since it had none for Socrates.* Moreover, matter (*hyle*) is ontologically absent in

I got this insight from a footnote by A. H. Armstrong to *On Intelligible Beauty* in the Loeb edition (Vol. V, p. 258).

the dialogues, since Socrates, who is certainly experienced in this-worldly badness, takes the upward way of knowledge, the way of virtue, rather than the plunge down into worldly-wise and cognitively obscure places.* There, I conjecture,

There is a pedagogical principle of real urgency at issue here: Should education, from kindergarten through college, be designed to involve students in current problems, their conceptualizations and solutions (usually found in current publications) or present them with the theories and traditions of liberal learning, usually found in un-current books? Otherwise put: Is an intellectually demanding education properly antecedent or is it ancillary to practical activity? I think the former.

matter would be at home, a principle of evil, as it will later be for Plotinus. In any case, the imagination is left ontologically unprovided by Plato, and so will it be by Plotinus. Yet there is a lot to be learned from *On Intellectual Beauty* (V 8).*

A short essay, "On Beauty" (I 6), serves as a prelude to V 8 in that it tells what beauty is: In the Neoplatonic system the Intellect is derivative from the Good and *is* Beauty. Thus it is "immediately Beauty" (I 6, Sec. 1, 27); Intellect and Beauty are identical. Inciden-

tally, the funerary urn of Keat's "Ode on a Grecian Urn" speaks as
a Neoplatonist: "Beauty is truth, truth beauty."

I want to sneak in here, once more, the understanding of beauty
that most immediately speaks to me: Beauty is and bestows visibility, *sightliness* (*lampron*, Plato, *Phaedrus* 250 c). What is beautiful
draws by its looks and repays looking; it shines. It is supersensory
in the double sense: exceedingly ocular, yet also originating from
beyond the eye.

This Beauty which *is* the Intellect, this non-sensory beauty,
is specified in this way: It is beautiful in all its parts. Is it then
spatial? No, because space degrades; it is the venue of lesser
being. The explanation jibes with the exposition of spatiality
given above, here by Plotinus:

> And by so much as it stretches out, going into matter, by so
> much is it weaker than that which remains in oneness. For
> everything that distances itself from itself, stands away from
> itself, . . . if its strength is in beauty, then it diminishes in beauty
> (V 8, Sec. 1, 27).

So to become spatial is to materialize, and becoming immattered is, in Plotinus's understanding of matter as badness, to
deteriorate in every property including beauty.

Then comes the Neoplatonic esthetics: Plotinus observes,
as I did above, that if works of visual or dramatic art copy
nature (and are therefore to be despised), we should, he says,
remember that natural things are themselves imitations. But
actually the arts "don't simply imitate what is seen, but run
back up to the reason-principles (*logoi*) from which nature
derives." In other words, the arts and crafts look to the forms,
not to nature, and their works are realizations, incarnations of
intellectual models, the forms.* Here's a consequence: Art is

Arthur Schopenhauer revives this esthetics in *The World as Will
and Representation* (Vol. I, 1819, Chs. 37, 49; Vol. II, 1844, Ch. 34).
To my mind, he relies too much on a convenient term: *Anschaulich*,
"visualizable," is the German version of "intuitable." To be sure,
the Platonic forms, the ideas, are apprehended (ultimately)
through intuition, direct insight, rather than through understanding, step-wise reasoning. But they are only metaphorically visi-

ble. Starkly viewed, they are precisely *in*visible, non-sensory, hence a-spatial. So here we see, as Kant would say, a subreption, a filch-ing of the solution to the inverse of the old problem, how sensory objects can participate in ideal models; this time it's how ideal models can be called down to participate in works of art. At this point, an unsympathetic reader might ask: Why not chuck tran-scendence? The answer, not for this inquiry, would run along these lines: Give up a Beyond, a There, and neither the world's class-forming similarities nor humanity's thing-intending speech would begin to be intelligible—nor would our never-to-be-exorcized existential nostalgia be assuaged.

But as so often, an "And yet": The largest imaginative genre, the modern "novel," relies on a world of curiosity-inspiring *facts*, *news* of which, as the latest novelty, be it true or false, is avidly con-sumed (Lennard Davis, *Factual Fictions*, 1983).

higher than nature. Neoplatonism involves estheticism.

Plotinus, like Schopenhauer in the note above, is car-ried away by word-metaphors. Let me present an overview excerpted from "On Intellectual Beauty" (V 8) with an eye to the "originals of mental imagery" question. The eighth essay of the fifth *Ennead* shares the tone of others: part apologist's incantation, part initiate's rant. Hence the Neoplatonic frame and terminology are employed by Plotinus as for sympathizers and/or those about to be; I shall look at these teachings askance, so to speak, and my abstract will be an outsider's take.* I'll

Let me say here that I am continually drawn to and repelled by the *Enneads*, drawn to the intellectual comprehensiveness, repelled by the iterative *Schwärmerei* ("romantic zealotry"). And the style isn't exactly elegant—though I marvel at what I take to be his word-coinings.

intersperse my précis with comment. (The first number refers refers to a section of V 8, the second to its line.)

Plotinus regards this subject as on the edge of the sayable (1, 6). He has plenty to say, so I think—and this is corrob-orated later—that he means something of great importance. What he is setting forth is an invitation to an *experience*, and, moreover, an ultimate experience. He describes the final step of the ascent, when the visionary no longer sees Beauty at all, sees it, that is, as one sees an other, "since he has come to be *in* beauty" (11, 21). It's a consummation that has an erotic aspect of penetration (though maybe not; I suspect these devotees of the intellect of being a little priggish).

Now comes the esthetic theory, which requires speaking of the Platonic *eidos*, the "form." There was the weakening already described that is consequent upon a being's self-distancing (1, 28), "falling into space," I would say. The arts then reverse this fall as they "run back up" to intellectual principles (*logous*, 1, 36). So they do not imitate what they see in nature.* In fact, natural items are, as has been said, themselves

> This is an intentional or unintentional rejection of Aristotle's theory in the *Poetics* that all poetic productions are mimetic, imitative, as the treatise makes clear, of life and its world (1447 a 16).

imitations. I think Plotinus is implying that if artists copied nature they would produce exponential degradation: imitation upon imitation. He adds that what goes for the arts goes for all the productions of nature. I infer that, at least in this essay, Plotinus takes the arts as a model for nature—esthetics precedes physics—and that is to my purpose, since it means that mental imagery becomes crucial.

And so to the *eidos*, "form." The first thing Plotinus says is that the form is in the mind of the artist. What, I ask, is its way of being there? It comes, he says, through the eyes, leaving mass and size behind, and there it moves the soul; it is form only (2, 23 ff.). So the *eidos* is *seen*, for what else could it mean to come in through the eyes, and it is *all* that is seen. More: The *eidos* brings along its own place, and consonant with an Aristotelian reference cited above, that place is the intellect, *nous*; it is the *topos eidon*, "the place of forms." This is donegality in transcendence: the environmental essence discarnate, the non-sensory Donegal with its indwelling figures, the forms. Nor is a spatial reference missing; Plotinus uses not only *topos* but also *chora*, room, Intellect as place is the ground of the forms; it itself is its own place "which runs along with it . . ." (4, 28), with some elements of extension.

The forms in that realm are not "axioms," acceptable propositions, such as introduce Euclid's *Elements*, but beautiful statues.* They are such as one might imagine to be in the souls

Agalma is the lovely Greek word for a statue, literally "delight, glorying, exultation." Socrates says to Meno, a vain man, that beautiful people rejoice in having images made of them (80c)—but so do even moderately good-looking ones.

of wise men, not painted statues but real beings (5, 24). What are these beings like? Plotinus refers to Egyptian temples in which statues, that is to say, images, are used rather than words, one image per thing. "Thinking these up" (*epinoia*), summoning them, is quite impossible; whence would they come to one who'd never seen them? (6, 10). In these lines we have, I think, a familiar description of mental imagery, and Plotinus will continue in this vein, but first he reminds us that in our cosmology "Here" is not intelligible to us because *we* think in those terms but because Here is disposed as are *things* "There" (7, 37).

He means that the world is not intelligible because *we* construct it to be so in our thinking, but because it images the beings of a world beyond, which are eminently intelligible.

What then is the Beauty There? He says, "It is what primarily comes to be present to view (*thean*) by being form and vision (*theama*) of the intellect—this also is most adorable for seeing" (8, 6). He refers to Plato's *Timaeus* in which a Divine Craftsman models our world on a paradigm, an *idea* and its loveable beauty (8, 11).

Then comes a really interesting passage, a description of the inception of a mental image—for it becomes increasingly clear that, intentionally or not, that is what Plotinus is describing: "Let there be in the soul a luminous image of a sphere," first the container, the place, the exterior sphere, and then the imagination (*phantasia*) of the sun and the other stars follow straightaway, then the earth, the sea, and animals, some entities staying still, others moving, all inside a diaphanous, a transparent, sphere (9, 1 ff.). That is exactly one way of learning to see our world: first cosmology (the diurnally turning container with its fixed stars), then astronomy (the orbiting planets in the middle place), then meteorology (the disorderly zone of shooting stars), and geography (the Earth fixed at the center, our place). But now comes the theological complement. Plotinus says: "Hold on to this, and take another such sphere into yourself and remove the mass. Remove also the places and the image of matter within you, and don't try to take in another, smaller in mass, but call on the god who had made the mental image (*to phantasma*) which you have and pray for him to come" (9, 8 ff.).

Plotinus had introduced these instructions by bidding us "take into our thinking (*dianoia*) this cosmos without any confusion, gathering all into one" (9, 1 ff.). But to me it is clear that he slides from thinking to viewing. He says that Being is longed for because it is the same as the Beauteous (*to kalon*), and the Beauteous is lovable because it is Being (9, 41). If Beauty and Being are convertible in a sentence, they are in fact identical, and if so, the more immediate question for me is what this betokens for visibility: Must Being be a vision, that is, *beautiful*, to be Beauty? It's, once more, an old question, whether transcendents are *qualitatively* what they ground *transcendently*.*

E.g., whether Justice is just.

Again, Plotinus's language says yes; so he soon will speak of the vision (*theamatos*) of virtues like Justice that differs from its imitation here below. The imitation, "running over the extension [*megethos*] of the whole," is discerned by those who have already seen many lucid visions (10, 17 ff.). This gathering of visual references ceases when the visionary is no longer looking *at* the Beauteous, but has now penetrated *within* it (11, 19 ff.).

Our cosmos is a beautiful image (*eikon*), and it imitates a beautiful archetype. So it is wrong to try to destroy it, since it exists by nature as long as its archetype remains. Plotinus ends as he began: He must, he says, use this language from his need for signifying (12, 13 ff.). The ending of the essay implies that the intellectable place (*noetos topos*) has not been satisfactorily explicated (13, 4). And that seems right to me. Whether intentionally or not, Plotinus has slipped, driven by his language, into implying that the Platonic forms behave/are? like mental images: spatial and sized, receivable but uncontrollable, matterless but sensory, shapely while evanescent.

Plotinus tacitly refers us to the essay "That the Intellectual Beings are not Outside the Intellect, and on the Good" (V 5). Here he eschews all attributions of sensory perception to the intellect because its objects are of it, within it, and so not really objects such as sensory perception presents (2, 5). Consequently, intellectual Beauty is downplayed because, as internal to its possessor, it is now invisible to him (12, 18). Moreover, the realms of sensory perception and mental apprehension are now clearly distinguished: He who wants to "see" intellectual beings must let sensory perception go (that is, the seeing we need not put between raised eyebrow quotes). Moreover, he who wants to "see" beyond intellectual beings, so as to rise even higher in the Neoplatonic system, must let even those go (6, 18 ff.). In brief: "Don't believe that intellecting . . . is seeing" (12, 4).

Here's my take: Plotinus has really fallen—my guess is from his own experience—into sometimes thinking that forms can be in the human mind as mental images, though, of course, he knows better. He and Schopenhauer pull down the Platonic ideas into the field of the imagination, so they become available as the archetypes of art. Plato would not turn but whirl in his grave. Mental images, in their unstable, feeling-imbued, eminently imitational quiddity, are almost the antithesis of the intellectual beings, the forms. Moreover, this Neoplatonic non-answer simply nullifies my question. Usually, when the thought of transcendent beings—a thought short of an experience—is lodged in our minds, we understand that we are to apprehend them in the mode of mortals. There may be intellects capable of purely noetic "contemplation" (*theoria*) but most of us must envision just to think. Plotinus is describing an eidetic experience, which means that the mental form is not just attributionally transcendent but actually so—that we are, for that moment, *theophorai*, "godbearers."

Mental imagery and its origins could not be more grandly described. So back down to earth.

Q. Idealists on Originals

My problem must now be what, very particularly, it means to be an image—to work out what is imagehood or imaginity or imaginativity, to coin some much-needed terms for, in turn, the quality or essence of a *product*, an image, or the *agency*, the imagination.

So-called idealistic philosophy is the first, and perhaps last, recourse. There are many varieties of idealism, among them Neoplatonism, with overt references especially to Plato's dialogues *Phaedo*, *Phaedrus*, and *Timaeus*. Among the ancients, I have already taken up Plotinus. Of the Renaissance Neoplatonists, I shall refer to Nicholas of Cusa and of the Romantics, to F. W. J. Schelling. These later idealists tend to be German and system-makers, neither of which attributes is much to my point, except for some interesting terminology. What they have in common is the attempted identification of realism and idealism, or perhaps rather the absorption of the former into the latter.

Idealism is the teaching that ideas, the kind of items we have in our minds, the kind that can be "subjective," are the ultimate beings rather than "objects" like immattered things external to us. Realism then gives the external side the prior-

ity. The identity thesis, the notion that thoughts are things
and the converse, spawns, as you can imagine, extremely
high-toned ontologies that I often can't quite follow and, in
any case, don't need for this inquiry, which stops on a rung
below such efforts.

Let me now quote two passages that seem to me to begin
to deal with "imaginity." The first is from Nicholas of Cusa's
dialogue *Of the Globe Game.**

My translation is from a German text, thus twice removed from
the Latin text, *de Ludo Globi* (1463), Bk. II:

Albert: . . . For I see quite certainly: Since the image
(*Abbild*) has nothing unless it be from its original (*Vorbild*), and also, that just as there exists only one original of all things, this is in all things and all things are
in it. It is a clear proof: when I have seen the original's
oneness (*Einheit*) in all different kinds of images, then
you have led me to a sublime vision.
Cardinal: You perceive well with your spirit that there
cannot be an image if the original is not in it.
Albert: For sure.
Cardinal: In what way, however, is the image an image
when it is not in just this, its original? For if the image
is outside its original, how can it then still remain an
image?
Albert: Nothing prevents me from realizing this too. For it
is absolutely necessary that the image be contained in
its original, or else it would be no true image. Therefore I fully realize that an original is necessarily in the
images and that the image is contained in the original
or is in it.
Cardinal: . . . Thus no image is smaller or larger than the
original. Therefore all images are images of the one
original . . . It is also not necessary that, because of the
manyness of images, there be many originals, since one

is sufficient for infinitely many. For in accordance with its essence, the original, of course, precedes the image, and just so: the oneness, which is the original of all imaged manyness, precedes all manyness.

And even if there were several originals, even so the original-unity would nonetheless precede that severality. Thus those many originals would not be first originals in the same way, but images of the one first original. Thus there can be only one first original, which is in all images and in which all images are.

Albert: You have now shown me what I wanted to see. For nothing prevents me from seeing: Oneness is the origin of all manyness, and from that I discern the oneness of the original for all images.

First some terminology. The German for "original" and "image" is *Vorbild* and *Abbild*, *fore*-picture and *from*-picture respectively. So a *Vorbild* is a *prototype*, model, *original*, while an *Abbild* is an off-picture, derivative, copy, *image*.*

> Add also *Urbild*, "archetype," to go with "prototype"; the prefix *ur-* betokens incipience.

The interest lies in the implied priority; the problem is—no longer "semantic" but philosophic—whether the precedence is merely temporal or value-laden: Is the original (from Latin *oriri*, "to arise, to be born") always earlier in time than its image, or logically prior or of higher value, and if so, is it because of its rarity, its uniqueness or its thicker substance, greater thereness? Is the *Ab-* prefix a fall-off, as German *Abfall* is "garbage"? There are problems and questions here to take us deep into human matters.* And, to end with, a query

> Examples. Problem: Are "heroic" and "ordinary" equally respectable as models—a practical problem in a democracy with a resolution to be prayed for. Question: Types seem to have grades of exemplars, but do forms? The type can be represented more or less

well: a flawed hero. Forms are not represented but instantiated; can that be done idiosyncratically? I mean, can forms impart distinguishing peculiarities other than their very being?

about *Einheit*. I've kept away from the Latinate pair, unity/multiplicity, because I'm not sure what Nicholas means. Is the origin of origins an *Einheit* as unique or as uniform?* Is the

> Nicholas is surely in the first instance speaking theologically or Platonically—of man being made in God's image or the world imaging the Forms. But I think he is also explicating all image being. It's a pity that so thought-laden a passage is so obscurely expressed.

original to be honored as being the only one over many copies, or is it to be admired for being through and through self-same, while the image is to be understood as in its very essence, self-dirempt, self-separated—with a crack in its being stemming from its being un-original (see below).

The *Globe* passage asserts, above all, something to me unexpected: original and image are *reciprocally contained*, mutually included. What can Nicholas mean? It is an important claim to him, since it is a probative example of the one-in-*and*-over-many thesis that is needed for his system.

Since the image has nothing that does not come from the original, and is said to be identical with it in size, yet posterior in time and/or dignity, we are entitled to ask: what might it be that differentiates them qualitatively? And to that Nicholas gives no answer, although to me it is a main question.*

> Unless we say that more seniority bestows honor—but not all image-viewers have classical Chinese sensibilities.

On the other hand, his claim of identity through mutual containment and size-wise coincidence are food for thought. As to the equality of size of original and image, this understanding makes sense to me: copies have no necessary size; a portrait can be wallet or wall-sized, and a mental image cannot easily answer the question "What are your dimensions?" except as measured by a ruler which is itself a mental image subject to the same problem.*

> For external images it's not quite true that they are magnifiable or reducible at will, because of the question of resolution: even a sharply outlined shape, for example, is fuzzily contoured when enlarged.

What then does Nicholas mean by the image being "contained in" (*enthalten . . . in*), the original and the converse? I think he must mean that there is something we can call the "imagery-content," and what can it be but the object—scene or setting, living being or thing, that is being imaged, a content that comes from, or *is*, the original. It occurs, to be sure, in two different modes: *as itself* in the original and *as copy* in the image. Or better, according to what I've just said, *as the original*, and *as a self-derivative* (so to speak) *in* the image. That is to say, it is without an underlay as an original, but in need of a support (such as marble, canvas, paper—anything) as its image. So in an original, object and content coincide, but in the image they have fallen apart. Hence to say that original and image are mutually inclusive is a quick-and-dirty way to speak of the object in both modes at once, as itself and as imaged. Then the conversion from original to image has already been achieved and the problem is moot.*

> I should remind myself that Nicholas is making his interlocutors speak of pictures (though, of course, it's not just paintings) and that makes his understanding of imaging as mutual containment more intelligible.

What is lurking behind Nicholas's treatment is the question (a vexed one) of similarity—sameness-in-difference (treated above), with an emphasis on sameness. It is helpful to remind myself that the sameness is obvious in imaging, but the difference—what makes an image an image and not a second original—is more problematic.

In fact, sometimes an image is a second, a secondary original: the exemplar, example, of which latter English "sample" is the short version.* A sample is a curious original—so to

Latin *Exemplum* is the fundamental term; exemplar is more specific; it is derived from a Greek word, *exomplarion*, "sample."

speak, a democratic original picked out of a mass of look-alikes to serve as a showpiece, but not itself superior to its mates, except perhaps in being, as it were, more flawlessly ordinary. Thus "sample" is fraught with human interest, even pathos: Pick a child, usually afflicted with some sorry condition, make it into a poster child, and it loses the very anonymity for which it was chosen and gains an empty celebrity, poor kid. Or pick some essentially ordinary adult, though with one virtue, say that of being diligent, turn him into a hero (as the Soviets liked to do), make his name a byword, say Stakhanovite, and there goes his privacy and, I imagine, the peace of mind attending his anonymous ordinariness, poor man. So a sample is an exemplar of ambivalence, neither original nor image, but both at once.

Replicas, incidentally, suffer from equal existential confusion. Say a genius-type forger produces a perfect replica of a van Eyck painting. It has gone at auction for three million. Then an equally gifted chemical analyst, unpersuaded by the fifteenth-century canvas, recognizes the original van Eyck in a junk shop and, back in the laboratory, discovers that the replica was, in fact, done in 1929. Major price-plummeting—O, what a fall was there! And yet the replica was, to the viewing eye, indiscernibly different from the original—and paintings are, after all, for viewing, not for titrating. To me the fact of the denigration of replicas, even under conditions of perfection, is indirectly revealing: an image does have, at least is felt to have, an independent image-character, independent, that is, of its content. "Replica" has a somewhat denigrating connotation because it is an image, but an image in concealment *as* an image. A replica is an ethical chimaera, neither truly an original nor candidly an image, yet both at once, in a precarious way.

In *living* with images most of us, I imagine, care more for the sameness, but in *thinking* about them we're more interested in the difference.*

> Not always about the sameness either; I, for one, would rather see a touched-up photo of myself than a warts-and-all snapshot (not my particular blemish, to be sure).

One last point. Nicholas makes the Cardinal draw the conclusion that all the images are of the one original. That makes sense, as set out above, for the cosmic application. But for images within the world, I don't see it. The identity claimed was vertical (original to image), but why would it therefore be horizontal (original to original)? Couldn't two images with the same content have diverse originals?*

> For example: Two lookalike cousins, to me spitting images, yet of different parents.

Now to Schelling's *Bruno, or On the Natural and Divine Principle of Things* (1802).* These brief passages, to say it

> My reference is to Pt. 1, Vol. IV, of the *Gesamtausgabe* (1861), pp. 237, 238.

upfront, propose an antithesis to the *Bruno* quotation, namely the absolute separation of image and original: This passage belongs to that type of exposition, noted above, that presents the problem as if it were the answer. Let it speak for (or against) itself:

Lucian: What do you call simply and what do you call relatively opposite?

Bruno: "Relatively" opposite I call that which can stop being opposite in one or another Third, and become one. "Absolutely," however, I call that of which this cannot come to be thought. Think of two bodies of

opposite nature which can mix with each other and
thereby can bring forth a Third, and you will have one
example of the former. Think of the object (*Gegenstand*) and its picture reflected from the mirror, and
you will have an example of the other. For can you
think of a Third in which the picture could ever pass
over into the object, the object into the picture, and
aren't they just through this, that the one is object,
the other picture, necessarily separated eternally and
absolutely?

Lucian: To be sure.

. . .

Bruno: Think only of what you have already thought,
and tell me whether you can think of a more perfect
unity (*Einheit*) than that between the object and its picture, although it is simply impossible that both should
ever come together in a Third. Necessarily, therefore,
you posit them as united through something higher,
in which that through which the picture is picture, the
object, object, namely light and body, are themselves in
turn one.

With the last sentence Schelling levers the problem into his
system, where I shall not follow.

These two passages from *Bruno* do seem to offer a theory
of original-and-image: 1. They are an irreconcilably diverse
unity, a paradox. 2. A "Third" would be needed "in which"
the one might pass into the other. 3. No such Third is thinkable except in the mysticistic terms of the system.

I want to understand the preposition "in" and the "third"
thing which mediates by apparently offering a venue for
mutual absorption. Schelling is clearly thinking of sexual
embrace and the resulting child as an example of the Third.
He is also making the most of the German word for object,
Gegenstand, "what stands against," a meaning of recalcitrant

opposition. If here it denotes the original, then the Third "in" which the union, the melding with the image, might—reluctantly—take place would be the bed.*

> I'll soon abandon this decoding.

But for original and image it is precisely the case that no such union, no such bedfellowship is by their definition? by their distinct essences? possible. So the problem of their transition into each other is crisply but unresolvedly stated.

What is this absolute opposition that is said to mark the relationship to each other of original and image? Why dwell on an incidental, if powerful, item in *Bruno*? Because it makes me reflect on relationality in general. People declare themselves "in a relationship," yet the term has, sometimes, a devastatingly different meaning for each of its termini. But logically long before that, any relation, even a wholly satisfying one, is fundamentally vulnerable to the query: Is it a bond or a split, a togetherness or a distancing? "Relation" is perforce an inherent duplicity, a distinction that is at once remotion and connecting, withdrawal and intimacy.

People rejoice in being the oracles of the obvious, so they announce: "Humans are social beings." Is that most binding relation conducive to tension or to comfort, to fear or to safety?*

> And further questions: Who and what counts as society? Only people, or God, oneself, books, animals, trees?

Back to thinking about images as related to originals. I am sympathetic to the notion of a necessary third being needed when radically different entities or ideas are to be related. So for instance, it is paradoxical yet common to hold two antithetical ideas in mind at once: "When my love swears that she is made of truth/I do believe her, though I know she lies, . . . (Sonnet 198). This paradox is resolved in a lower realm: he credits her "false-speaking tongue" because he, knowing it to be false, construes her to be implying that he is, although past his prime, a youth with young thoughts. On a higher level, such a paradox is resolved by drawing on the duplicity of self-consciousness—that I am double and must, perforce, sometimes speak out of both sides of my mind.*

> To be a self is to be at once a unit and a relation—a self-relation.
> Thus it is to be an incarnate paradox, a paradox resolved by the
> fact of being existentially embodied, saved by a fact, the fact of life.

All that said, what understanding of the original-and-image relation might convince me that they are "necessarily eternally and absolutely separate"?

One answer might be that the original is terminally fugitive and so unavailable for conjoining. Thus every proposed accessible original turns out to be itself an image, while the inaccessible ones may, in a practical mode, be called pipe dreams. I mean the very originals I'm after, those whose images are the figures or settings of fiction. Another answer might consider the difference in existential dignity between the pair original/image as a social bar in the ideal realm, so to speak. But the most fundamental dissociation between the pair, this necessary and incompatible pairing, is the uncircumventable secondariness of one member. This is an inferiority not just in *dignity* but, more fundamentally, in the very definition that is here more than a word construction, a dictionary entry, but rather captures *essence*. What are the elements of image-inferiority or original-superiority? And, it now occurs to me, how are these related to similarity, which is the background condition of all imaging?

The *Bruno* passage confirms my sense that the notion of similarity is problem-ridden and that the fact of similarity is a great question: What is involved in being alike but not the same? Are there any two things in *our* world that are truly identical, or any two that are utterly different? Isn't similarity the most global comparative condition we live with? And at once lucid like the ether of heaven and swampy like the bogs of hell. Getting it clear is desirable, because I would like to see what makes images imitations, that is, what in their essence requires it.* But it would be a diversion from the question *what*

> It is so easy to imagine a counterworld in which a painter was con-demned/enabled to set up an easel in a meadow and paint a sky-scraper, and a painter who actually put a meadow on canvas would be feted as wildly original—and the perceptual world that went with this eradication of similarity. Then the question of originals would again be moot.

mental images are similar to. Nonetheless, here is a brief try at saying how imagery has a peculiarly intimate relation to similarity. Recall the explication of similarity as sameness-in-difference. I think that imagistic similarity is fascinatingly peculiar. The difference-element of imagery is its dependent, derivative, secondary character—its *inferiority*. This imita-tiveness is, however, the very condition for *originality* to come into its own, for the original to be carried over into mundane time and earthly space, and so to have its manifestation, its epiphany among us.

So back to the question. Maybe no particular idealist sys-tem will yield an acceptable answer, but some sort of recourse to transcendence might. Meanwhile, by way of signing off, I'll try to collect what I learned from the *Globe Game* and from *Bruno*.*

> Schelling, I imagine, named his leading interlocutor Bruno for Giordano Bruno, a rebellious spirit of the early sixteenth-century Renaissance, an early Copernican, and, not entirely coincidentally, a serious reader of Nicholas of Cusa. This Bruno is clearly an ava-tar for Schelling.

There are no answers, but clarifications of the elements to be considered, all concerned with relative ranking. The fur-ther the inquiry goes, the more these are involved with each other, but to begin with, they need to be isolated. So here:

Is the original

> prior in logic,
> earlier in time,
> greater in value,
> higher in dignity,
> better in quality

than the image? The answer usually tacitly assumed is yes. An original outranks an image in everywhich way. But next, closer consideration, more attention to circumstances and cases, modifies this judgment.

It sounds logical to say that the original is the condition for the image's existence, that we could not think of an image without having an original in mind. But if you carefully consider the experience, it's the other way around: It isn't until you've apprehended that "this is an image" that you begin to think of something else as its original. In other words, originals aren't born, any more than are mothers; the child makes her a mother and the image makes the original an original.*

> It's not even quite right that nothing is by birth, that is, by nature, an original, absent an image, and it is not nonsense to speak of an "inimitable" original. A being does not have to originate to be an original. It is enough to be itself not derived, and so we call people who aren't like others "originals." In sum: an "original" is a two-faced critter: looking backward, self-born, underived, looking frontward, spawning lookalikes.

Does the original precede the image in time; is it earlier? Often. It would be a peculiar portrait that was painted before the sitter was born. Sometimes they are simultaneous, as when a student receives her diploma at graduation, and the father's camera is rolling. And sometimes, rarely, the image precedes, as when you dream of a happening and then it happens.

Is the image greater in value than the originals? Well, nobody thinks, I hope, that a photograph of me is more valuable than am I myself, but lots of people would pay far more

for a painting of a pair of old shoes by van Gogh than for
the shoes.*

> Though if that pair turned up and were authenticated, they'd cost
> plenty.

Is the original more to be honored, of higher dignity than
the image? As always, it gets complicated. Consider, once
more, a made image, say a not-so-bad statue of a very bad but
toppled dictator. Even the worst human being is invaluable,
not in the sense of being beyond any affordable price, but in
the basic sense of being inherently incapable of being priced.
The statue of a toppled dictator probably in turn deserves
some respect as being of some historical interest.* Someone

> And probably some more for having itself been toppled, as hap-
> pens nowadays.

might want to argue that the image has more dignity than its
original. In some countries people salute or bow down before
the ubiquitous images of the Leader. But then the personage
himself is probably even more highly honored. People line the
streets for his limousine.

So, generally speaking, more dignity attaches to the original than to the image, but that is, it seems, more related to
the intrinsic stature of the original than to its mode, that of
being an original. In other words, the attribution of honor lies
more in the honorable content than in the "in person" firstness, thereness. But even as I write it, it seems banal to say
and not quite right either. For surely quite often the original is
more vivid, more distinct, than the image.

So the above is what I've come to see by thinking about
these two, totally opposed, understandings of the original/
image relation, namely that 1., each must be "contained in"
the other and that 2., they are so radically different that they
can never "pass over into" each other. What can be more
thought-provoking!

Finally, is the original better in quality than its copy? Well, some copying degrades the original: an art student's rendering of a Great Master; more rarely, however, the copy greatly outdoes its original: a builder's execution of the architect's model.

R. Vico's Imaginative Universals

Giambattista Vico conceived the notion and invented the phrase "Imaginative Universals" and its associated idea of "poetic wisdom."*

> Set out in the *New Science* (1730/1744, second and third edition). Donald Verene, in the beginning of his chapter on "Imaginative Universals" (Ch. 3) in *Vico's Science of Imagination* (1981), says that *sapienza poetica* would nowadays be called "mythic mentality." The phrase is illuminatingly chosen and reflects (not well) on academic locutions: it's patronizing, as Vico's isn't; it introduces an abstraction (mentality for wisdom), as Vico's doesn't; it has an agentless adjective (who's being mythic?), while being *poetic* belongs to poets.
>
> In the *New Science* Vico will establish a science of history. Recall that Galileo called his book *Two New Sciences* (1638); it established, just about a century earlier, the science of mathematical physics (mechanics and local motions).

The term, *imaginative universal*, is head-raising. To begin with, it sounds self-contradictory: Universals are either abstract (that is, "drawn off" from sensory particulars) or substantial (beings from a non-sensory realm). Imaginative items can be expected to be quasi-sensory: quasi-visible-audible-tangible. So "quasi-sensory abstractions" might be a description for "imaginative universals." It will be interesting to see how Vico means the phrase.* He has three terms for his central

> I found this phrase, together with the two alternatives mentioned below, collected in Verene's book. Notice that "imaginative" doesn't turn up in the Latinate Italian. In English the *phantas-* words are used for the wilder imagination, such as produces phantoms and phantasms, *etc.*; fantasy belongs to both, the sober and the exuberant, imaginative realms. It's a world I like slighting, see above.

Image-words emphasize the representational character of the imagination, through the Latin cognate verb for imitating, *imitari*; phantas-words derive from the Greek verb *phainein*, "to show" or "shine." Of course, Greek has a perfectly good word for image: *eikon*, "likeness."

notion: *caratteri poetici*, *generi fantastici*, and the above mentioned *universali fantastici*. They have as their opposite *universali intelligibili*, as one would expect.*

Although the interest for this part of my inquiry lies in the formation of the notion of imaginative universals set out in Vico's *New Science*, I found in his *Autobiography* (Part A, 1725) a long note on a subject of importance to every teacher (we style ourselves "tutor") at my college, St. John's College in Annapolis and Santa Fe. We maintain an all-required Program that includes four years of mathematics. It is, especially in the earlier years, predominantly geometrical, for both pedagogical and philosophical reasons, these being, of course, connected. In a different part of this inquiry I have had something to say of the space in which figures are inscribed and the way the geometric imagination works.

This preference for spatial mathematics implies a postponement of students' confrontation with the symbols of algebra, an involvement which effects the severe reduction of the role of *visualization* through figures and its replacement by *operation* with formulas, in brief, a transition from concreteness to abstraction: forms to "formulas," see above.

Vico's note, referred to above, mounts an attack, nearly three hundred years ago, on "the algebraic method," used to teach youth "the science of magnitudes" because, among other harms, "it obscures their imagination."

The deep transformation in the nature of mathematics and its science, physics, which may be understood as being the model of the concept-formations that constitute the spirit of modernity, was laid out by Jacob Klein, Tutor and Dean of the College, in *Greek Mathematical Thought and the Origin of Algebra* (German 1936, English 1992); to those who read it, it became a grounding work for the Program. A detailed exegesis of Klein's book and of its relation to Husserl's work was provided by Burt C. Hopkins in *The Origin of the Logic of Symbolic Mathematics* (2011).

So the retirement of the visual imagination involved in the early teaching of algebra corroborates the relevance to my inquiry of Vico's note.

The role of the *imaginative universal* is to make his new science possible. So first, what is it? It has an illuminating instantiation, namely myths, which Vico calls "imaginative genera" (*generi fantastici*), that is, imaginative class-concepts. They are the counterparts of intellectual universals, the class-concepts we are used to dealing with; the imaginative universal names its own cognitive source, the imagination.*

> Verene makes the point that this imaginative class, myth, is not Euhemeristic (discussed above), not a rationalization of the gods as divinized kings. They are not poetic interpretations of events but their directly intelligible form as apprehended at a historical cognitive stage of human beings, their "way of making intelligibility."

It is a way, temporally bound, of apprehending the world. It is immediately evident that the imaginative universal is devised to become a historical principle, a foundation for erecting history into a science, a new one. I say "devised" because it's a problem whether such a cognitive chimera can be "discovered."

To say briefly how this imaginative universal functions in a rational history capable of yielding a new science: It belongs to a *first*, and earliest mode of human cognition, characterized by having "the power to assert identities, not similarities" (Verene). Human individuals and mythical figures are simply and confidingly merged.*

> Once again, identical/same : similar/other emerges as a fascinating range of relations. See Bruno passage, end.

To me, this way of knowing can indeed be viewed as a power: the ability to apprehend imaginative products *not* as representational, symbolic, imitative, imaginary, but *as one, as same*, with their originals. It is, however, but a stage in which history reveals itself as having a development toward human rationality.* Our stage is the "intelligible universal" under

> Here a reader would rightly say: "proto-Hegel!"

which class extensions are collected by the fact that their members are similar to each other. That implies, we can see, that universal and instance can no longer be identical, since the universal is a unity but similars are, perforce, several.

The "power" of the imaginative universal is, in fact, a deficiency. I think it is even worse—an impossibility, because, as I've noted, the very phrase is in its terms contradictory: being imagined and being universal are at odds; an image is, as Plato's stranger in the *Sophist* would say, in important aspects precisely *not* what a class is.* If we try to express for ourselves

One might say in Vico's behalf that his word for the source of poetry is not imagination but fantasy, which obscures in its etymology of "showing" the secondary nature of the imagination's images.

the character of such an imaginative universal, we will come up with phrases like this: types with proper names, quasi-sensory categories, classes impersonated, paradigm with peculiarities, ideals with warts—absurdities.

And yet. I can't resist mentioning that angels are like imaginative universals in this crucial point: Each individual angel is its own species, as Thomas Aquinas shows (*Summa Theologica*, Pt. I, Q. 50, Art. 4), though, of course, I don't know whether they exist. But there is another group of beings that I do know to exist: the figures of fiction.* And they too seem to me the

Which, to be sure, remains to be proved—no, made plausible, see Chapter Four.

very exemplars of this logical absurdity: type and individual in one.

Think of some of the characters you care for and about, say Petya Rostov and Huckleberry Finn. Each is unforgettably *sui generis*—an apt term because it says: "his own genus," *and* it is used to say "terminally individual"—truly *imaginatively universal*. The fruitful confusion goes even further: Though each is one distinct type-and-individual, yet they are more than brothers under the skin—they are one and the same imaginative universal, Boy Incarnate, Male Child: latent and warmhearted, proud and worshipful, bold and faithful.

Yet, why only fictions? Aren't we ourselves, human beings, imaginative universals? Externally we stand for something that it takes abstracting language, categorical words (universals), to express, and we do it by being our colorfully various selves. Internally we think thoughts, but—almost always— only upon producing images.*

> When Aristotle asserts that "the soul never thinks without an image" (*On the Soul* 431 a 17), he is opening the door to just the thought above.

I can't refrain from noting another similarity. Word is that Heidegger could not issue the already announced completion of *Being and Time* because he was finally unable to assimilate the atemporal being of things to the temporalized existence of humanity. So for Vico: while his imaginative universals, necessary to kickstart history, are presented as a radically different way of thinking (though still thinking), who doubts that there was still a world of *realia*, of brutely thingly things not amenable to myth-being? For me it follows (as it preceded): Thinking is thinking, everywhere and everywhen—or else ages and places can communicate, exert significance, only in double talk. But though the paradoxes behind self-contradiction are often deep, that's only as local truths. As universals, they are devastating to determinacy and require levering into a higher consistency.*

> Pertinent example: An image *is* what it *is* not; here the levering into a realm of paradox, "where the Law of [Non-]Contradiction is superseded," is itself the explanation.

Vico's "imaginative universals," which are the most confounding—and the most interesting—take on the imagination's products, serves as a fitting finale to this long chapter, devoted to the inquiry into the essence of images and especially of mental images—except for (always more) two confirming commentaries:

S. Corroborations

It is far more feasible to gather and cite testimony about the arts that sideline the question of originals than to find support for inquiries into their intended effect. In sum: not originals but origination attracts comment. *Per contra*, a wonderful quotation from a fine novelist: ". . . just the imagination . . . 'As if imagination were not the medium by which *super*-reality is perceived.'" (Rosamond Lehmann, interviewed by Shusha Guppy in *The Art of Fiction*, No. 88, Issue 96, 1985.)

I'll use as main reference that anthropological masterpiece of "thick description," Clifford Geertz's "Deep Play: Notes on the Balinese Cockfight" (1972). These fights are plausibly regarded as an art form. Thus, if you set aside the Balinese particularities, you can learn what art as art might be. That, in Geertz's interpretation, leaves the cockfight and its betting in a class with *Macbeth*, *Lear*, and *Crime and Punishment*, the class of art per se. As such, they all have this common effect: they can serve as a "sentimental education"; they allow the viewer or reader "to see a dimension" of his own subjectivity, to "open his subjectivity to himself." So the question is not "Whence the model?" but "What's the effect?"

Call this—certainly attractive—view the soft evasion. Then there are the hard ones, held by the "positivists" of the mind who have gotten down to brass tacks, to whom the imagination is an "encoded voluntary simulation system"— and other such brassy equivocations. Positivists are reductionists of the mind: All mental motion is monotonic, goes single-mindedly in one direction and with one voice; never imagines what it hasn't pieced together from atoms or fragments of sense-experience; never thinks doubly or even triply in harmonious schizophrenia; never judges yes, no, maybe, all at once; is never attracted and repelled simultaneously— in love and quite heart-whole, smitten and undamageable, free and bound. Could there possibly be such crystalline, see-through souls?

On the other hand, there are unintended benefactions. I
cannot think of a more convincing corroboration that a possible fiction's reality can receive than a retelling by a fine writer
who is also an acute reader. A special and daring case is
Thomas Mann's *Joseph and His Brothers*. A less voluminous
but even more meticulous case is Pat Barker's filling-out of the
Iliad, *The Silence of the Girls* (2018). It is a first-person novel,
and the teller is Briseis, queen of Lyrnessus, a dependency of
Troy. She is now in the possession, a slave of, Achilles, the
conqueror of her city, awarded to him as his prize. Agamemnon, who is the Greek army's overlord, has been awarded
Chryseis, but has to return her to her father, Apollo's priest,
forced by the intervention of the latter's god. Agamemnon
indemnifies himself by, in turn, seizing Briseis from Achilles—and so, with Achilles, the only Greek capable of taking
Troy, sulking inactive in his tent, begins the *Iliad*.

Briseis, brought up to practice silence as a main woman's
virtue, is the right person to speak, since she thus knows the
two chief Greeks, all too intimately. In the *Silence of the Girls*
she tells the inside tale of the tents in these last weeks of the
ten years' siege before the fall of Troy.

The novel is beautifully realized as an independent fiction.*

> One reviewer calls it a "feminist" novel. It does the book no honor
> to degrade it into a tract and to denigrate Briseis, who is, not by
> force of an ideology but by the power of her nature, a woman to
> reckon with. So good a novel about so plausible a woman can't be
> an "-ist" book.

But its corroborative force lies in the attentiveness to Homer's text, for Homer tells by insinuations, intimations, innu-
endos—the most sophisticated writer I know of.* Let me give

> I'm persuaded that *one* poet (call him Homer) was the final com-
> poser of *both* epics and that they were *written*.

some examples of Homer's obliquity and Pat Barker's attention to it. To me the most neck-tingling case is the Homeric
fact that Achilles thinks that he has killed Patroclus. On hear-

ing the news of Patroclus's death, Achilles sobs "I have lost him," but he uses a verb that can also mean "killed." Recall also that when he avenges his friend by thrusting his spear through his killer's, Hector's, gullet, what he sees is a head wearing his own helmet with its face-hiding cheek and nose pieces, in which he last had sent Patroclus into battle, having allowed him to wear it: His spear is going *both through himself and his other self.**

> Reading Homer is largely *envisioning*; he is the consummate caller-up of mental images.

Silence conveys this intimation as a very delicately handled fact: When Patroclus runs off into mortal danger, Achilles, fearing the worst in his tent, cries out Patroclus's name. Patroclus, on the battlefield, miraculously hears it, and, distracted for a moment, is killed by Hector.*

> Those who tolerate magic may take this episode that way. It's also perfectly good psychology—miraculous past magic.

Another keenly observed relation: Anyone must wonder whether the two friends are lovers. *Silence* has it, it seems to me, exactly right and says it more explicitly than does Homer. Theirs is the apotheosis of friendship: intensely physical but not, or only quite incidentally, erotic.

Silence also picks up on a subtheme: Patroclus's moments of self-assertion, his silent but powerful disapproval of Achilles' withdrawal from battle and—fatally—his conversion from alter ego to identity, once he's in Achilles' armor, plus his consequent fatal disobediences as he sweeps over the battlefield intent on himself taking Troy.*

> Two modifications of the epic by the novel mark a difference between the two genres: the inexplicit indication of epics and the explicit narration of novels. The lesser modification: Agamemnon is a prime ass, shown in the follies of his generalship, reported by Homer in his epic, and his stultifying sexual practices told by Briseis in her novel, which, incidentally, allow him to swear, when

required to do so, that he has not lain with her "as is the way of men and women"; as Briseis knows, that's only literally true.

The other, more global, difference is the absence of all the Olympians in *Silence*. I think that, again, genre considerations prevailed; a barracks novel like *Silence* requires vulgarity, and in the Muses' epics, vulgarity is not an option. Homer's people can be earthy and rough-tongued, but vulgar, never.

The point of this section was to show how a subsequent retelling, and, particularly, a novelistic expansion, can thicken the indices of factuality around the primal image so as to bring it closer to, and to corroborate, its actuality—and thus make the thought of a causal source, an origin, more plausible.*

> The thoughts above were about the enhancement of narrations by fiction. But here's a real curiosity: the imaginative realization of the greatest *philosophical* utopia in a 718-page trilogy, Jo Walton's *Thessaly: The Just City, The Philosopher Kings*, and *Necessity*—Plato's *Republic* in which image-making is proscribed, very extensively imagined. It is a pertinent practical commentary on this undertaking that Plato himself tried it and gave up: the dialogue *Critias*, perhaps deliberately unfinished, was intended to fulfill Socrates's desire "to see his works moved" (*Timaeus* 19 b).

T. "How it actually was"

I recall my father talking to me—I think I've got this reasonably right—of the German historian von Ranke who famously said that the historian's task was to discover "how it actually was." Here's a question: Is the novelist's task different?

I have a quarter-shelf of fiction, novels, even poetry, retelling, amending, expounding the Homeric epics.* Do they know

> Expanding seems to be of the essence. Novels are by nature long, expansive—the greatest ones are the biggest. Irène Némirovsky speaks to my point in her notes to her own wonderful novel *Suite Française*. (It was to have been a long novel, but she was deported and died in Auschwitz in 1942.) She says, citing *War and Peace*: "Expansion. That is the idea the novelist must cling to. Not completion. Not rounding off but opening out." I think I might know what she means. I've thought—and said to our students prepar-

ing to write the great American novel—that when you're on the
last day of a well-structured novel, you will know what they're all
doing the next day—and decade.

more or otherwise than the Muse told Homer? Or didn't he
have time to tell? What do their authors know and how, and
most puzzlingly, about whom? For example, there is that
fine novel, *The Silence of the Girls* (2018), just considered.
Its heroine is a passive figure in the *Iliad*. I found myself saying, "Yes, yes," and sometimes "Where'd that come from?"
Well, passages eliciting the latter sort of comment were sometimes made-up fill-in by the author, but those that called forth
assent seemed to be observed—but *what* was looked to?

The particular aspect of this question here is why there is,
at least to me, a reality-enhancing effect in such second or
further tellings, as if they confirmed the actuality of the first
book, thus turned it into a document, so to speak.

The most spectacular case I know, also mentioned above,
is a much grander work, Thomas Mann's *Joseph and His
Brothers* (1933–42). The source book is Genesis. By my reck-
oning, the Joseph novels take sixty-some times as many pages
as does the Bible to give the fleshed-out account of father
Jacob, the eleven other sons, and Joseph, the favored one.*

The account in Genesis takes around thirty pages of my Scofield
Bible; the Stockholm Edition of *Joseph and His Brothers* is 1,822
pages long.

Speak of expansive! And here's an odd but telling circumstance: the *Old Testament* presents itself as history, fact—
but the circumstantial detail-laden account is a story, fiction.
Well, of course: the further off in time the event, the more its
detail deserts memory and relies on imagination.

So with each new telling the images gain life-likeness, in
two ways. First, alternative tellings induce an impression of
aspectual or perspectival seeing: You can view the same figure or setting with different eyes, so to speak, or from differ-

ent perspectives—and either of these enhances the impression that we live in the same, real world with them. Second, each supplementary telling accretes a "thicker" description, and thus allows figure and scenes to approach the sensory plenitude of reality.

Therefore, if you have a novel-writing friend whose book you want to help become world-viable, pick some characters who are recessive and give them a coming-out telling, a piggy-back novel.*

> I think the phenomenon I'm talking about is in fact behind the pleasure we take in character-continuity over several novels. To be sure, there is always something more to be said about a well-conceived character, but there is also the satisfaction of giving the earlier figure retrospectively a future.

A half-playful, retractable answer to the question whether historians and novelists should both be engaged in finding out "how it actually was": Yes, but the venue of the research is different—and here it gets interesting, because for both it's got the same name. It's called *the past*. But it is a different past.

I should know, since I was a sort of historian in my youth, a grass-roots historian, to use an inept locution. For the grass of the Greek past (for me the eighth and seventh century B.C.E. of Attica) is utterly gone, and it was sherds of pottery, broken cooking pots tossed into disused wells, and lovely painted pots put into well-tended burials, that survived. So we sorted the trash, collected fragments, restored the shapes by gluing (this last-stage wasn't done by me; the excavation had specialists). Then we looked, described, compared, brought to bear whatever sensitivity of the eye we possessed on identifying workshops' styles, painters' hands, decorative conventions, applied complex dating inferences—and finally knew a lot about a little: how they boiled their beef, buried their children (affectionately known by the excavators as potted brats), and, low to the ground, how they saw the world. Had someone asked me: "Could you see the grandeur that was

Greece coming in this humble archaic junk?" I would have
grown eloquent. That was, however, not a cherished ability in
a very young acolyte among these down-to-earth, sober worshippers of the *realia*, which were all that really *existed* of a
past that they were recovering. For, to quote the inevitable
Goethe, what they really wished to do, without my help, was
"to seek the Land of the Greeks with the Soul"—*das Land
der Griechen mit der Seele suchen.* So I held my peace.

That's the archaeologists' bygone. And then there is the fiction writers' past. To be brief: The former look with the soul
and find by the spade. The latter look with the soul and find
by the imagination. For the first, the past comes from broken
ground, for the second, from productive memory. And what
comes thence is not real, thinglike, but it *is* actual, true—
more or less. And so my great question has morphed: What is
imaginative truth? That's for the last chapter—more a provi-
sional than a final answer.

CHAPTER FOUR

Do Feigning Images Have Originals?

Alles Vergängliche
Ist nur ein Gleichnis;
Das Unzulängliche,
Hier wird's Ereignis; . . .

All that is transient
Is but an image,
Here insufficiency
Achieves eventhood; . . .

Faust Part II, end; my accurate
but unlyrical rendering.

I have to smirk. I take down a German book now and then, and it will sport that obligatory Goethe epigraph—almost always. I shake my head, and here I'm doing it myself. But there it is: This German national drama, in losing battle with my admiring love for Albion's *Paradise Lost*, ends with the perfect quotation for this chapter, in which push comes to shove.* This final *Chorus Mysticus* proclaims that there is a

---

* I grew up thinking that *Faust* was a collection of quotations. I was an American by the time that I actually read it, as a teenager: utterly familiar and completely alien.

venue where the insufficiently actual becomes wholly so, and supplies the predicate for this realization: Temporal being is image-like, so the realization is original-like. It's too good to pass up, though a bit *ex post facto*—I'm thinking of earthly eventuations and the Chorus is singing of heavenly eventualities.

Now, near concluding, I'm reconsidering this whole enterprise and driven to cook up excuses. I've got five.

A. In Defense (Greek: *Apologia*) of My Inquiry

First, though I've not come across a published inquiry of this sort, I would bet that somewhere, in someone's folder, reserved and preserved, some fellow-soul has done and deposited exactly the same essay. This unknown friend was probably much younger and therefore cared more about being thought kooky. So I'm thinking that I'm not the only one, at least in my imagination.* The more so since it's nine months

> There is, in fact, a book that is on the brink of being explicitly concerned with originals, Raymond Prier's *Thauma Idesthai: The Phenomenology of Sight and Appearance in Archaic Greek* (1989). *Thauma* means "wonder." *Idesthai* is an infinitive of the verb "see" in the middle voice (active: *idein*), a grammatical form which signifies that its subject both performs the action on an object and is itself, somehow, reflexively affected by the sight. (The same goes for *phainesthai*, middle of *phainein*, pertinent to "fantasy," lit up in itself and lighting up the world.)
>
> Thus the phrase *thauma idesthai*, which occurs frequently (and with variations) in both Homeric epics, is interpretable as meaning that the object is wondrous, a marvel to behold, *and* that there is a special reflection of that wonder in the viewer: the object is radiant (*lampron*—the very term Socrates uses to define beauty; see above). Prier describes this kind of vision as being "for oneself and itself," both *by* the subject and *for* the object. The object itself, as eliciting such viewing, he calls a *proto-object* or a *proto-eidetic reality* ("eidetic" here means "vision-endowing"; the whole phrase is reminiscent to me of Vico's "imaginative universals").
>
> For my inquiry, the above interpretation of *thauma idesthai*, "a wonder to behold," signifies that in Homer's world the originals have descended from their transcendent seat to dwell in objects

of beauty—the phrase is often applied to humanity or divinely crafted artifacts, like Achilles's shield—which are thus proto-objects, primary as embodying the prototype and doing it superlatively, *not* as Platonic forms, but as quasi-sensory Firsts.

Prier regards as "non-modern" this double-viewing, this sight at once externally of the object and, again, internally, by way of a recognizing awareness; thus it signifies that the object is received as an intimation of a higher provenance.

But why "non-modern" when it can happen anytime? Haven't many of us wondered what it was that cast a golden glow over Homer's description of things, venues, events, people, both terrible and beautiful? Here's an answer: They are proto-objects, poetically drawn-down originals.

into COVID-19, and, along with other sensible elders, I'm locked up and looking at my books: six- to eight-thousand lamellated solids full of speech. What actually goes on in there? Do the image-beings that dwell in these curious habitations come from some Beyond of originals? How do they issue from their dwelling's mode of dead trees and speak to, lodge in, me? Time to face it!

Second, lest someone say that there's too much explained about something best left to its own devices, I have come to think: anything the worse for being exhaustively examined isn't worth much.*

Where we say "exhaustive" with a whiff of denigration, the Germans say *gründlich* as an accolade: "getting to the bottom."

Third, one's love, my love, for fictional beings can be conditional on Mondays, Wednesdays, and Fridays, and absolute on the other days including weekends. "Conditional" means that disillusionment is possible; on the next reading the character may seem more a fiction than a being—the worst fate that can befall a fictive entity. "Absolute" means that I've fallen in love with the creature, and though its author, its divinity, may not have done well by it, I'll stick with it. And here's an odd fact about fictions: They're intended to derive part of their fascination from the flaws deliberately inflicted on them by the author. But sometimes the author fails in the craft of attributing flaws, the figure goes flat or unrealistic, and yet we, having become engaged, help the author out by interpreting the authorial defect as expressive of a real debility.*

> Use of "unrealistic" makes me think of the pair *real/realistic*. What is the difference, which, if rightly articulated, must tell something pertinent to this inquiry? *Real*, I've reminded myself several times, means "thingly, thing-like." What about *realistic*? It goes, in ordinary use, in two directions. Applied to action, it means "seeing reality clearly, sensible." But applied to art it means fulfilling some requirement of verisimilitude, adequately rendering facts. And as ever, a question immediately arises: What kind of demand on art is it that it should seem real? Why should we *wish* it to be so? How *can* it be so, being art? The novelistic genre is the particular venue for realism. I'll do my best to phrase the question really suggestively, but first, Aristotle said long ago: "All human beings delight in imitations" (*Poetics* 4), so the imitational aspect is explained. The remaining question is: Why is the real particularly pleasing in imitation? It used to be a given that it was the *ideal* that art imitated to please. So the answer depends on what is meant by "real," and that is the *ordinary*. Then, in brief: the genre of the modern novel appeals to a democratic public that likes to see itself depicted. Here's the unanswered question: What kind of art can make the ordinary deeply engaging? Incipient answer: the art that knows how to magick ordinariness into humanity.

Fourth, the explanations do not make things plainer but drive them into deeper perplexities as they proceed. For example, *donegality*, the notion that atmospheres can have essences, is at least not only true to my experience but, what's more, is strongly felt by writers, some of whom I've cited. Yet no logical sense can I make of it, since a vapor, no matter how meaning-fraught, is just not capable of the degree of delimiting definiteness that is the chief feature of essentiality; it's a notion that keeps you from seeing the trees for the wood.

Indeed, donegality is not the only notion that is chimeric in this way; so is originality itself. For to be an original is not to be a certain kind of thing—nothing is just an original—nor, when all is said and done, to exercise definite functions—an original may never actually produce copies or may turn out, viewed from a higher level, to be itself an image.

My fifth, last point is not an excuse for this inquiry but an acknowledgment of its helpful effect on the inquirer: I've learned that *some* things often said and generally believed are just not so.* I've come to see that it can't be true that beauty is

I'm sure of my democratic bona fides. I tend to think that what my fellow-citizens keep saying and believing is probably sensible (and that even includes the intellectuals), but not invariably.

in the eye of the beholder. It's in the object and the behold-ers *recognize* it, even in its ugly occurences, some more dis-cerningly than others. I learned this from thinking about the distinction between a beautiful original and its less? equally? beautiful image, possibly even a deliberate fake. This engross-ing question (and many others) would be moot if beauty were subjective.*

There is a famous pot, a funerary urn, I think, that got an ode written to it, Keats's "Ode on a Grecian Urn." This vase (I guess it merits this more elegant appellation; archaeologists say "pot" of what's on their shelves)—this vase finally bursts out in speech: "Beauty is truth, truth beauty." The object is acquainted with Ploti-nus. Who knows, it may have contained his ashes, though it would take more provenance-tracing than I'm prepared for to tell if that's possible.

Anyhow what could the thing mean by this saying and the claim that it's all I need to know? Plotinus labors mightily to establish a beauty that is intellectual, thus capable of truth. This Sosibios Vase, as drawn by Keats, is very moderately beautiful itself, so why is it drawing attention to beauty? Here's a guess: The meaning of the urn's utterance lies in the complete convertibility of subject and predicate. So I think that beauty here stands in for visual-ity, truth for verbalization: The urn is asserting that its own looks and the poet's words are adequate to each other. He can speak of a handsome artifact and it can respond by being receptive to being descriptively absorbed by speech: pot and poem are "commensura-bly convertible." The pot's dictum is not nonsense, as one scholar claims, but very significant: Speech can render sights, sights can speak to us. They have a mutuality *in fact* that—I think I've shown—we have *no reason* to expect.

How to put the question! I can't ask: "Do such originals exist?" because I've committed myself to existence as meaning "being here and now," yet if they were here and now, they couldn't serve as the originals of *imaginary* images. In fact, their being, once more, is terminally ambivalent: They are neither here nor there, yet they appear as lusty, solid burghers of our world. Odysseus *in* the *Odyssey* is bursting with virility, Odysseus *beyond* the *Odyssey* must be more so; in fact he has procreated over centuries and continents, because there's many an Odysseus-lookalike bestriding the world. I've run into them (and away from them).

So I must face it and accord them a highly special original-of-images-being, as I've delineated it. Here's a first feature I would attribute to them. I've met some *natural* aristocrats in my life, ennobled not by letters patent bestowed by a palace but by a personal character developed by themselves.* It seemed

> Of course, that's upside down. They weren't ready-made natural aristocrats whose character I observed, but I noticed their conduct and thought: There goes the real thing.

to me that they were marked, first, by being perfectly natural, neither diffident nor pretentious and, second, by their inoffensive reserve, a *noli me tangere*, a courteous privacy. Just so originals seem to me: The thought of them has a certain natural obviousness, and yet they avoid easy access.

B. THE REINSTATEMENT OF IMAGE BEING

Aristotle, in his *Poetics* (1448 b, Ch. iv 6), says something that obviates, simply disposes of, a question that fascinates me: What makes an image an image? What is image being? Since he regards all drama as imitative, he explains, as mentioned above, the viewer's pleasure as a delight in the kind of learning that is recognition. We see a character and say "That's him, that's Odysseus!"—a satisfaction. But what if the viewer "has, by chance, not been in the condition of pre-seeing (proeorakos)"? Aristotle means "hasn't seen the original before-hand?" Then, he says, the imitation "will not provide the pleasure insofar as *it is an imitation* [my italics], but by reason of the execution. . . ."

In other words, an image has no independent image-force, independent of our knowing it to be an image. I think that's totally wrong, but it poses a challenge: think out what an image, presumably *ipso facto* an imitation, is in its very own being—content withdrawn.*

> When my godson was four or so, I took him to a children's play, whose venue was a dark forest—which was a little too scary. At a point, Chrissy was scrunched up against me (the seat arm was up) and comforting me with the incantation "It's just make-believe; it's not for real!" He was denying the power of images *as* images, in this case, to de-scarify!

I'll give it a try right now. Three main content-independent attractions of image-viewing offer themselves: *ontological teasing, supine biddableness, interpretative incitement.*

The philosophical teasing arises from the paradox of image-essence, the togetherness of Being and Nonbeing, the paradox of the *being* of its contents: "That is my kid (or my cat)," upon which we must say "Isn't it cute!" But also, of the *not being* of its subjects, so that, were we offered a copy of the picture, we would gratefully put it in our wallet, while, were the content-subjects real, we would return either of them, if offered (at least the cat). I think this existential duplicity, this extension and retraction of the promise of presence, exercises a certain seduction.

The biddableness, the docility, lies in the enforced passivity of an image, the impotence of its depictions: Put your hand up against a lion's open maw and no incisor will gnaw you; even the worst of imagined humans can't materially harm you. In an image *as* image, no matter what the producer's intention, the content is physically powerless.

The incitement, the arousal, of the desire to cull meaning

lies in the imagery itself; it arises from its *specific incomplete-ness.** To look at an image is often to feel impelled to articulate

> I'm now thinking of *qualities* that images often lack (rather than of the ambiguities of their *existence*), such as a principle of motion (life), a solid dimension and its coloration (materiality), and a soul that thinks, wills, and feels (consciousness).

the meaning it was intended to skew or hide, to clue out how it is implicitly framing the world of which it is an excerpt, even to divine how one might gain entrance into it.

C. The Truth and Primacy of Originals

Why does this topic, the being of originals, become an issue, a preoccupation—a question? What in our humanity might make one of us burrow into this notion of an original?

To me it seems that the terminal inquiry concerning inanimate things and animate beings—objects we *have* before us—will, inevitably, concern such originals. Thus the ultimate questions concerning internalities, such as possibly partite souls and reflective, "back-bent" selves—the subjects we *are* within us—must be, for the former, the souls, "What is their model, whence come their looks?" and for the latter, the selves, "What makes them move, what brings them alive?"

Objects and subjects are hence, it hardly needs saying, interdependent. Beings, objects, arouse desires (or aversions) that move our souls, affect us, as subjects. These desires are of two sorts; one sort is that for possession in various modes and is called *appetite*, the other for knowledge of various kinds and is called a *question*.

Thus feeling and thinking are not, rightly considered, by nature at odds (though that is a common preaching). They are, rather, harmonious. For both are ultimately desires that consequently arouse the willing expenditure of effort.*

> Why then does love not always issue in knowledge? Because love functions duplicitously. It gives us the inside knowledge that

comes from intense attention, but it also inserts a filter, that very love, between subject and object. This is one reason why people say that beauty is in the eye of the beholder—another is that tastes just differ. Here's a difference between "in love" and "love": In the former, that filter beautifies; in the latter, it's a high-resolution magnifying lens, and the beauty had better be in the object.

One last time on "real": *Real* is, recall, from late-Latin *realis*, from *res*, "thing"—thus "thingly."

And an observation on the frequent, perfectly factual dissonance of passion and reason. It seems to me not to arise from some natural misfitting of these two human capabilities, but because passion has picked the wrong object. Sometimes everyone sees that beforehand but the one impassioned; usually everyone is wise after the fact—*ex post facto* insight. I think we're just not up to the situation, and our comfort has to be in the very fact that there is, after all, a right and a wrong choice.

Back to *real*, one more point: From *real* we get to *realize*, "to make real, to turn into a thing." Here is an example. A beauty, a thing of beauty, in particular a deliberate work of art, arises (I am paraphrasing Schelling from Copleston, *History of Philosophy*, Vol. VII, Ch. vi) when an object is so perfectly in accord with its idea that it can be said *literally* to realize it. Thus in a beautiful object we see *a notion made into a thing*. Is it intelligible?

This concept seems to me to carry Platonism way beyond itself. Now the forms, the ideas, rather than being responsible for the appearing world, which imitates or participates in them, themselves descend into appearances. The original is now melded with the individual thing; the forms have fallen down to earth.

So, in sum, the question concerning originals is as natural to us as an interest in our genealogy, our family history. We expect the latter to reveal the genuineness of our generation, our birth, and to guide us to the discovery of our elders and betters. It's analogous for these originals.

And now to the questions to be asked about the originals of our fictions, and the demands to be made on their originality. The encompassing question is: What is imaginative truth? That sounds like a contradiction in terms, since the imagination is generally taken to be an agency for "making things up."

It is indeed such a contradiction, unless it turns out that the imagination fictionalizes only secondarily, but is primarily a receptivity. Hence the question immediately turns towards the originating originals.

But which way round? Is it because the imagination is receptive that we must ask what it receives? Or is it the reverse, that we apprehend fiction as news from somewhere and of something? I think we are alive to the product before we regard its producer and to the object before the subject.

And why originals rather than some higher-order tale-telling, storytelling ratcheted up into the Muses' home, to Parnassus in central Greece or Olympus high up in the north, or deposited in myth-preserving Hades, the underworld at the edge of the world?* Or kept in the memories of bards or in

> Odysseus visits Hades, there to find the heroes and especially the heroines of Greek myth (*Odyssey* xi). The mode of being characteristic of Hades, fleshless spatiality, bodyless appearance, has exactly that notional ambivalence which I have been attributing to imaginative originals.

books held in libraries? Well, because of the infinite regress that would result if the source of stories were stories. There has to be some sort of reality to make a beginning and a backstop. And also because, unlike empty time and featureless space that have within themselves no principle of definition, distinction, or destination, the imaginative field is continual and not continuous, punctuated and not monotonous, multiform and not homogeneous. And yet it is not archetypal but derivative—its very name and that of its product, *imagination* and *image*, is cognate with *imitate*, and so denotes them as copyist and copy, hence as having an original.

Original, then, implies a sort of firstness, but what sort? Is it a temporal primacy, being before in time, plain earlier?* Or

> Time, incidentally, also has its originals or something analogous: moments. An example is to be found in Geertz's account of the Balinese cockfight. The event reproduces the temporal mode of Balinese life, an "on-off pulsation of meaning and vacuity." So each match is an intense display of furious aggression and bloody mayhem, an isolated, unique moment, neither connected to, nor repeat-

able by, any other fight, distinguished as an original by its temporal pointillism. Onlookers drift in and out, but the fight clearly lodges in the spectators' imaginations—multiple images of what the Balinese most fearfully evade in the human realm: manic explosions.

is it primacy in rank and dignity, which we intend when we praise "originality"? Or is it generative origination, the power to spawn similars, copies? Is its dignity in its uniqueness, its being a one-and-only, as opposed to the permissible multiplicity of a copy? On the other hand, can there be a solitary original, *sui generis*, the only one of its kind? Are originals and copies of the same kind to begin with, and what is their common kind?

This is the budget of questions that I've looked into, for example, the list of original-priorities presented above. Here, as so often, is an addition, an afterthought: Perhaps originals are even distinguished from copies in respect to place. Originals tend to have a place—in a frame, in the safe—while copies fly all over and become litter, ending up in the wastepaper basket, throwaways.

D. A Reprise of the Ancients

This attempt to let push come to shove will, once again, begin with two deep but ultimately unhelpful approaches to the question of my chapter title concerning the originals of feignings.*

> Why are the ancients, represented for me by Plato and Aristotle, generally deeper than the moderns? The third party to this claim are the Stoics, the proto-moderns of antiquity, because of their novel representationalism, the notion that the world is ours insofar as it comes to us in impressions, re-presentations. They don't figure in this inquiry because for impressionists the question concerning imaginative originals is drowned in the global question whether a real world is required as the original of our impression-images. Berkeley's *esse est percipi*, "to be is to be perceived" (*A Treatise Concerning the Principles of Human Knowledge*, 1710, ¶3) actually implies a negative answer: our impressions, our mental images, require no back-up realities, no originals.

My answer is this: The great moderns, so I think, are the systematizers. But an idea, when worked into a system, be it organic
or mechanical, becomes a part, hence leveled by its participation,
its functional duties. The great ancients are exuberantly unsys-
tematic, though maybe the Stoics not so much and the Neoplatonists not at all—they fill in "Plato" furiously. Hence each topic,
as it comes under scrutiny for the non-systematizers, preserves its
pristine wondrousness. The deliberate systematizers, the Neoplatonists, go completely mystical in compensation.

So then, first, a brief final reprise of Plato's *Sophist*, this
first onto-logical, this "Being-accountable" *analysis of images
as images*, and the consequent *condemnation of the use of
images in the Republic*.* In the *Sophist* (240), an image is

Consequent: not meant temporally.

accounted for by a melding of the forms Being and Nonbeing,
and the latter is radically reinterpreted from Mere Nothing to
Otherness, Difference, relational negation: Not-this-but-that
(25 b). Thus, as self-same-*and*-other, an image is marked as
belonging to a class of entities that are a difficulty to themselves. In the human instantiation, there are fellow souls who
tear themselves apart just by being what they are, and distress
others in being difficult to live with and impossible to get away
from.* This analysis has the virtue of illuminating images

A perfect example is the anti-hero of Marilynne Robinson's masterpiece *Jack*.

as images, but for my purpose, the inquiry into *imaginary*
images, it has the defect of saying nothing concerning the
content *as* image-content: whence and of what?

Then, second, the *Republic* (Books II and X) does indeed
focus on this content, to proscribe it, first, for being too exclusively engrossed by morally reprehensible but stimulating
figures and settings, by fascinating badness, instead of making excellence look lovable (Book II) and second, for its very
unoriginality, its falling away from the thing itself to appear
as its own imitation (Book X). And thus, antisymmetrically

about the nearly precise numerical center of the scroll, the book, there is a higher approach.* There is a new proscription,

> Exactly where the philosopher-ruler and his/her education are introduced.

not because of content but for the very derivativeness, the imagistic occlusion of the original by the privileging of its images. But in neither book is the imaged figure at issue.

Next, third, Aristotle, whose *Poetics* is a tactfully inexplicit attack on Plato, argues not only that image-recognizing does have its *own pleasure* (which Plato's Socrates would agree to while terming it psychologically corrupting) but that it is, in fact, a *learning experience* (which Socrates would deny). Aristotle, as well, is not interested in the beings behind the fiction. That actually is to be expected. He is writing before the advent of the novelistic genre and so is most interested in *drama*, Greek for "deed." Thus he duly regards *plot*, the plan of action, as prior to the characters, the mere executors.*

> I was opportunely reminded by Daniel Rodriguez, an alumnus, that as Aristotle (in Ch. 6) puts the *mythos*, the plot, before the *ethos*, the "character" of the characters, so novelists—the good ones—delineate figures to themselves or their readers and then let them loose to act out these assigned characters (*onomatopoeic*: "a mark scrrratched on them"). Fictional figures are thus split-minded, *schizophrenic*: They have no self-determination at all by the very fact that the author may have written the freest of wills into their character. So these plot-shaped beings are not suscepti-ble to fully-rounded personhood.

E. THE SECULAR FAITH REQUIRED

Soon I want to enter into the most surprisingly revealing anal-ogy of image-originals that I know of: *angels*. But first—this seems the place—a word about faith. For faith, or perhaps better faithfulness (not a dogma but a disposition), is a need-ful ingredient of this inquiry. I am not, to be sure, thinking of religious doctrine, and I am certainly not inclined to believe in angels just because I begin to see a solution in their nature. I can do even better—more, I want to say, devotedly: not belief but the genuine agnosticism I have laid out in Chapter Three.

Among my friends there have been declared agnostics. On closer acquaintance, it turned out that they meant by that self-appellation to fend off others who attempted conversions on them: "Go away, leave me alone, I'm an agnostic," meaning "I'm already a convert to the class of those interested in not being interested"—a form of ostrich-behavior. An a-gnostic for real, however, I'll say again, is an "alpha-privitive [a grammarian's term for the negating prefix] knower," a non-knower—a *genuine* agnostic. It's not that I don't care; it's that I'm ignorant.

Neither ostrich-behavior nor, while I'm at it, a very discriminating distaste for select groups of my fellow citizens, is proscribed by our constitution—and so permitted.* What

* My favorites for disfavoring: intellectuals and bureaucrats. That means people only when they turn themselves into types.

the First Amendment does proscribe is—I'm happily repeating myself—"abridging freedom of speech," and in establishing this near-sacred right, it seems to me, Article 1 does imply a *shadow-right* that protects the inclination not to utter determinately. Thus it is not, I think, humility that keeps, say Socrates, from asserting an expertise—humility being, in any case, a cringe-making virtue, this creeping "close to the humus," for me, a deep-seated revulsion. It is rather a form of arrogance, no less a sort of vice for being camouflaged.—No, arrogance does not fit a model-worthy philosopher either; call it rather a humanely softened stand-offishness. All this is in defense of my faithful agnosticism. I just don't know, though I wish I did, and that to me has potent consequences: the effort to be a knowledgeable non-knower. It is the very condition Socrates models. Unlike fictive images, real persons (me) have real originals (him), albeit the imaging is neither in the mode of visibility nor of dogma but of just this—faithfulness.*

> *Re* religious dogma: Dogma understood as an approved teaching seems to me to warrant attentive listening. As an intended imposition it seems to me an incitement to cunning withdrawal or open resistance. Yet I have respect for fellow souls who have it in them, as I haven't, positively to submit, without lacking the grit, if necessary, negatively to resist. To me that's a *double* gift I don't have.

The willingness, however, to submit to some very odd notions that urge themselves on me, when, to use a handy but misleading phrase, all roads lead to Rome, so that without those ideas things can't be got to come together—this faithfulness to things thought out, I do have. And it now makes me take account in all seriousness of my experience: The figures and scenes of epics and novels rise to the level of realities outside their text.* Such faith-propensity is needed especially

> Why not drama as well? Because, whether I am a reader in an armchair or a spectator in a rowchair, of the four great genres, epic, lyric, drama, novel, the drama is most naturally incarnate and so least suggestive of originals. For, though the actors are impersonators pretending to be a scripted character, they remain ineradicably real people who bring along much personal detail that trumps their craft. Here's an example. Paul Scofield's impersonation of Thomas More, a hero of mine, was so plausible that in the London staging of *A Man for All Seasons* he transfixed me for three nights in a row, so that I left my snickering traveling companions to their own devices, to revel in the impersonated company of a man who combined devout surrender with cunning resistance. But, of course, Scofield appeared in various movies that I saw as well, and I recall the sense that Thomas More had been hijacked and disguised. So much of him had been incarnated in this particular actor that, had I met him in Hades, I would not have acknowledged him. So I began to think about this problem: How far can even the most controlled and crafty actor suppress his/her natural incarnation so that a very precise new self-image can take over? How recessive can a real original make itself?

because a certain perversity acts up: My very desire that the case for originals should win may stand in the way of self-persuasion, where there is just about enough reason to sub-

mit. No, the psychic liberality of letting scruple yield to trust
should reign.

I'll add two more notes to these virtues of temperament:
First, the vividness of a conception, not the gaudy but the
demure kind, should be allowed its not so trustworthy persuasion, and second, an equally weak recourse, the testimony of operatives in the arena should assume weight. I'll
add three final ones here. Edith Wharton (to me the American Jane Austen) speaks in her autobiography *A Backward
Glance* (1933) of "the strange beings who command me to tell
their stories"—this is a really delightfully complex analysis of
the novelist's work: the characters eventuate and assume that
the author knows the plot in which they're implicated. Whatever Edith Wharton was thinking, her words say that there
are beings and then, no matter how much the being's character determines the tale, it has an element of contingency:
the being/the story. This duality speaks to the verisimilitude
of novels, their lifelikeness. We have our story, an element of
which, going like a figured base beneath it all, says: "This
continuo could have supported an other tale."

Then there is Alice Walker's lovely novel *The Color Purple*
(1982), which concludes with an epilogue, one line on the last
page, addressing her characters: "I thank everybody in this
book for coming. A.W., author and medium."

And finally, my special love, W. P. Kinsella's baseball novel
Shoeless Joe (1982; Shoeless Joe Jackson was implicated in
fixing the 1919 World Series). Here a mysterious announcer's voice says to Kinsella during a game, I think in Fenway
Park: "If you build it, he will come." He builds the diamond
on his Iowa farm, using up a cornfield. Shoeless Joe and his
teammates duly show up as ghosts on the edge of the carefully rolled turf and become incarnate as they step onto it.*

When I served as dean, this sentence was pasted on the door-
post of the Dean's Office door (which was almost always open). Of

course, I didn't mean Shoeless Joe and his Black Sox teammates. I meant Plato's Socrates and George Eliot's Dodo and the like. They came as well.

Above, I was collecting the features of originals and the modes of their existence. Now I want to ask: What demands can be made on such originals *as* originals? I answer that they should project a sense of "the buck stops here," that there are no returns in going behind or above them. Do others share my sense, in the face of a fine fiction or any sort of work excellent in craftedness, looks, significance: This isn't yet *it*. Something is *showing itself forth in* these works, *from behind* their appearance? They are a front, perhaps for a something that has discharged what I am viewing and has withdrawn to stand off and behind, leaving a trace of itself.*

> It is probably this sense, this intimation of an archetype that is already an experience, though a nameless one of childhood, one that opens the way to *very* occasional glimpses of transcendence and eventually supports the willingness to read some very obscure books.
>
> "Archetype," German *Urbild*, can be used to cover sins of fuzzy thinking, as in an otherwise charming book, Hesse's *Narcissus and Goldmund*; the latter speaking: "The *Urbild* of a good work of art is not an actual living figure, though it might be the occasion for it. The archetype is not flesh and blood, it is of the spirit. It is a picture that has its home in the soul of the artist." And Narcissus explicates: "This 'archetype' is to a T exactly what the ancient philosophers call an 'idea.'" Well, it's exactly *not* that; it's a quasi-visual, a mental, image, whereas an idea, at least the Platonic kind, is, albeit apprehended with the mind, not subjective but actual and non-visual (though I considered above that for some Neoplatonists it may have involved a de-materialized but sensory vision). A consideration here is that in Narcissus—whose name, that of a self-enamored mythical being, doesn't seem to fit this very austere monk—Hesse has invented a figure that in general, if not here, exceeds Hesse himself in acuteness.

Next, an original should project, for all its uniqueness, a potency for numerical increase,* for propagating and spawning,

> With some exceptions, see above.

a professional fecundity, a readiness to "be fruitful and multiply"—or less figuratively, a capability for being copied. All that lies in the notion of an original. Moreover, an original needs to be accessible to a comparing inspection by which to assert its primacy, while maintaining its mystery; it must be able to descend into the copy while remaining distinctively aloof.

I am inquiring into the possibility of objective beings behind the story; let me first cite a great storyteller's attempt to grapple with this perplexity by producing a subjective chimera: an abstract spirit—more thought-provoking than solution-producing.

F. The Storytelling Spirit

Peal of bells, surge of bells, *supra ubem*, over the whole city, in its airs overfilled with clangor.

So begins and ends a book by Thomas Mann, *The Holy Sinner* (*The Chosen One*, 1951). The bells are celebrating the cortege and crowning of a new pope, the Chosen one, the Holy Sinner. Here's the problem: All the bell ringers are out on the street celebrating; the bell ropes hang slack and unpulled. Who's ringing every bell in Rome's seven dioceses?

The answer is: it is the *Spirit of Storytelling*.

He it is who says: 'All the bells were ringing,' and consequently it's he who is ringing them. So spiritual is this Spirit and so abstract, that grammatically he can only be spoken of in the third person, and it can only mean: 'It is he.' And yet he can coagulate himself into a person, namely the first, and incarnate himself in someone who speaks when so impersonated and says: 'I am He. I am the spirit of storytelling.'

And that is, to be sure, not Thomas Mann, but one Clemens the Irelander, a monk, who now begins to tell the scandalous story of the Holy Sinner.

Mann is, playfully, to be sure, offering an answer to the

question, thus corroborated as askable: "Who gives life, who gives sensory presence, to the characters of a fiction?" It is not a human author, but a spirit, an abstraction—that is, universal and impersonal—that incarnates itself, impersonates itself, in a human being.

Try to pry this apart—it boggles the mind. Storytelling, feigning, fiction-making, is a life-bestowing incorporeal but impersonateable abstraction! The action this spirit performs, a world-creation really, takes place, however, in a book, a written story. And, of course, it takes a reader, myself, yourself, to revivify this written life, to release it from the mere letter, the mere literariness, of *The Holy Sinner*, a book.

Is it all just tricksiness? No, I think Mann means something, means to give an answer to my question: Whence originate the figures? Never mind that here they're pealing bells: "They're talking, all of them at once, all interrupt each other, even themselves."

He intends to avoid this crudely curtailed answer: Clemens is the creator of the tale, or worse, his brain is. So Mann interposes the Spirit of Storytelling, supra-human, im-personal, dis-carnate. The time frame is indeterminately medieval, so Christian.

This Storytelling Spirit is, I think, the Christian counterpart of the Olympian Muses that Homer calls to his aid: "The man—tell me, Muse, of him, the twisty one"—that's Odysseus. So Clemens, too, receives the Spirit that tells him the story. Neither the Muse nor the Spirit tell a new story; it is a fresh re-telling, a renovation that takes the burden of innovation off the teller and with it the suspicion of making things up.

But there's a difference: The pagan merely passes on the tale he's been told, while the Christian does that and something extra—he creates a world.* I mean by "extra" that the

---

It's my understanding of the *Odyssey* that it lacks this extra and is, indeed, wholly realistic. I mean that Odysseus, as I said above, the

first teller of his "odyssey," is also its "poet"—its *poietes*, "maker"—
not maker-up. And what he tells of are his piracy and brigandage
and various other depredations undertaken on the way home from
Troy, as well as all the women he fell in and stayed with—and all
the real islands and strange palaces, tucked-away harbors and wel-
coming whore-houses in which he prolonged his return to his true
allegiances, his wife, son, and island home. But he has a poet's soul
and artistry as great as Homer's, and so he tells his, sometimes
sordid, adventures so poetically that there's nothing in them

> But doth suffer a sea-change
> into something rich and strange (*Tempest* I ii 400).

tale is not only lifelike in itself, but comes with a warrant: a
Spirit, an intercessor, who has not merely humanly poetic, but
divinely creative, power—and so brings forth a heaven and an
earth *without the need of an original*: *ex nihilo*—a neat and
nihilating answer to my question. But I resist that shortcut to
nowhere, that question-nullification.

Next comes a true marvel, a real answer, with one draw-
back for me: I haven't got that *little* plus it takes to believe in
angels.

G. The Angelic Analogy

To turn back, then, from Mann's subjective attributions of an
original's nature to the objective analogy with original-prop-
erties—back to the angels. In the *Summa Theologia*, Thomas
Aquinas offers a long disquisition on the nature of angels (Q.
50 ff.), on which, in the absence of personal experience, I shall
draw. Then I'll follow the paradisiacal angelic inventory with
the analogous one for imaginary originals.

ANGELS

1. begin as creations, but do not end.
2. have a life but do not age.
3. do not change.
4. do not live in passing time yet are compatible with its
   passage.

5. have their own paradisiacal temporality, between eternity and time, the *aevum* (Q. 10).*

> A history and analysis of *aevum* is given in Ernst H. Kantorowicz's *The King's Two Bodies: A Study in Mediaeval Political Theology* (1957), Ch. VI 1. A point of special interest to me is Kantorowicz's claim that *aevum* is conceptually similar to the Aristotelian *eide*, which are "immanent actualizations of the separate types." To me that puts *aevum* and Aristotelian *eide* both in the chimeric class of yoked incompatibles. I must not apologize for not working out the donegality of Aristotelian forms and of angelic *aevum*, for, if I had written the required three pages of joyfully pedantic polemicism, I'd have to say sorry for inflicting them on a conceivably less chimera-fascinated reader.

6. are each *sui generis*, fixed in its own intelligible species, yet can make considered choices.
7. assume bodies to express their nature, bodies that are, however, incorruptibly incorporeal.

FICTIONS

1. are made, come into being and are given whatever mode of existence they have, by an artful author, but they do not cease to be. Thus Gilgamesh and Enkidu, those poignantly faithful friends, appeared first in the *Gilgamesh* perhaps four thousand years ago, but are still perfectly present to me.
2. never age, but are now of such ages as they were when conceived.
3. do not change between my encounters with them (except as I have changed). The books in which they live are ineditable (except for a new edition or as a frightened author may be driven by censorship. Thus Dostoevsky's *Demons* had its beating heart ripped out when the terrible chapter, telling of Stavrogin's crime, "At Tikhon's," was suppressed). Published books are, properly, ineditable.
4. do not live in progressively passing, historical time, yet are perpetually relevant to any time—if their book is great.

5. have, therefore, their own paradisiacal time, their time-bubble. Recall that *paradise* means "a walled safe-haven," the wall-part, *dheigh-*, meaning dough, that is cement, being also related to "feigning": significance-accumulation! This bubble-time is *aevum*-like, between passing time and still eternity.

6. are, as Vico termed it, each an "imaginative universal," at once an intensely, will-endowed individual *and* more a universal than any historical person, as Aristotle claims (*Poetics*, Ch. 9).

7. are, in good books, persuasively embodied. I mean through thick description—which does not need to involve much wordage: some very great novelists achieve descriptive density with concision. For example, here's Jane Austen describing *Persuasion*'s Anne Elliot: "her delicate features and mild dark eyes" (Vol. 1, Ch. I). Yet these bodies do not age except with their author's permission, nor emit even the faintest "odor of corruption"; in fact, in many novels no human being of consequence dies. Great contrary case: the corpse of Father Zosima in *The Brothers Karamazov*, who emits this "odor of corruption," shocking his devout young acolyte into a spiritual revolution (Book VII, 1).

All the above was fun to work out, but, in truth, for little return on originals; they're just not in it, neither construed as angelic nor as fiction-originating. Nor would Thomas have welcomed my angel/fiction relation; angels are, for him, too prepotent in reality. Yet there is a real illumination in this curious exercise: Its lesson is that *creation* and *making* are in truth deeply different. God created the angels, needing no matter, regarding no model—*ex nihilo*, out of nothing. Human authors need both. So for the Biblical Creator there is no question of originals, for human makers it persists.

Here is a helpful text: Thomas Mann's *Doctor Faustus* (1947, Sec. XIV).* A club of young students of theology, including

> The hero's life is in its phases almost precisely, numerically, par-
> allel with Nietzsche's. (I've done the math.) So Leverkühn's story
> is hybrid, part "indigenous," part "immigrant" (see above), as the
> whole novel itself is hermaphroditic: a historical novel, a factual
> fiction.

the novel's hero, a composer and, earlier on, a student of the-
ology, has a get-together. Leverkühn has played for them, improvising on the piano. A naive young colleague is flab-
bergasted by Leverkühn's answer when asked what that was he's just performed: "Nothing." He demands how the future composer can claim that it's nothing when he's just played it. The youngster means to ask: How can you play what hasn't preexisted, what has no prescriptive score to read off? Then ensues a theological disputation *re* God's exclusive power of *ex nihilo* creation and the fact that:

> human creativity had finally to be recognized theologically as a
> distant reflection of the divine power of creating beings, a reso-
> nance of the all-powerful call to becoming, and the productive
> inspiration as coming, after all, from above.

The scene is uncanny because Leverkühn's improvisation is an intimation of his later composing which is, ambivalently a denial and a corroboration of human creativity, of producing absolute novelty, that is, from nothing, from no pardigm. For Leverkühn—whose name says that he "lives boldly," will sell his soul to the devil for years of creative production, of creating a new music. So indentured, he does not really produce in the earthly human mode but is absorbed into the united realm of heaven-and-hell. Evidently human creativity requires such soul-indenturing contracts.

But from the modes of bringing fictions into being, back to the fictions themselves, and now to the question *whence* they come into books. Here are two apt terms, already laid out above, with which to think of provenance: *indigenous* and *immigrant*.* "Indigenous" are the figures born and bred

Terence Parsons, *Nonexistent Objects* (1980), Ch. 1.

within the book, "immigrant" are the figures that come from *outside*, from active people in the world, who have real originals that they mirror, with varying degrees of verisimilitude, the hybrids mentioned in a note above. Add to this population those figures of myth, those public authorless stories whose figures were for Vico a period-characterizing thought-mode, the imaginative universals, as yet another kind of fictive being. But even much later, myths are thought of as having a clarifying function, shaping happenings by "arrangement and hierarchy."*

Richard Weaver, *Ideas Have Consequences* (1948), Ch. 1.
   The story of Oedipus, as mythical as it gets and shaped into hieratic drama, is a well-fitting parallel to the fate of Job, probably not even a Hebrew, yet absorbed into Sacred Scripture. In Weaver's terms, the Oedipus myth can be seen as *arranging* the events of his life into a drama, *Oedipus the King*, enacting the eventuation of a terminal paradox: Without doubt, Oedipus has committed patricide and incest, albeit unknowingly, and this story is developed by gradual revelation, rearranging the king's life. But the story also develops a *hierarchical* aspect by showing the god's oracle as supervening on Oedipus's own final judgement of his innocence (in *Oedipus at Colonus*, e.g. 966). It says: You did the deed; you must pay. And, like Job, who is subjected to suffering by his God, but will neither concede guilt nor blame him, he is rewarded. Job gets a life back, albeit a new one (to me, an inhuman compensation!). Oedipus's life ends not in death but in annihilation. There are no remains to be buried and he is not among the shades in Hades, as far as I've heard (*Odyssey* xi 271). He's undone, gone—nowhere, relieved of *all* being.

The immigration status of mythical figures moving into authored works of art—can they really become citizens?—is questionable, but perhaps that of bona fide immigrants is even more so. These figures are not touched by the question of origins since their originals are easily discerned in the real world, plausibly documented, historical.* So Napoleon in *War*

> Here's an interesting fact told me by my colleague Louis Petrich:
> In all of Shakespeare's so-called history plays, all of the characters
> are immigrants, that is, from the real world, but one—Falstaff.
> He's indigenous, a true-born son of the imagination. Wonderful
> question: Why?

and Peace, Lincoln in any number of Civil War stories, Shoeless Joe Jackson and all the ghostly Black Sox in Kinsella's
Shoeless Joe or the movie *Field of Dreams*—they all have
their indubitable origins in real people. But once again, it gets
muddled: verisimilitude butts in. Does an ineptly executed
or deliberately falsified depiction change an immigrant into
a native? Can ineptitude naturalize immigrants? How much
does intention count? To my mind, you can deviate if you well
know the straight and narrow; if not, it's not deviation but
errancy. But then again, does the author's integrity matter if
the work be good?*

> These quasi-moral questions arising in the realm of that highly
> respected lie-telling called fiction are at once risible and engross-
> ing. One example: Is a young writer, say a student of coura-
> geous incompetence, more promising than one of conforming
> competence?
>
> Here's another. I preach the virtue of plagiarism to students
> (when they let me), yet I'm against shoplifting. Why? Both activi-
> ties filch what the owner values. But stealing supine stuff deprives
> the owner of possession, the power just to control or actually to
> enjoy. Our thoughts and their emitting words are, on the other
> hand, neither controllable nor consumable, but are given potency
> by propagation. Example: You shouldn't tell students things but
> incite them to tell you. Yet if, in a moment of lost self-control, you
> have pontificated, and the bespoke student (so to speak) goes and
> tells others, even without attribution, am I, who sent my thoughts
> in the world, not the beneficiary? In general: Isn't learning from a
> teacher, be it in person or through a book, approved plagiarism?
> Do we want to call learning misappropriation? Above all: Can one
> steal what is invaluable?
>
> On a few occasions words have been said to me, or I have read
> them, which seemed familiar because they were mine. Mine? Well,
> happily no longer. I gave them away. What was the point of this
> long expectoration? To discourage the thought that the search for
> originals is an exercise in sourcing, in credit-giving.

H. Hades, the Home of Originals

Here's a penultimate thought for which a possible reader will not like me the better. I want to apply what I said above to my death: I haven't got a clue what comes next, after my body's certified decease. There's no place to look it up. And even if, Hamlet notwithstanding, who thinks that death is an "undiscovered country from whose bourn / No traveler returns" (III i 80), such a revenant did turn up—why would I believe his travelogue?* Death has a large topology, as I imagine that

Hamlet's dead father did, in fact, just that: turn up (I i 41).

venue, and I may land in a very different place from his. But I must be allowed to draw on the benefits of true agnosticism. If I truly can't know that there is a post mortem on the other side of dying, I also don't know that there isn't. That side of my ignorance entitles hope, gives room to imaginative expectation, even if I contemplate the worst possibility. Here *Paradise Lost* does the imagining for me; in Satan's realm, Hades/Hell, they carry on as we do at my college, also built on rising ground:

> Others apart sat on a hill retired,
> In thoughts more elevate, and reasoned high
> Of providence, foreknowledge, will and fate,
> Fixed fate, free will, foreknowledge absolute,
> And found no end, in wand'ring mazes lost (Book II 557 ff.).

Long before Milton (and Dante) visited this realm, Odysseus did; he as well went down not as a permanent resident but as a one-day visitor (*Odyssey* xi). In xxiv Hermes brings down Penelope's unwanted suitors, slain by Odysseus. So Homer went down there, once with Odysseus, once with Hermes, and once for good. Socrates, for whom I would be willing to brave Hades, would not arrive until 771 years after Odysseus's descent.*

Here's the math. The traditional date for the fall of Troy is 1183 B.C.E. Odysseus, as far as we know, quite soon after began his odyssey, his return, taking 20 years to get home. The final 7 years were spent lost to the world, with Calypso on her island. (Her name means: "I will hide [him].") So he arrived in Hades 13 years after leaving Troy, in 1170 B.C.E. Socrates died in 399. Subtract 399 from 1170, and 771 years separate Odysseus's arrival from Socrates'. But he's there now. I feel close to both of these souls, but given eternal togetherness, I'd prefer Socrates.

Here's a subject for musing;* it bears on the venue of originals.

> Turning muddles into wonder and wonder into musing is, I believe, a respectable mission in life. Wonder is the hinge here because it means both marveling and considering.

When heroes' corpses are burnt they turn into shades. What kind of transmogrification has occurred? Shades are certainly not angels, but they surely are now originals, and share angelic properties. In Hades they live in a temporality neither of present/past/future and forward passage, that is, *time*, nor of the standing now, the *nunc stans*, that is, *eternity*, but of the *aevum* described above; thus Hades is like Paradise (albeit antisymmetrically), and if you descended you would see the aboriginal originals—who are indeed imaged in epic and dramas. It is really strange that, be it Homeric Hades or Miltonian Hell, the underworld seems more livable than the celestial venue. But that's probably because I'm imagining *living* there. *Post mortem* it might be, as I've said, more congenial up in Heaven.

When Odysseus arrives at the mouth of the underworld and summons the shades, he gives them blood to drink and they grow ruddy (xi). Here's an interpretation: the first work of all epic poetry and novelistic prose is *to incarnadine*, to help the originals live among and for us, all redd up as they used to say.

Am I ready with an answer to my question? Are there originals?—No, there's always more prelude to a proof: What is, in sum, the essence, the originality of an original *as* an original? What is it without which an original is sterile as a mule? Well, the answer is in the question. Apart from its particular content, an original lives up to its name when it begets, bears, spawns—orginates. When all is said and done (and I think I've said plenty) this is the primary demand on an original. It is

1. copy-able/imit-able/image-able
2. copy-prone/imitation-prone/imaging-prone.*

> Most of these terms are not dictionary words but I imagine they've been used by somebody.

I mean that originals *can* be copied *and want* to be copied.* To anthropomorphize here—originals as desiring to be

> Not all, as I've said before. There are solipsistic originals.

parents—is unavoidable: there is something in these originals that demands imaging.

How can that be? My first thought, to go with the etymology of "original" as that which *has arisen, is born* (Latin *oriri*), is unhelpful. The origin of originals, their family, may be in Hell as defeated rebels or in heaven as created angels, but for us, I will now conclude, they are *postulates.**

> I didn't say "nothing but." Let the exacting Latinate locution pass by unregarded for now.

More prelude: What does it take to be copyable (a real word), what is that capability? It's a question prior to that about art and artists, the making and the makers of images, and rarely asked in public—though surely in many a soliloquy or private colloquy.

I. Radiant Visibility

It takes, I think, *visibility* (and, *mutatis mutandis*, audibility, tangibility, *etc.*). Without raising the vexed question concerning theories of vision—how the sensory intake is converted into the visual experience—I want to try a phenomenological approach.*

> Phenomenology describes, as meticulously as the observer can detail it, conscious experience. Insofar as the brain subserves seeing, the account is given in neuroscience. But there has to be a reliable experiential account for the science to go to work.

I experience, I'm pretty sure, seeing at the site, *at the object.* The more I'm giving over to looking, the more it feels that way: a beloved face is a sight-magnet. So ocular viewing takes place *before* the eye, confronting the organ of sight. Now shut the eye.* It turns out that seeing has also conveyed sights *from*

> The fact that ears have no lids must bear on the image analysis of audibles. First guess: auditory images have fewer indices of being images. Even birds are fooled by man-made bird calls, but who takes a picture for its original? What *is* the image of a piece of music? Can non-experts tell a really good electronic transmission from a live performance? On the other hand, we do have silent mental images of pieces of music.
>
> One consequence of lidless ears: We are self-trained in shutting out auditory perceptions *in their presence*, to degrade them automatically. What effect does that have on our image-recognition? Just ruminating: Not much; after all, we are similarly trained in *overlooking.*

the object, the mental image. "Mental" means "*in* the mind." What's "in" mean here? Not "in" the brain, because nobody has ever recorded an image there.*

> That I know of. Ages ago I saw brain images of macaque monkeys who'd been shown concentric circles around a radiating center; fuzzy sectors of circles appeared. I don't know where that went.

What is behind these experiences? For me, then, the crucial notion is *visibility.* What is that capability? Is it in us or in the object? Surely in both; it is supplied by the object and received by us. Our cognitive constitution is *receptive*, which has to mean that, however the organic and neural functions are understood, something comes to us sensorily but not bodily. And that's an image. So it is *our way of being*—to be involved in discerning originals from images. To be an embodied human being is to live with, to be implicated in, the original/image duality.

What specifically human circumstances attend on this condition? There is an aboriginal duplicity in our view-love. Recall Socrates's understanding of beauty as shining (*lampron*, *Phaedrus* 250 b). To be truly visible is immediately also to be beautiful, to be attractive.* Perfect visibility conveys not

> And to be beautiful is to be *both* luminous *and* to illuminate, to be *lampron*, to be a lamp.

merely verifiable looks, accurate images, but it irradiates them. I mean that it does not "touch up" the object but simply makes it luminous—as is. And that appears to me to be *imaginative truth*—coincident with *perfect visibility*.

We love to look, and we recoil from the "unsightly." But consider the German word for "shine," *scheinen*. It signifies *both* the glow, the beauty, emitted by objects that have true visibility *and* their falsifying seeming. This apparency (an obsolete word herein revived), this duality, may be due either to their intended and crafted deceitfulness or to their inherent distance from, worse, their obscuring of, the thing itself, their screening of reality—not unlike the way a cloudily transparent, delicately decorative screen works in a dressing room. As for the beauty, however, it invites and draws regard and respect, two words that each mean *both* looking and esteeming.*

> Thus the function of the Olympian gods in epics is explained. No one looks to them for the salvation of his soul, never (I guarantee it) do they help the heroes do anything human beings can't do for themselves. Their special function is to *watch*, like Helen and the elders on the walls of Troy. Better to be under the regard of a hostile god than to be unwatched: human splendor requires it. Gods watch humans; they also play with them, and sometimes it's dire: "They kill us for their sport" says pagan Gloucester (*King Lear*, IV i 39). The epic heroes are always under their regard and shine

the more. I get the impression that among the Greeks before Troy there was just one ugly man, Thersites, and he was the first democratic man—unheroic and plaintive (*Iliad*, II 211 ff.).

I conclude that this very visibility must be complexly conceived. It is an object shining *in itself* and thus shining *to us*.*

Recall *phainein* and *phainesthai* above.

As shining for us it is beautiful. For to shine, to be egregiously visible, is convertible with being beautiful. Moreover, when the subject receives *from the object* an image that leaves the object behind, an image that the subject now holds *within its memory*—this reciprocity of thing and soul, this very duality, is, I guess, our first experience of original and image.*

Convertibility of shining and being beautiful: I believe Socrates partly because, as so often, the experience of the opposite, ugliness, is corroborative. Neither is looking drawn to unsightliness, nor is the ugly being fully capable of being seen: It is deficient in form or overlain with accretions. But you might say there is that *belle laide*, the attractively ugly person, primarily female. Well, there starts romanticism: deviance redeemed as eccentric originality. But no, there's Socrates himself, ugly as a Silenus to the superficial glance and beautiful to a more penetrating look (*Symposium* 221 e ff.).

First experience of original and image: I seriously believe that the early experience of mental imagery as opposed to perceptual reality is incipiently philosophical.

This is the moment to recall two sets of notions central to this inquiry. One set is *donegality* and *aevum*. Both of them are mongrels of thought, notional hybrids. One, *aevum*, lies between time and eternity, the progeny of an incompatible conjugality—a bubble-time for fictions. The other, donegality, signifies an impossible marriage between space and substance—an atmosphere with essence.

The other set is, first, a group held together by its Indo-European root *dheigh-*, which makes paradise, dough, figure, effigy, fiction, and *feigning*, all cognate; then a second group around "imitate," cognate with *image*.

Both sets, in their variety-in-unity, served to work out the nature of an image, without which an original would be unintelligible *as* an original. For as I've just claimed, a true original is, in its very being, to be understood as originating images.

For originals to function as originators they must have a world capable of similarity. So once more, in conclusion:

J. SIMILARITY: SAMENESS-IN-DIFFERENCE

Recall the English teacher who assigned this for homework: Write sentences illustrating the distinction among "same," "identical," and "similar."* I shall try to hand it in to her,

> From Katharine Weber, *Still Life with Monkey* (2018), about a man who was paralyzed in an accident and is given a capuchin monkey as helper. His wife is musing about how to compare him to his twin brother.

because these terms are most pertinent to image-inquiries. And I'll add "different" on the right-hand side of the list, not just for symmetry, but because it figures in the delineation of similarity: sameness-in-difference.

First, a reordering: identical, same, similar, different—in ascending order of difference; I can see that at a glance. So, "identical": These two are identical twins; you can't tell them apart, and there is *no daylight between them*. In your mind, they meld into one. To call them identical what you say of one you will have to say of the other.* Next, "same":

> So truly identical twins don't exist.

More accurately, these two sisters look very much the same, but to say that, you have to be able to tell them apart— as they *are* in number (each is, in herself, one, and two only when taken together), in place (one's here, the other there) or in time (each one was then, or is now, or will be going about her own personal business). Sameness involves comparison, hence difference.* "Similar": it is etymologically cognate to

> Consequently "one and the same" is not a logical idiom; one thing alone can't be the same, except as self-same, *i.e.,* stable. "Same-*like*": *-lar* or *-ar* signifies "of a kind, like that kind."

"same," but with a difference: "same-like." Neither are these twins *quite the same,* as I said, *minute distinctions turn up,* the brow of one has two thought-lines engraved on it, the other two and a half. *Similarity* being *sameness-in-difference,* similar beings are differently same. It's the most wonderful paradox that has ever shaped a world, see below. Finally, "different" is global to this sphere of comparatives.

Resumé: I naturally use "identical" to mean indiscernibly different. Immediately a problem turns up: Isn't there a contradiction here? Mustn't we speak, with Leibniz, of the "identity of indiscernibles," meaning that the two have indeed conceded their duality and collapsed into one? So identity, I concluded above, should, properly speaking, be used only of self-sameness, the abiding sameness of one: "One is one and all alone," sings the Christmas song cited elsewhere—"and evermore shall be so." It is a word of gravity, applicable to an Origin, the incomparable, unique, ultimate original in those philosophical theologies that provide for one.

Next, "same," which appears to be properly used when items are compared under the assumption that they are received as distinguishable. Shakespeare has a problem: What new thing can he say to express his love?

> Nothing, sweet boy; but yet, like prayers divine,
> I must each day say o'er the very same, . . . (Sonnet 108)

It's witty, touching, and true—love's language tends to the formulaic and repetitive; why not (naughtily) redeem it by pointing to its—quite comprehensive—sameness with prayer?—adoring, imploring, divinizing, in short, ritualizing.

So, finally, to "similar," "same-like," "same-in-kind," in which the identity is somewhat abridged to be reasserted, now involved in a relation: identity-in-difference. The problem is saving the notion from the overt self-contradiction of its formula. As I've already said, this, the most significance-fraught of the three terms, depends for its integrity on the constitution of the world: Each item, be it thing or setting, must have _a subject_, an underlying receiver, platform, frame, scaffolding, to which are given, on which are loaded, to which are applied, multiple _accidents_, "fallings-to." Each item has either all the same properties as a putative other (including number, position, time) and that makes them collapse into _identity_.*

Which here act as property—dubiously but necessarily.

Or, the two items being somehow distinguishable, say in number, so as to be comparable, all its remaining properties are found to be the same, and that accords the two _sameness_. Or it has some of these properties in greater or lesser degree, or it has other properties, and that bestows _similarity_. At what point similarity morphs into difference or otherness is a matter of judgment, and thereby hangs many a human tale.*

It's another reason why I added "different (or other)" to the right of the list: identical, same, similar, different. Irresistible observation: "different" does signify "other," but Other is the new interpretation of Nonbeing given in the _Sophist_ (257). Recall that Image there is constituted of Being and Nonbeing (240), as it is now found between identity and difference. Serendipity!

"We've grown apart" is a sadly conclusive inference, but who did the distancing, or induced it by standing still, and who became different and did it by losing or gaining many trivial or one consequential property—that is a matter for many a wakeful night.*

And the many small distancings are probably harder to bear than some single, unforgiveable transgression, which at least bestows the comfort of focused righteousness on the transgressee.

Here is more on the significance of similitude, almost a paean. Were the world not a venue of similitude, it must needs be either one of homogeneity or of chaos—*either* all the same, down to the minimals of existence and therefore absolutely uniform, even ultimately contracted into that least, ultimate individual, that atom without an inner division, and terminally unmanageable in speech, because all items—were there any—would need their own name, each being radically other from the others—and that would be the *or*: cognitive chaos.*

And utter disaster for Gulliver's academicians of Lagado, who have abolished words and carry sacks, presumably of typical things, to signify their meaning (III v); they would have to carry all the items in the world.

Awareness would oscillate between uniform tedium and frantic frenzy. No one could ever be company with his like (because you would need an infinite search to find him—and then fail), or be compared with his other (because each would be other in another way); a hut and a mansion would not be "shelters" in common, and 17 Wagner St. could probably not have 19 as its anti-symmetric wall-partner. Perhaps we do live in the best of possible worlds—ontologically speaking.

Similarity is full of further complexities and perplexities: of kinds and size, of priority and precedence, of reciprocity and mutuality, of stability and ambiguity. A register of problems for various cases of similarity would be, though big, not entirely boring. Images, however, are the paradigm case, the incarnation of conceptual Similitude and its question of questions: How came we to be given a world so similarly constituted, so through and through Oppositional and yet so compacted of Same and Other, to our cognitive advantage and our intellectual engagement? An attempt to pursue this question would lever this inquiry into a theological disquisition, which I'm not up to.

Could there be an image without an original, an originating image that had no "Imaged Itself" behind it, in its background?

As ever: Yes and No. *No* is easily and uninterestingly disposed of: "Image" means, by definition and by common use, imitation, copy, re-presentation, all marked by likeness. So no such image.

Yes is more subtle. Take Picasso's portrait of Gertrude Stein. She (or someone) complained that it didn't look *like* her. He is said to have said: "But it will." I suppose he meant: People will learn to see as I do. But even today, looking at this purported portrait (from Latin *portrahere*, "to draw forth," much like "delineate"), we wouldn't wish these exact looks on any woman. Yet we would say that, although this quasi-representation was *very* original, a work of art, it was also somehow an image; we do recognize her; it *is* a depiction, especially if it's got a label—but the likeness component is low.

So there *can* be an original image as well as an imaging original. Here the nature of likeness or similarity, cognate with "same," so a modified sort of sameness, comes front and center.* You can tell that this notion of "same but not quite"

Now is the moment to mention that "similar" is cognate with "same."

is tricky; careful English teachers of yore used to beat it into you: there's no such thing as "more unique," unique is absolute. So why isn't "same"? Well, because it's inherently comparative, while unique—"only"—is "one and one and all alone and evermore shall be so."

But first, as I've said, an image being an entity, but likeness primarily a quality, images fall under the notion of likeness; not so the converse: there are other likenesses (now used substantively) besides images. What might they be? Perhaps non-intentional images, such as offspring are to parents? Well, according to my guru-poet, offspring can be *very* intentional images: "Die single and thy image dies with thee" (Sonnet 3), he says, once more, and advises procreating.

This line of thought raises yet another question: Is intention part of the *essence* of imagery? Are the various non-intentional, natural or accidental, images perhaps exactly what I'm looking for?—likenesses that are not, speaking accurately, images, even though they have some image features, such as diminished dimensionality? It seems to be a supportable usage distinction. Not very significant.

But there may be several more interesting uses for "like." One I've already mentioned; it gets to me because it has the makings of human vexation: the resemblance of offspring to parents, visibly the same blood but like only in looks. Then there is non-pictorial and non-visible likeness, such as underlies *analogy*, a verbal device that can be used in logical mentation: ana-logical reasoning, in which the same logic is carried "through" (Greek: *ana*) from one subject to another, thought to be similar, a huge territory outside this book.*

> Ana-logy can be thought of as a cognitive mode opposed to analysis, that pries the subject apart, or loosens it "up" (also, *ana*).

Here, finally, is a brief analysis of likeness or resemblance.*

> I consulted my colleague Stewart Umphrey's book *Complexity and Analysis* (2002).

First, it comes in degrees, which I think of as "self-comparative." One object can grow to be more or less like its former self. Second, it is comparable as between like objects—it is "other-comparative"; one object can be more or less like another, either to begin with or over time.

The first relation is symmetrical; when *one* human being changes, then the former and the present self have both grown unlike each other, though only the older self has changed, albeit, one hopes, not too much. For that would be self-alienation, involving not only our external features, but, what might be worse, our internal extension over time, our memory. That way madness lies.

The second relation, of likeness *between* objects, say human beings, is verbally symmetrical, either having grown dissimilar to the other. But it is, sometimes devastatingly, dissimilar materially, as when one has outgrown the other, be it in excellence of character or worldly prosperity.*

> A consideration of this problem is the stuff of novels: how to conduct a friendship if a longtime friend has fallen behind you *or* you've outdone him in worldly reputation and prosperity? The two cases are likely to be different: he's probably responsible for the first condition, you for the second, so the latter case makes kindness both more apt and more spontaneous. *Neither* of these are, however, really going to happen frequently, since worldly involvement is, often, adverse to mental growth, while practical ineptitude is, sometimes, the concomitant of inner plenitude.
>
> Aristotle treats, with great subtlety, the most serious case, when a friend deteriorates in moral excellence, in character. I take him to be saying, in sum: "Get out, the sooner the better—unless you think you can help"; he's not explicit, but his words seem to wink: doubt you can! (*Nicomachean Ethics* 1165 b).

The most telling characteristic of likeness or resemblance is *identity-in-difference*, sameness in dissimilarity (since the definition of "different" is "unlike" or "dissimilar"). You can see that this dog is chasing its tail, which is to say that "identity-in-difference" is not so much an explanation as a reiteration of the problem. This problem is, in fact, already present in the word "similar," which is composed of the cognate for "same" and an ending "-ar," meaning, as I've said, "of a kind with," and so "relating to" or "resembling"; this latter means "somewhat the same," "exhibiting similarity."

As so often in this sort of problem, what is presented as the explanation is really a statement of the deep question: What thought-frame for our world makes it possible to say that some items in it are the same (identical) but not really so (different)?

I think the most straight-forward answer is that, as we see things, they are indeed compacted of different "properties," features that *belong to them*, or "accidents," features that *befall them*. The latter often means: befall them accidentally, that is, inessentially. We are apt to think of things as being similar, identical in their difference, when they differ in inessentials but are essentially the same. Here's a prime example, though contentious: people differ biologically in certain, presumably superficial, physical features, called racial, but are generically identical, namely human—thus under certain aspects similar, under others the same.*

> In the Platonic dialogue *Sophist* a deeper analysis is given of diversity, one that is rooted in an account of being, in *ontology*, rather than in the use of words, in *linguistic analysis*. Curtly put: the dialogue contains an inquiry into the deep meaning of Otherness and finds in it the principle of universal relatedness, of connecting difference (255), I'll introduce the chief political term now current in America: *Diversity* rightly, that is, ontologically, understood as Otherness, is the dialogue's source of togetherness.

K. POSTULATED

Are there, then, originals for these images, the forms fiction takes, its works? Here is my underwhelming but, I think, sensible answer: Yes, there must be. How do I know, having not yet access to heaven or hell, where I have claimed would be their home? My reply lies in the mood of my claim: There *must* be originals. I mean: They are *postulates*. A postulate is, literally, a demand made of the interested participant in the enterprise to grant a proposition or a possibility, so as to allow an activity to proceed. The most enabling formal statement of a postulate I know comes from Euclid's *Elements*; it is his first postulate and has not only mathematical but also human application:

> I command that it be granted me
> To draw a straight line from any point to any point.

It's clear that if you can't just do that without any precondition, you can't do anything geometrical, nor clue out the shortest way to various accomplishments. And so I think that without granting myself faith in image-originating originals without postulating them, nothing I care for is intelligible, least of all fictive imagery.

Let me say it once more, in conclusion: The originals I have postulated are not forms, ideas, or universals, but mongrels unwelcome in straight-laced philosophy: at once discarnately transcendent *and* sensorily mundane, dwellers in that notional middle place between heaven and earth—which is descriptively identical to Paradise.

Is the postulate-answer, as they say, a cop-out? Well, I'm in respectable company: Kant, who says in the *Critique of Pure Reason* that we must *postulate* God because without his power the moral law will be untenable. I'm doing for esthetics what he is doing for ethics.*

In all modesty.

To conclude:

... the truest poetry is the most feigning ...
(*As You Like It* III iii 17).

What does Shakespeare mean? I'll interpret, *parti pris*: *The most veritable imagery* ("the truest poetry") *imitates originals* ("is the most FEIGNING"). *Ipse dixit.*

FINIS

Index

Index